Men of Property and Intelligence

The Scottish Electoral System prior to 1884

Michael Dyer

SCOTTISH CULTURAL PRESS

First published 1996
Scottish Cultural Press
PO Box 106, Aberdeen AB9 8ZE
Tel: 01224 583777
Fax: 01224 575337

British Library Cataloguing in Publication Data
A catalogue record for this book is available from the British Library

ISBN: 1 898218 22 6

The publisher wishes to acknowledge subsidy from the Scottish Arts Council
towards the publication of this volume

THE SCOTTISH **ARTS** COUNCIL

Printed and bound by BPC-AUP Aberdeen Ltd

Contents

Maps

Also published by Scottish Cultural Press:

Capable Citizens and Improvident Democrats: The Scottish Electoral System 1885–1929, Michael Dyer (1 898218 23 4)

Jacobite Clans of the Great Glen: 1650–1784, Bruce Lenman (1 898218 19 6)

Jacobite Risings in Britain: 1689–1746, Bruce Lenman (1 898218 20 X)

Parish Life in Eighteenth-Century Scotland: A Review of the Old Statistical Account, Maisie Steven (1 898218 28 5)

Scottish Lifestyle 300 Years Ago, Helen & Keith Kelsall (1 898218 06 4)

Scottish Burgh Surveys, Historic Scotland [for full list of Burghs covered, their ISBNs, etc contact SCP]

For the complete SCP catalogue, please contact the publishers at the address shown at the front of this book.

Acknowledgements

The author wishes to thank Pamela Strang and Dr Lawrence McLean, Dept of Geography, Aberdeen University, for their help in the production of this book.

The author also acknowledges with thanks the financial assistance received from the Carnegie Trust for the Universities of Scotland.

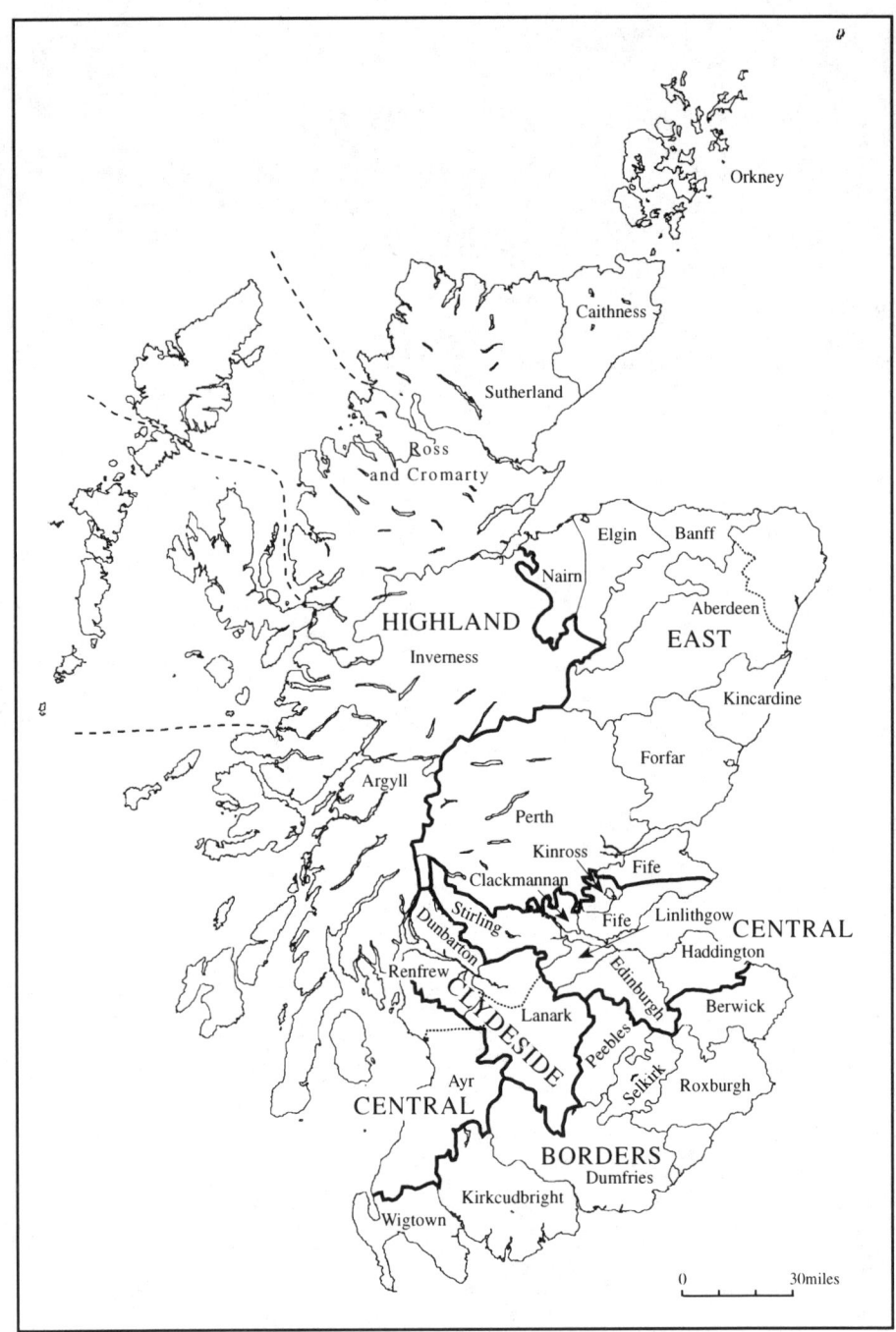

Scottish County Constituencies, 1832-1884

Definition of Regions

Any system of geo-political regionalisation is likely to produce a disputed classification on both geographical and political grounds, and this scheme is no exception. The task is particularly difficult when searching for a system sufficiently robust to cover a lengthy period, because economic and political change suggest different classificatory schemes at different times. As far as possible I have tried to anticipate such problems without changing the basis of the classification in order to assist comparisons over time.

A second problem is that the burgh districts sometimes have their constituent parts in different regions. In Chapters 3 and 7, where they are so dispersed, I have divided their influence proportionate to their share of their respective District's electorate in each region. In Chapters 4 and 8, however, where such fine adjustments are not possible, the Districts of Burghs have been allocated to those regions in which the majority of their electors resided.

Briefly the rationale behind the system is as follows:

The four major cities merit isolation because they are different in character from their surrounding areas; Leith is included with Edinburgh in Chapters 2 and 5 because it is part of the same metropolitan area, though it was necessary to place it in Central in Chapters 4 and 8; the Highlands and Islands cover the Crofting Counties; the East covers the mostly rural counties between the Moray Firth and the Firth of Tay; Clydeside is restricted to those counties directly bordering on Glasgow; the Borders are those counties bordering on England and Peebles and Selkirk; Central includes all the remaining constituencies in the central belt from Ayrshire to Fife.

Regions 1832–1868

Aberdeen	(1)
Dundee	(1)
Edinburgh/Leith	(3) [excluding Leith, Chapter 4]
Glasgow	(2)

Highlands and Islands – Orkney & Shetland, Caithness, Sutherland, Ross & Cromarty, Inverness-shire, Argyll, Wick Burghs, Inverness Burghs (greater part), Ayr Burghs (lesser part).

East – Elgin & Nairn, Banffshire, Aberdeenshire, Kincardineshire, Forfarshire, Perthshire; Fife (notional half, Chapter 3) [all Fife, Chapter 4], Perth, Elgin Burghs, Montrose Burghs, St Andrews Burghs, Inverness Burghs (lesser part).

1

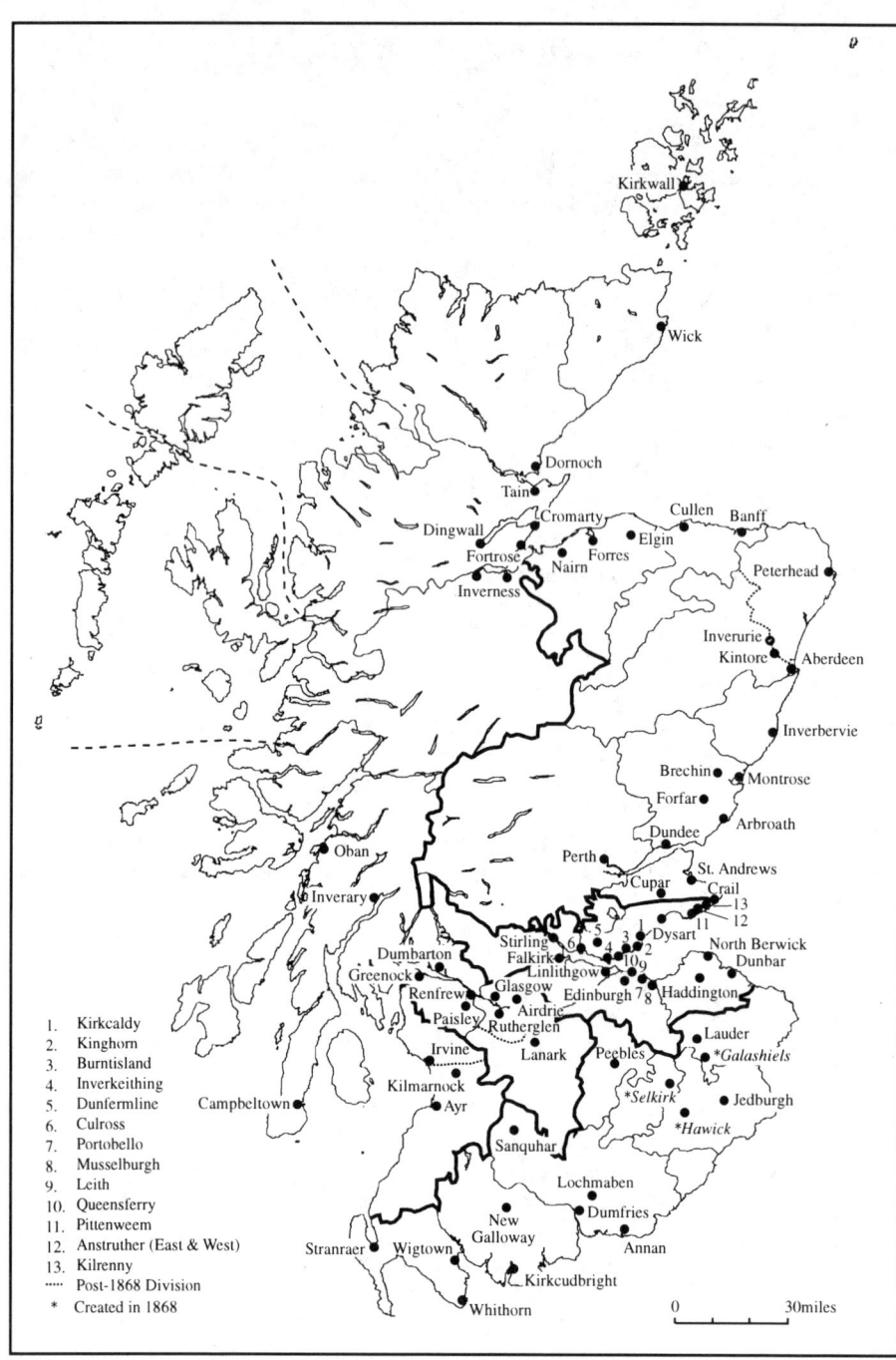

1. Kirkcaldy
2. Kinghorn
3. Burntisland
4. Inverkeithing
5. Dunfermline
6. Culross
7. Portobello
8. Musselburgh
9. Leith
10. Queensferry
11. Pittenweem
12. Anstruther (East & West)
13. Kilrenny
···· Post-1868 Division
  *   Created in 1868

Scottish Burgh Constituencies, 1832-1884

Central – Bute, Ayrshire, Stirlingshire, Clackmannan & Kinross, Fife (notional half, Chapter 3), Linlithgow, Haddingtonshire, Midlothian (Edinburghshire), Stirling Burghs, Kirkcaldy Burghs, Falkirk Burghs (greater part), Kilmarnock Burghs (greater part), Ayr Burghs (greater part), Haddington Burghs (greater part) [Including Leith District, Chapter 4].

Clydeside – Lanarkshire, Dunbartonshire, Renfrewshire, Greenock, Paisley, Falkirk Burghs (greater part), Kilmarnock Burghs (lesser part)

Borders – Wigtownshire, Kirkcudbrightshire, Dumfries-shire, Roxburgh, Selkirk, Peebles, Berwickshire, Dumfries Burghs, Wigtown Burghs, Haddington Burghs (lesser part).

Regions 1868-1884

Aberdeen   (1)
Dundee   (2)
Edinburgh/Leith (3) [excluding Leith, Chapter 8]
Glasgow   (3)

Highland : As 1832–1868.

East   : As 1832–1868 + Extra Seat for Aberdeenshire.

Central : As 1832–1868 + Extra Seat for Ayrshire.

Clydeside : As 1832–1868 + Extra Seat for Lanarkshire.

Borders : As 1832–1868 but with Peebles-shire and Selkirkshire combined, and Hawick Burghs added.

1 Introduction

Electoral systems are an important area of study, for not only do they reflect on the values of the political system in which they operate, but also play an important role in the management of political development and the process of nation-building as they evolve from traditional to modern forms.

In his seminal work, *Citizens, Elections, Parties*, Rokkan describes electoral arrangements as reflecting 'tensions between three concepts of representation: the numerical, the functional, and the territorial,' (Rokkan, 1970:165). In traditional systems the numerical is of least importance because representation is based on corporate rather than individual identities, in particular on the functional distinction between the commercial concerns of municipalities and the agrarian interests of landowners. In this context the member of parliament acts as an ambassador for his constituency rather than the representative of a national party. Traditional systems are also associated with a territorial distribution of constituencies that reflect historical accumulation rather than a currently prevailing spatial distribution of either electors or population. Both the functional and territorial aspects of traditional systems are associated with a diversity of franchise qualifications and methods of election. The numerical aspect, of course, becomes more important as the process of democratisation gains pace, so that the principle of one vote one value advances the arguments for equal electoral districts, and, with the growth of political parties, for the introduction of proportional representation. Democratisation leads to the standardisation of electoral procedures, the individuation of voting through the secret ballot, and the replacement of corporate and territorial particularisms by a national political identity.

The focus of this study is on the evolution of the electoral system in Scotland, and the process by which procedures inherited from an independent Scotland were gradually rejected in favour of a uniform system encompassing the whole of the United Kingdom. In that respect, the development of the electoral system is part of a more general process of incorporation, encompassing a wide range of Scottish political and social institutions, from local government, education, and the provision of welfare, to political parties, trade unions, professional associations, and pressure groups. The degree of incorporation, of course, has been by no means uniform – the Kirk is mostly independent, though subject to parliamentary legislation and judgements of the House of Lords; the legal system enjoys a high degree of autonomy, though the laws to which Scots are subjected have become less divergent over time from those governing the English; and the development of the Scottish Office provides an element of administrative devolution of varying effectiveness. It is, nevertheless, the case that the most important influences shaping the lives of the Scots and English have become increasingly similar, and those which convey distinctiveness, especially religion, have become more marginalised. Undoubtedly some of these developments can be traced back centuries, but the impetus initiated by the Reform

Act of 1832 in undermining Scotland's historic constitution has played a major role.

The democratisation of the electoral process sheds a particularly instructive light on a contemporary political question: namely, the apparent paradox, frequently noted by political scientists and politicians, between the willingness of Scots to describe themselves as Scottish rather than British, and their overwhelming propensity to vote for unionist parties. Apart from the general observation that the significance of ethnic identity depends on the social context to which it is applied, and that there is no necessary connection between the ethnic nation and the political nation, why the two remain separate in Scotland's case still invites explanation. A major factor has been the dissonance between the values supported by the *ancien regime* inherited from an independent Scotland, underpinned by the electoral system, and the aspirations of the new urban middle class of the early nineteenth century. Consequently, the link between nationalism and liberalism, in which the freedom of the nation and the realisation of individual citizenship rights become intertwined, was not a feature of Scottish politics. Instead, nationalism was a weapon employed by Tory romantics and reactionaries to portray reform, extending across a whole range of institutions, as the betrayal of Scotland's constitutional heritage enshrined in the Treaty of Union. As a result, the United Kingdom not only became the agent of change, but, as the champion of liberal democracy against a discredited legacy, the nation to which the Scots gave affective political allegiance. Similarly, the new mass electorates after 1885 looked to a progressive Westminster parliament to weaken the economic and political control landlords had continued to exercise in the counties after 1832, and to satisfy demands for welfarism, which local elites were either unwilling or unable to deliver. Thus, democratic integration was also the integration of the Scots into a British political identity.

The development of the electoral system in Scotland might be seen as falling into five phases, punctuated by the Treaty of Union, the Reform Acts of 1832, 1868, 1884/5, 1918 and the equalisation of the adult franchise in 1928.

1. Traditional

This relates to the period before 1832, when the system was based on arrangements developed prior to the Union, but modified to accommodate reduced representation in the United Kingdom parliament. Territorially, Scotland had an allocation of seats bargained between the Scots and English commissioners in negotiations leading to the Union Treaty. The manner of their distribution, franchise, and electoral arrangement were left to the determination of the last Scottish parliament. Representation rested on a functional distinction between counties and Royal Burghs, which had its origins in an estate-based parliament. It was a measure of the landlord-dominated polity, that two thirds of the seats allocated to Scotland were awarded to the counties, whose franchise was based on a feudal system of landholding, though somewhat extended at the Restoration. The determination of burgh elections was confined to members of the close corporations. The system was more exclusive than that of England in the eighteenth century, because it contained no mechanism whereby sections of the new middle class could be incorporated into the county electorate, and the burghs eschewed the principle of popular election altogether. Even on the eve of reform there were barely 3,000 Scottish electors overall. Burgh representation was completely corrupted, and the functional foundations on which it was based traduced by ministerial patronage. The counties were also vulnerable to manipulation by the government, though a small number of landed magnates were not without influence. Scottish members, both from the burghs and counties, were mostly landed gentry, mostly closely related to members of the House of Lords, and noted less as ambassadors for their constituencies than lobby fodder for the administration, whatever its political complexion.

2. Transitional, 1832-1884

This period covers elections under the First and Second Reform Acts. Differences remained between the Scottish and English electoral systems, Scotland requiring its own distinctive legislation in both 1832 and 1868, and the functional distinction between county and burgh continued to be reflected in their respective franchises. Nevertheless, the franchise provisions in the burghs were substantially the same as those south of the border, especially from 1868; and differences in their respective county franchises were much reduced, though the proportion of county residents enfranchised in Scotland was significantly lower than in England. The Celtic periphery was effectively excluded from the reforms. The moves towards a greater standardisation of the franchise was not reflected in the approach to redistribution, and Scottish backbenchers, who had little independent control over changes to the voting qualifications, exerted considerable influence in the shaping of redistribution both in 1832 and in 1868. Consequently, conservative influences ensured that virtually no attempt was made to address the maldistribution of seats, which meant that county interests continued to dominate parliamentary representation overwhelmingly.

Reform in 1832 ended ministerial influences over electoral outcomes, which, in the absence of national parties, (slower to develop than in England), transferred considerable power to local political leaders. The nature of the franchise and open voting rested great power in the hands of landowners, (often non-voting aristocrats), so that before the general election of 1874 county electors had little independence; but in the burghs from 1832 onwards voters enjoyed a considerable degree of autonomy. Between 1832 and 1865, in both county and burgh constituencies, a high proportion of returns were uncontested, so that participation, even amongst the enfranchised, was restricted. From 1868, however, turnout greatly increased, and there was a significant decline in uncontested returns. In the fifty years after 1832 the burghs were Liberal almost by definition, whilst Whig and Tory landed proprietors shared power in the counties. Despite an overwhelming Liberal victory in 1880, most members of parliament were drawn from the landowning class, and to that extent they had more social affinity with members elected before the first reform act than their successors returned in 1910.

If the traditional system could be described as Tory in its bias, the 1832-1884 electoral arrangements could be seen as part of a wider Whig project designed to placate the urban middle class, while leaving the polity as a whole dominated by rural landowners, whose county power bases were largely unaffected by radical changes in urban life and politics.

3. Standardisation 1884-1918

The franchise and redistribution acts 1884/5 applied to the whole of the United Kingdom, standardised voter qualifications, and marked the end of the Whig constitution of the previous fifty years. Scotland's proportion of seats was broadly in conformity with her share of the population, although their distribution continued to favour rural areas to the detriment of Clydeside. The functional distinction between county and burgh remained for the purposes of redistribution, but the equalisation of the franchise reduced its importance. The division of the cities also marked a shift away from functional representation, because it questioned the notion of there being a single corporate interest. In partisan terms, the contrast between burgh and county became less important than differences between geographical regions.

Post-1885 developments marked a major change with the past, because the creation of a mass electorate stimulated the growth of national parties, the development of a modern bi-polar party system, and incorporated Scotland within a British system of representation. Indeed, the central issue of the period, under pressure from the greater prominence given to Irish Home Rule through the enfranchisement of the Celtic peasantry, was how national identity(ies) might be redefined in such a way as would incorporate the new mass electorate. With the reduced influence of local elites and local issues, the ambassadorial aspects of representation became subordinate to party identification, and the social backgrounds of MPs changed markedly as landowners deserted the Liberals. Unopposed returns virtually disappeared, and participation by the electorate was high.

4. Democratisation, 1918-1928

The introduction of manhood suffrage in 1918 and the realisation of adult suffrage in 1928 fundamentally altered the principles on which the franchise was granted, turning it from a privilege to a right; and although functional representation continued to be recognised in the distinction between burgh and county constituencies, redistribution was based principally on population (later electoral) size. On the other hand, new territorial considerations emerged, for although the principle of pro rata representation was sustained, the danger of Scotland losing seats was avoided by explicit recognition of the need to overrepresent sparsely populated areas, and the cultural distinctiveness of the Outer Hebrides was also recognised. Registration was greatly simplified as qualifications to the general provisions were removed.

Not only did the 1918 franchise treble the pre-war electorate, but redistribution shifted representation firmly towards the industrial areas in the west. The effect was to recast the party system through the rapid rise of the Labour Party, and occasion a process of realignment between elements of the disintegrating Liberal coalition and the Conservatives. Both the class-based and differing ethnic characteristics of these alignments incorporated the new electorate in parties which transcended the border, thereby consolidating the working class into the

United Kingdom as completely as the gentry and middle class before them.

5. Post-Democratisation

Changes to the electoral system since 1928 have been largely marginal, and concerned more with removing anomalies, such as the three combined university seats and the smattering of business voters, than embracing new departures. The most important changes have been the introduction of periodic boundary commissions – a necessary corollary of democratisation – and the reduction of the voting age to eighteen. The introduction of an instruction to boundary commissioners that Scotland's representation should not be less than seventy one, indicates recognition of a need to recognise the national sensitivities of the Scottish electorate. The abolition of county councils and municipalities in 1974 finally led to the end of functional representation in 1983, though local government boundaries have continued to provide the structural underpinning of redistribution schemes. The survival of 'first past the post' as a means of settling electoral outcomes as a crucial feature of the system, however, indicates how persistent traditional features of the electoral process have been.

Although changes to the electoral system are not so readily recognised as major variables in developments in the party system over the last sixty years, as they were following the major reform acts, it may be argued that it wasn't until the 1950s that the realignments caused by the 1918 Act were finally completed; and although the Scottish National Party (SNP) was the first significant party to have grown without a major change to the electoral system, the consolidation of its position would be much assisted by the introduction of proportional representation. The Nationalists, nevertheless, underline the point, as did the Irish Nationalists before them, that while the processes of standardisation and democratisation may have played an important role in the integration of Britain, it could only do so, and continue to do so, within a certain historical and social context.

Men of Property and Intelligence deals principally with the transitional stage of the Scottish electoral system, when the Scottish arrangements still remained distinct from the rest of the United Kingdom. Particular emphasis is placed on the attitudes and impact of Scottish politicians on the reform process, as expressed in the correspondence of Henry Cockburn with Kennedy of Dunure, and in House of Commons debates. Analysis of the electoral system makes reference to various Parliamentary Papers. In making use of a variety of secondary material, I am particularly indebted to FWS Craig's compilation of electoral statistics; W Ferguson's thesis on *Electoral Law and Procedure in Eighteenth and Early Nineteenth Century Scotland*; RM Sunter's *Patronage and Politics in Scotland, 1707-1832;* JI Brash's *Scottish Electoral Politics, 1832-1854*, for its discussion of politics in Midlothian and editing of Horne's election surveys; the mine of information found in IGC Hutchison's *A Political History of Scotland*; and FB Smith's, *The Making of the Second Reform Bill.*

The period between 1885 and 1929 is covered in an accompanying volume, *Capable Citizens and Improvident Democrats.*

2 *The Inheritance*

It is reported that the first Earl of Seafield, the last Lord Chancellor of Scotland and leading negotiator in the discussions preceding the Treaty of Union of 1707, on signing the Act after its contentious progress through the Scottish parliament declared, 'Now there's ane end of ane old song.' If that air was the voice of Scotland's 'independency and soveraignty' (Lockhhart: 222-3) then few today would argue it was extinguished in 1707, and more would protest that the earl[1] hardly did justice to the success of his own labours, for the Treaty of Union and its associated statutes ensured that numerous aspects of Scotland's social, economic and political peculiarities survived.

Of particular concern here is the considerable latitude afforded to the Scottish parliament in determining the character of its nation's future representation at Westminster. That the Scottish parliament alone in 1707 established the qualifications of candidates, the manner of their election, and the constituency pattern adopted for returning both the 45 commoners and the 16 Representative Peers to the United Kingdom parliament, and that it should have been decided to leave the franchises for electing members from the counties and burghs substantially as they were, meant that the polity represented by them, constituency retrenchment not withstanding, was that of ancient Scotland.

The Scottish system of government and its parliamentary traditions were significantly different from those of England, and had important implications for the development of its electoral system. Whereas, by the end of the seventeenth century, the English parliament was sovereign, the Scots parliament had legislative rivals in the Privy Council, the General Assembly of the Church of Scotland, and the Convention of Royal Burghs. Furthermore, whereas the English parliament met in two separate chambers with a strict division between the Lords and Commons, the parliament of Scotland, composed of three (latterly two) estates, assembled in a single chamber. The first estate, the Tenants-in-Chief, became divided between the Lords of Parliament or Nobility (aristocrats summoned by personal invitation), and the Smaller Barons elected from the shires. Until 1689 the Clergy formed a second estate, while a third estate consisted of representatives from most of the Royal Burghs. Finally, there were eight or so officers of state, ministers of the crown, who if they had entered parliament as members of an estate ceased the connection on appointment. The corporate nature of the Scottish parliament was reflected in the preamble to statutes, viz., 'His Majesty, with the Advice and Consent of the Estates of Parliament' (Terry: 1905, appendix). More importantly, the incidence of direct taxation was levied on estates rather than individuals. The Royal Burghs, for example, paid one sixth of such taxes, and it was the duty of their Convention to determine the proportion borne by each of its members (Pagan: 53).

The feudal nature of the Scottish parliament helps to explain why the franchise provisions for electing commissioners from the shires (the sub-estate of Smaller Barons) and the burghs were highly restrictive. In the counties the qualifications were archaean. Until 1661, the shire franchise was confined to forty shilling free-holders of the Old Extent, (a valuation of the lands of Scotland undertaken during the reign of Alexander III towards the end of the thirteenth century), which in 1667 ceased to be a source of taxation. Furthermore, in recognising the Superior (i.e. the original or immediate vassal of the King) as the qualifying owner, the franchise was often denied to those who had corporeal possession and pecuniary interest in the land. As Crown lands were not assessed under the Old Extent, tenants of Crown lands and church lands acquired by the crown were also denied the vote. The County Franchise Acts of 1661 and 1681, after which there was no further reform until 1832, went some way to increasing the electorate, particularly amongst tenants of crown lands, by extending the vote to possessors and feu-holders of estates valued at £400 Scots annual value. The provisions, however, only applied to those lands where for various reasons the Old Extent could not be ascertained. Rait considered that these two statutes must have substantially increased the county electorate, (although he offered no figures), and Ferguson that the £400 franchise latterly constituted a majority of county electors, (Rait: 215; Ferguson, 1957: 58). Nevertheless, the numbers still remained extremely small. As late as 1832 there were less than 3,000 enfranchised in the shires, and many of them were no more than nominal electors. Only during the brief Cromwellian union, when the franchise was based on the possession of an estate, real or personal, valued at £200 per annum, had there been an attempt to anticipate the changes of the nineteenth century. Burgh representation was determined by an even less popular process. There the selection of a member lay in the hands of magistrates (councillors), self-perpetuating oligarchies since a law of 1469, which, in seeking to end the influence of the mob on the electoral process, had disfranchised the burgesses, and vested in the magistrates, themselves, sole power to nominate and replenish their numbers. Non-Royal burghs, Burghs of Barony and Regality, sent no commissioners to parliament because they were represented through their superiors.

Although most provisions of the franchise were not materially changed by the Union, steps were taken to deny the vote to Jacobites and their potential sympathisers. Roman Catholics were disfranchised, and several oaths might have been required of an elector before he was allowed to exercise his right (Adam: 354-7). The most basic test was the Oath of Allegiance: a simple promise to 'bear all true allegiance to His Majesty King George,' but The Assurance involved a written renunciation of the claims of the pretended James the Third. If desired, those requirements could be reinforced by the Oath of Abjuration, a more lengthy version of The Assurance that made specific reference to the maintenance of a Protestant monarchy, and by the Test Oath, which denied the vote to those who in the previous year had twice attended an Episcopal service where the officiating prelate had failed to take oaths of allegiance to the government, or failed to pray expressly for the King, his heirs and successors. More meritoriously, oaths were introduced to discourage bribery and the registration of nominal and fictitious voters, which were reinforced by an act of 1743 directed against the making of votes based on the Old Extent (Ferguson, 1957: 58). During the reign of George II further legislation was enacted to remove recipients of government patronage, especially those connected with the customs and revenue, from the voters roll. The impact of these measures did little to change the broad parameters of the system, but any one of them could (and did) have a crucial impact on a contested election, because electorates were so small.

The constitutencies represented by the commissioners of shire and burgh fluctuated considerably. It was as late as 1681 before the number of counties sending members to parliament was finally fixed at 33. In the 1640s, the Stewartry of Kirkcudbright fought a battle to retain its separation from Wigtownshire, and to avoid the fate of Tarbertshire, which had been swallowed up by Argyll a decade earlier. Only in the seventeenth century did Sutherland and Caithness become recognised as separate shires, and the independence of Ross from Inverness ratified. It was as late as 1690 before the number of commissioners returned by each county at the time of the Union was determined, when the larger counties secured additional representation to the two commissioners all shires, except Kinross, Cromarty and Clackmannan, had formerly enjoyed (Table 2.1). The major impact of these latter-day changes was to shift the balance of representation between counties and burghs significantly in favour of the shires (Terry, 1905: 207).

Table 2.1: County Representation 1690–1707
(Total Seats: 88)

4 Seats Each	3 Seats Each	2 Seats Each	1 Seat Each
Aberdeen	Argyll	Banff	Clackmannan
Ayr	Renfrew	Bute	Cromarty
Berwick	Stirling	Caithness	Kinross
Dumfries		Dumbarton	
Edinburgh		Elgin & Forres	
Fife		Inverness	
Forfar		Kincardine	
Haddington		Kirkcudbright	
Lanark		Linlithgow	
Perth		Nairn	
Roxburgh		Orkney & Shetland	
		Peebles	
		Ross	
		Selkirk	
		Sutherland	
		Wigtown	

Royal Burgh representation was almost entirely controlled by the Convention of Royal Burghs. Before qualifying to send a commissioner to parliament, most burghs had first to be admitted to the Convention, which was far from automatic, for while membership involved a willingness to share the tax burden imposed on the third estate, membership also granted assistance in the protection of the monopolistic trading rights implied by incorporation (Ballard; Pagan; Mackie & Pryde). Consequently, a new applicant for membership could rely upon the opposition of other Royal Burghs in its immediate region. As Pryde (1965) recounts: in Galloway 'Whithorn encountered the fierce and sustained opposition of Wigtown' so that having become a Royal Burgh in 1511 it was not admitted to the Convention until 1574 and to parliament before 1641. Stranraer, incorporated in 1617, in like manner, 'owing to the fierce and prolonged opposition of Wigtown, it was not admitted to Convention until 1683 or Parliament until 1685'. In the north, Inverness strongly opposed the admission of Cromarty and Fortrose; while Wick, having been made a Royal Burgh in 1589, 'in encountering the sustained hostility of other northern burghs... was not admitted to Parliament or Convention until 1661.' Similarly, in Fife, Crail opposed, though without success, the admission of Anstruther Easter, Anstruther Wester and Kilrenny in the late sixteenth century. There were few examples where exclusion was self-imposed as in the case of Kirkwall, which, having received its charter in 1486, 'through remoteness, oppression, and poverty...delayed its enrolment by Convention until 1669 and its first appearance in Parliament until 1670.' Members of the Convention were frequently in conflict with one another. In Fife, for example, between 1363 and 1370, the merchant guild of Cupar, 'was in dispute with St Andrews, and its possession of a tolbooth;' and there was a long history of struggle between Burntisland and Dunfermline, who each challenged the right of the other to be a Royal Burgh. It was, therefore, hardly surprising that while in 1707 there were 210 Burghs of Barony, a mere 66 Royal Burghs were represented in parliament, and nine of them had been created after the Restoration (Smout: 146).

Following an act of 1672 which deprived the Royal Burghs of their traditional trading monopolies, their privileges were much undermined, and the advantages of incorporation for the more indigent burghs became increasingly marginal. So much so that Cromarty, having only been enrolled in parliament for the first time in 1661, was permitted to stop sending and supporting a member after 1672.[2] In 1685, the town even ceased to be a Royal Burgh, successfully pleading to be released from the financial burdens which membership of the Convention entailed, and thereafter became a Burgh of Barony. Nevertheless, reluctance on the part of the Convention to lose too many tax payers meant that such a merciful released was denied to other supplicants.

The number of commissioners sent by each Royal Burgh to parliament varied before 1619, but an order of the Convention of that year fixed the figure at one each, with the exception of Edinburgh, which was permitted a second, so that there were 67 burghal members on the eve of the Union. Thus, the total number of Commissioners elected from the shires and burghs was 155 in a parliament of 232 returned in June 1705 (Terry, 1905: 3).

It was clear from the start of negotiations leading to the Union that any amalgamation between the two nations would necessitate the submission of Scotland's parliamentary traditions to those of England, and a substantial reduction in the number of Scottish representatives in the new United Kingdom parliament. Recognising the difficulties necessarily involved in any scheme of union for the Scots, the pro-union commissioners sought to leave as many details as possible to determination by the Scottish parliament. Thus, while the total number of Scottish Commoners and Lords in the new parliament had perforce to be decided bilaterally, their method of selection could be (and was) left to the Scottish parliament for resolution.

The delicacy in fixing the number of Scottish representatives provoked the only formal conference which took place between the English and Scots commissioners, and its proceedings were secret. The only previous experience the conference had before it was the Cromwellian union, which had granted Scotland 30 seats in a Commons of 400 (Table 2.2), but the Scots argued it was no precedent 'because he [Cromwell] was arbitrary' (Defoe: 106), and the estimation of prosperity and population levels was mostly a matter of speculation (Smout: chapter XI). According to Defoe, taxation would have allocated Scotland only 13 members out of 526, while population would have afforded 171 in a Commons of 684. The agreement to settle for 45 Scottish MPs out of 558 seems to have been a compromise born out of a desire by the pro-union commissioners not to prejudice the success of the general negotiations.

> After the Commissioners sincerely and candidly applied themselves to one another, debating not only the reasons and proportions on either hand, but the temper and circumstances of either nation...and to consider not only what was equal, but also what was likely to take place in the minds of their respective Parliaments, which were to debate them (Defoe: 166).

Table 2.2: Scottish Constituencies during the Commonwealth, 1654–1660 *

A. The Burghs (10 Seats)

1. Edinburgh two members.
2. Dornoch, Tain, Inverness, Dingwall, Nairn, Elgin, Forres.
3. Banff, Cullen, Aberdeen.
4. Forfar, Dundee, Arbroath, Montrose, Brechin.
5. Linlithgow, Queensferry, Perth, Culross, Stirling.
6. St Andrews, Dysart, Kirkcaldy, Cupar, Anstruther Easter, Anstruther Wester, Pittenweem, Crail, Dunfermline, Kinghorn, Inverkeithing, Kilrenny, Burntisland.
7. Lanark, Glasgow, Rutherglen, Rothesay, Renfrew, Ayr, Irvine, Dumbarton.
8. Dumfries, Sanquhar, Annan, Lochmaben, Wigtown, Kirkcudbright, Whithorn, New Galloway.
9. Peebles, Lauder, Jedburgh, Selkirk, North Berwick, Dunbar, Haddington.

B. The Counties (20 seats) **

1.	Ross, Sutherland, Cromarty.	11.	Lanark.
2.	Inverness.	12.	Midlothian (Edinburgh).
3.	Banff.	13.	Berwick (Merse).
4.	Aberdeen.	14.	Roxburgh.
5.	Forfar, Kincardine.	15.	Selkirk, Peebles.
6.	Fife, Kinross.	16.	Dumfries.
7.	Perth.	17.	Wigtown.
8.	Linlithgow, Stirling, Clackmannan.	18.	East Lothian (Haddington).
9.	Dumbarton, Argyll, Bute.	19.	Orkney, Shetland, Caithness.
10.	Ayr, Renfrew.	20.	Moray (Elgin), Nairn.

*   Source: C. Sandford Terry, *The Cromwellian Union*, Edinburgh, 1902.
**   The exclusion of Kirkcudbright from this list according to Rait *The Parliaments of Scotland*, Glasgow, 1924, was because 'the advisers of the Protector seem to have accepted the convention of the burghs that the Stewartry was included in Wigtownshire.'

Ironically, for all the criticism of the Cromwellian settlement, the agreed 8.1 per cent Scottish share of the seats in the United parliament after 1707 was little more than the 7.5 per cent awarded by the Lord Protector. Nevertheless, the extra fifteen seats afforded by the latter union meant that a less radical approach would be needed in their distribution.

The Scottish parliament accepted the seat settlement by 114 to 73 against. Of the three estates, the nobility (43:23) were the most in favour, whilst the Smaller Barons (39:28) and the Royal Burghs (32:22) remained less enthusiastic. Opinion on this matter, however, proved less divisive than other aspects of the treaty (*Acts of Scotland*, XI: 388-9).

In searching for an acceptable scheme to recommend to the Scottish parliament for the distribution of the 45 Commons seats, the Scots commissioners were faced with considerable difficulties. The basic problem with the representation of Scotland within the United Kingdom, then as now, was that its area was disproportionately large in relation to the size and dispersal of the population. An added difficulty was that in 1707 there were substantially fewer than the present number of seats to allocate. A rational solution at the time of the Union argued for a scheme which recognised the differences in size between the various shires, as had been a feature of both the Cromwellian settlement and the reforms of 1690, in their different ways, together with a severe retrenchment in the number of burgh constituencies, as under the Commonwealth (Terry, 1902: lii-liv). In the context of 1707, however, the Scottish parliament could neither amalgamate shires on the scale of the Cromwellian settlement, nor agree to very large burgh groupings. Nevertheless, despite their cautious instincts, and a recognition that redistribution constituted a political minefield in which the opponents of the Union hoped the whole enterprise would explode, the commissioners could not avoid their difficult problem. In the event, the Scots parliament was persuaded, without a division, to follow the 'arbitrary ways' of Cromwell by agreeing a two to one division in favour of the shires. In most other respects every attempt was made to render a necessarily traumatic measure as palatable as possible by protecting traditional interests.

Although there were only 30 seats to distribute amongst the 34 shires, the county settlement, which like that for the burghs was carried without the request for a recorded division, was dominated by the principle of individual shire representation, and total opposition to amalgamation (Table 2.3). The one exception was Orkney and Shetland, where unification was traditional and symbolised the semi-colonial status of those islands. For the rest, the 26 largest counties based on taxation were each given one seat, while the remaining three members were shared between Caithness and Bute, Cromarty and Nairn, and Clackmannan and Kinross. Sharing involved the electors of Caithness, Nairn and Clackmannan each returning a member to one parliament, and those of Bute, Cromarty and Kinross to the next. This arrangement effectively disfranchised three counties in each parliament, but the member for an alternating county was constitutionally recognised as representing its fellow. Undoubtedly the major attraction of this novel solution was that it enabled landowners in alternating counties to control county membership in half of the parliaments, whereas amalgamation might have given them dominance in none. The Marquess of Bute, for example, would have had little influence if his county had been joined to either Dunbarton or Argyll, whereas an independent Bute afforded him a nomination county. The settlement, however, provoked strong criticism from James Sinclair of Stempster and James Dunbar, the commissioners for Caithness, who claimed that their county was valued higher than Sutherland, which had not been partially disfranchised (*Acts of Scotland*, XI: 420). Their complaint, however, fell on deaf ears, and Sutherland retained permanent representation. The electorate of the shires remained as before the Union, and eligibility to stand for parliament was restricted to those entered on the voters' roll, and continued to exclude the eldest sons of peers. If an MP ceased to remain a qualified elector whilst a sitting member, he was in most cases permitted to remain in the House for the duration of the parliament (Wight: 259).

Table 2.3: Scottish Constituencies 1707–1832

A. The Royal Burghs (15 seats)

(The order in each group presented in terms of precedence on the roll of the Scottish Parliament)

1. Edinburgh.
2. Tain, Dingwall, Dornoch, Wick, Kirkwall.
3. Inverness, Nairn, Forres, Fortrose.
4. Elgin, Banff, Cullen, Kintore, Inverurie.
5. Aberdeen, Montrose, Brechin, Arbroath, Inverbervie.
6. Perth, Dundee, St Andrews, Cupar.
7. Anstruther Easter, Pittenweem, Crail, Anstruther Wester, Kilrenny.
8. Dysart, Kirkcaldy, Burntisland, Kinghorn.
9. Stirling, Inverkeithing, Dunfermline, Culross, Queensferry.
10. Glasgow, Dumbarton, Renfrew, Rutherglen.
11. Haddington, Jedburgh, Dunbar, North Berwick, Lauder.
12. Linlithgow, Selkirk, Lanark, Peebles.
13. Dumfries, Kirkcudbright, Annan, Lochmaben, Sanquhar.
14. Wigtown, Whithorn, New Galloway, Stranraer.
15. Ayr, Irvine, Rothesay, Inverary, Campbeltown.

B. The Counties (30 seats)

1. Aberdeen.	16. Kincardine.
2. Argyll.	17. Kirkcudbright.
3. Ayr.	18. Lanark.
4. Banff.	19. Linlithgow.
5. Berwick.	20. Nairn *alternating with* Cromarty.
6. Bute *alternating with* Caithness.	21. Orkney and Shetland.
7. Clackmannan *alternating with* Kinross.	22. Peebles.
8. Dumbarton.	23. Perth.
9. Dumfries.	24. Renfrew.
10. Edinburgh.	25. Ross.
11. Elgin.	26. Roxburgh.
12. Fife.	27. Selkirk.
13. Forfar.	28. Stirling.
14. Haddington.	29. Sutherland.
15. Inverness.	30. Wigtown.

A number of schemes were considered regarding the possible distribution of the fifiteen burghal seats. In the end parliament concentrated on two approaches. The first envisaged the grouping of burghs into three, presumably with the intention of returning five members from each group (*Acts of Scotland*, XI: 421);

while the second, favoured by the Commission, envisaged fifteen groups each returning a single member. The latter course was adopted without a division. Edinburgh was to form a constituency of its own, but the remaining 65 royal burghs were gathered into fourteen groups on a geographical basis, each containing four or five members. No consideration appears to have been given to the possible suppression of certain burghs, still less to the inclusion of burghs which were not royal. That the constituencies no longer had to support their member financially undoubtedly negated the former attractions of disfranchisement.

In Edinburgh the electoral process remained as before, with the 33 magistrates chosing the member, but elsewhere the system of grouping necessitated modifications to established procedures. Whereas each burgh had formerly elected a commissioner, the magistrates in each council now had to appoint one of their number an elector. The electors once chosen met together in the Presiding Burgh, (each burgh in the group fulfilling the role in a strict order of precedence based on the Scottish Parliamentary Roll), under the chairmanship of the elector from the Presiding Burgh. In the event of a tie the chairman exercised a casting vote: a provision which was very important in groups of four. Prior to the Union, the commissioner of a burgh, by tradition and enactment of the Convention of Royal Burghs in 1574, was required to be a trafficking merchant or indweller of the place he represented, and as late as 1661 petitions against contraventions of this act were successful (Terry, 1905: 58-9). In 1690, however, the commissioner for Stranraer was permitted to remain in parliament despite objections to his non-compliance with these regulations, and strict enforcement of the law in this matter fell into abeyance. Following the Treaty of Union an attempt was made to revive the former qualification, it being 'generally understood, that a person who was to represent a district should have previously been admitted a burgess of at least one of the burghs of which it was composed' (Wight: 404). In 1774, however, the convention was again overruled, when Sir Henry Dashwood was permitted to remain MP for the Wigtown group despite his not being otherwise associated with the burghs. Thus, it transpired that the member for a Scottish Royal Burgh grouping merely had to render the necessary oaths of allegiance to take his seat in the House of Commons, a property qualification not being required.

Superficially there was a certain attraction about the grouping of the Royal Burghs. As Rait remarked, 'it was natural that the problem of reducing the number of Scottish representatives should have been solved by a rough geographical grouping of the burghs' (Rait: 227), and regarded 'cantonment' (Marchmont: 445) as justified by the similarity of economic pursuits undertaken by burghs within particular groups. It also made possible the retention of a traditional feature of Scottish political life. The problem, however, was that geographical grouping negated the very *raison d'être* of burgh representation, because in this context it is mistaken to equate similarity of economic pursuit as evidence of mutual self-interest. Burghs had sought incorporation because their burgesses regarded prosperity as deriving from the exercise of monopoly over limited markets. Geographically proximate neighbours, therefore, were natural enemies, as was demonstrated by the lengths to which some burghs had gone to deny others the benefits of incorporation. It was a violence both to tradition and perceived self-interest that Wigtown should have been given the same member as Whithorn and Stranraer; that Fortrose should have been lumped with Inverness; that Wick should have been cantoned with the northern burghs who had so strenuously opposed her membership of the convention and parliament; or that Crail should find itself in the same constituency as Kilrenny and the two Anstruthers. Both the concept of grouping and particularly grouping by region undermined what had been the essential justification and character of burghal representation.

A more practical objection to cantonment was the strict adhesion to groups of four or five burghs, because it made almost no concession to the disparities of population size, rejecting the flexibility of the Cromwellian settlement, which had placed all thirteen Fife burghs into one constituency and had joined Glasgow to only two other royalties (Pryde, 1950: 48). Had the Scottish parliament adopted either the solution of the Protectorate, or, even better, a system of multi-member constituencies, as was discussed in 1707, then later reform or amendment could have been made either by varying the number of burghs in each group, or by reapportioning the number of members representing each constituency.

The more long-term problem resulting from cantonment was that it made possible the survival of burghs which ought to have been suppressed. The difficulties of Cromarty were by no means unique in the late seventeenth century, and it was only the extreme reluctance of the Convention, which was firmly opposed to the loss of taxable members, that prevented Kilrenny and Anstruther Wester resigning their status. *A Report of the State of Royal Burghs of Scotland, 1691,* commissioned by the Convention, was evidence of contemporary concern, and indicated that a considerable number of burghs were in severe financial straits. Dysart, for example, is described as 'altogether without trade... it is evident what a poor and distressed condition this poor place is in, and how unable they are even to bare a small proportion of the stent roll, the two parts of the burgh being either uninhabited or ruinous;' whilst Dingwall 'has no debt because they will not get credit, there being no visible way how creditors could be paid by the public...it is visible they must of necessity quit and resign their privileges, unless the Royal Burghs fall upon some way for the support...without which it...is impossible for them to send a Commissioner either to Parliament or Convention.' The grouping of burghs, combined with the removal of the obligation to meet the expenses of the MP, pushed such problems into the background, ensuring the survival and protection of exiguous burghs, thereby establishing a precedent which was to carry much weight in 1832 and compromise the cause of reform throughout the nineteenth century.

The constituency settlement at the Union was radical in that the number of parliamentary seats in Scotland was much reduced, but reactionary in that it turned aside from the principles which had informed the county amendments of 1690. If the grant of 45 seats to Scotland in the United Kingdom parliament implied the notion of proportionality between the nations, that principle did not apply to the distribution scheme. One is inclined, therefore, to agree that 'with every allowance, it is hard to avoid the conclusion that the Scots Parliament could have done better as regards both shires and burghs' (Pryde, 1950: 48). By establishing individual county members for all as against the need to amalgamate the smallest and increase the representation of the largest, and by masking the problem of indigent burghs in groupings, the constituency settlement of

1707 was hardly a reform. Nevertheless, the apportionment of the Union was to remain the essential basis of Scottish parliamentary representation until at least 1885.

What most recommended the constitutional settlement, at least from the perspective of the unionist commissioners, was that it ensured a successful passage of of the treaty as a whole through the Scottish parliament. Failure to balance the interests of each estate or to offend too many powerful individuals could have jeopardised the whole enterprise, as the Earl of Seafield candidly admitted to Godolphin:

> We have made some progress in the act of constitution. We have divided forty-five commissioners betwixt the shires and boroughs, whereof thirty are to represent shires and fifteen the boroughs. And we have so ordered it, that each shire has a representative, and for this end we have conjoined the six smallest into three; and these are to chuse alternately. We hope also to get the boroughs so cantoned, as that their fifteen representatives shall come from all corners of the Kingdom…that this affair also is like to terminate so well, that the enemies of the union will be disappointed; for they thought to have made extraordinary advantages by this great alteration, that is made in our constitution by the articles of the treaty (Marchmont: 445).

Perhaps the most important feature of the unreformed electoral system was the smallness of the electorate. In 1788, for example, there were only 2,662 voters in all the county constituencies, ranging from 205 in Ayrshire to only twelve in Bute and none at all in Shetland, (conjoined with Orkney), 'on account of the state of land valuation' (Adam: 1). The median number enfranchised in the county constituencies was a mere 74. It was a measure of the intimacy existing between electors and their MP in some counties, that in Kincardineshire, where in 1788 there were just over 50 voters, it was the custom of the member to entertain those present at election time to dinner at the Mill Inn, Stonehaven.

Most county electors were independent landed proprietors, but there were several counties in which blocks of voters, often liferenters, were beholden to one or two magnates. Twenty-two of the 34 electors in Sutherland, for example, were controlled by Lady Sutherland and the Earl of Gower; Sinclair of Ulbster held nine of the 23 franchises in Caithness; whilst the Earl of Fife and the Duke of Gordon shared 87 out of a 122 electors in Banffshire, and 77 of the 178 registered in neighbouring Aberdeenshire. George Graham of Kinross controlled sixteen of the 26 votes in Kinross; Lord Elphinstone and the Duke of Montrose influenced almost half the electorate of Dunbartonshire; Campbell of Calder decided eight of the 20 electoral preferences in Linlithgow; and the Duke of Hamilton a third of those in Lanarkshire. There was a similarly small number of participants in the burgh contests, where only the councillors took part, and then, with the exception of Edinburgh, only indirectly through the selection of electors.

With such a small number of voters it was possible and necessary in a system where the determination of an election could hinge on the behaviour of one or two people, for party managers to focus their attention on individuals rather than groups. In 1788, for example, William Adam and Henry Erskine commissioned a report on all Scottish county voters in their attempt to strengthen the Whig opposition to Pitt and Dundas. Amongst the details considered worthy of mention were occupation, wealth, marital status, family connection, ambitions, personal obligations, local political leaders to whom the elector might defer, and general political disposition. Thus, for example, one Charles Hunter of Burnside, Forfarshire, was summarised as possessing a 'Moderate fortune. A large family. One of them sent to India by Paterson of Huntly who will have influence. Mr Douglas may also have interest. A half-pay Lieutenant in the Navy. Wants a Customhouse Yacht' (Adam: 152); John Davidson of Haltree WS, a Midlothian voter, was described as being 'obliged to Mr Dundas, to whom he is Deputy-Keeper to the Signet. The Crown Agent. Very rich. An only son in the Army. Pushing for a Clerkship of Session through the Dukes of Montagu and Buccleugh' (Adam: 112); and Sir James Grant of Grant, Aberdeenshire was presented as 'Very independent. His son by compromise with Lord Fife to come in for Moray. The son a lawyer. The family influenced by Lord Findlater, to whom they succeed, and by Henry McKenzie, Attorney in Exchequer, who married a sister of Sir James's. Of great weight and respect in the north' (Adam:11).

The means of translating such information into votes was patronage. Although the bulk of patronage lay in the hands of the administration in the form of judicial appointments, commissions in the army, chairs in the universities and treasury control over the allocation of posts in the customs and excise, jobs not always in the gift of the government party included cadetships in the East India Company, promotions in the Royal Navy and the appointment of Kirk ministers (Sunter). Additionally, a wealthy proprietor could have at his disposal positions associated with his private interests that could be used to obligate electors. Thus, while the system was biased towards the administration, it was still possible for supporters of the opposition to sustain an interest. Despite many of the positions available carrying low levels of remuneration, the relative poverty experienced by many of the restricted Scottish electorate combined with the fecundity of their families to increase the importance of patronage and the currency of even the most minor posts on the nomenclatura. Added to the affective ties of kinship and marriage, patronage translated social obligation into a formidable political weapon.

The importance of patronage to the Scottish electors served to strengthen the dependence of Scottish members on the administration. Under the skilful political management of Lord Ilay and Henry Dundas, who judiciously distributed jobs in return for support in the lobbies, ministerial manipulation of Scottish representation was particularly evident. If MPs resisted the blandishments of the government, their voters could always be bribed, particularly the burgh electorate, who had a markedly less developed sense of gentlemanly obligation to their MPs for services rendered than county voters (Sunter: Chapter 10). Not without justification did Francis Jeffrey remark during the Reform debates of 1832, 'The Representatives of Scotland [are]...of the court rather than what is called the country party, always found supporting the Minister and swelling the ranks of his majority' (*Hansard*, 1831: XII, 354).

Small electorates also meant that the outcome of contested elections could hinge on technicalities and procedural coups. In the counties, for example, the electoral roll was revised annually by existing electors at a Michaelmas Head Court, and at election time the return of a member was immediately preceded by a final revision of the roll. In managing an interest it was clearly important to control the registration process, and particularly so on election day. Such meetings began with the last elected member, (and failing him another in a strict order of precedence established in 1681), in the chair, who would supervise the election of a preses (convener) to conduct the rest of the business (Sunter: 154). The preses could then decide the order in which new applications for the franchise should be considered. By initially examining those favourable to his faction, the preses could turn a slim majority (perhaps depending on his casting vote) into a stronger one, which could then control the election by rejecting a significant proportion of applications from the opposition. At the Peebles by-election of 1732, where the two opposing factions went into the election meeting with ten votes each, the preses was determined by the casting vote of a doubtfully-appointed sheriff clerk. By controlling the revision of the register, the preses ensured his candidate eventually won the election by nine votes to fourteen (Sunter: 154-9). A similar process in the burghs could even turn a majority into a minority. At an election in the Inverkeithing group, the candidate supported by the presiding burgh was in a minority of three to two following the determinations of the various councils. At the meeting of the electoral college, however, the convener, (always from the presiding burgh), refused to accept the credentials of the elector from one of the majority burghs, and then used his casting vote, following a tied election, to deny their candidate (Sunter: Chapter 12). Other stratagems, apart from bribery, such as arrest for debt, kidnapping, (Sunter: 183,185) and even armed intervention (Ferguson, 1959) directed against councillors and nominated electors at crucial points in the electoral process, also added a certain piquancy to the electoral culture of the Royal Burghs.

Pre-Reform Scottish MPs were perhaps drawn more heavily than English members from the ranks of the landowning aristocratic families because the economic changes in the latter half of the eighteenth century and beyond made little impact on the social composition of the electorate (Foster). As late as the early 1830s, the lower house included FW Grant (Elginshire), W Gordon (Aberdeenshire), Hugh Arbuthnott (Kincardineshire), Lord Montagu Graham (Dunbartonshire), Anthony Maitland (Berwickshire), Sir Alexander Hope (Linlithgowshire), HF Scott (Roxburghshire), Charles Douglas (Lanarkshire), WR Maule (Forfarshire) and Freddy Leveson-Gower (Sutherland), who were all either the sons or brothers of members of the House of Lords; and others, such as Sir George Clerk (Edinburghshire) and James Balfour (Haddingtonshire) were married to the daughters of aristocrats. Alongside them were representatives of well established landed families such as the Sinclairs of Ulbster (Caithness), the MacLeods of Cadboll (Sutherland), the Adams of Blair Adam (Clackmannan), and the Agnews of Lochnaw (Wigtownshire), whilst the rest, including most burgh members, were returned because they enjoyed the backing of the nobility. It was not insignificant that the key to the voting behaviour of Scottish county members during the debates on the reform acts lies with the preferences of their relatives or patrons in the Upper House.

Although the unreformed electoral system in Scotland has been harshly criticised (Porritt), there is little to suggest it was significantly worse than elsewhere in the United Kingdom and Ireland (Ferguson, 1957; Sunter). In some respects, particularly in the balance between burgh and county representation, the Scottish system was arguably superior. Despite the tendency of Scottish members to support the ministry, the relationship was bargained rather than dictated, and both members and the government needed to respond to the needs of their constituents in order to retain their support. Some of the more negative aspects of the system derived largely from the Union. The massive reduction in the number of Scottish MPs negated the enlightened reforms of 1690, which had related county representation to size, and the cantonment of the burghs, coupled with relief from having to support the MP, removed the pressure on smaller burghs to seek disfranchisement. Indeed, it was not to be until the passing of the Third Reform Act that the apportionment of seats began to reflect the enlightenment of the late seventeenth century. The Union was also accompanied by an increasingly careless attitude towards the enforcement of existing electoral provisions, so that despite the Act of 1743, the degeneracy of the English system infected Scotland, too. The weakness in the Scottish system derived less from corruption than the narrowness of its franchise, for which the Scottish parliament was entirely responsible. Thus, at a crucial point in the economic and cultural development of modern Scotland large sections of even the upper middle class were denied active participation in the political process, and although that was to be formally remedied in 1832, it produced a middle class culture in which the arts of political leadership had a low priority, a deficiency which continues to haunt the Scottish polity.

Notes

1 The Lord Chancellor's attitude, recorded by the Jacobite Lockhart as 'despising and contemning,' was intended to dam Seafield, *Lockhart Papers*, 222.
2 It being the duty of the Royal Burgh corporations to pay the expenses of their commissioners to the Convention and Parliament.

References

Acts of the Parliament of Scotland, Vol. XI, 1702–1707, Edinburgh, 1824.
Adam, Sir CE, *A View of the Political State of Scotland in the Last Century*, Edinburgh, 1887.
Ballard, A, 'The Theory of the Scottish Burgh,' *Scottish Historical Review*, Vol. XIII, 1916.
Defoe, D, *The History of the Union between England and Scotland,* London, 1786.
Ferguson, W, *Electoral Law and Procedure in Eighteenth and Early Nineteenth Century Scotland* (Ph.D., Glasgow, 1957).
Ferguson, W, 'Dingwall Burgh Politics and the Parliamentary Franchise in the Eighteenth Century,' *Scottish Historical Review*, Vol. XXXVIII, 1959.
Hansard
Lockhart, G, *The Lockhart Papers,* London, 1817.
Mackie, JD, and Pryde, GS, *Estate of Burgesses in the Scots Parliament and its Relation to the Convention of Royal Burghs*, St Andrews, 1923.
Marchmont, AH, *A Selection from the Papers of the Earls of Marchmont*, London, 1831.
Pagan, T, *The Convention of the Royal Burghs of Scotland*, Glasgow, 1926.
Parliamentary Papers, *Reports from Commissioners*, Vol. XXIII, Session 1836, appendix, *A Report of the State of Royal Burghs of Scotland, 1691*, pp. 19–79.
Porritt, E & A, *The Unreformed House of Commons*, London, 1903.
Pryde, GS, *The Burghs of Scotland: A Critical List*, London, 1965.

Pryde, GS, *The Treaty of Union of Scotland and England*, London, 1950.

Rait, RS, *The Parliaments of Scotland*, Glasgow, 1924.

Smout, TC, *A History of the Scottish People, 1560–1830*, Glasgow, 1969.

Sunter, RM, *Patronage and Politics in Scotland, 1707–1832*, Edinburgh, 1986.

Terry, CS, *The Cromwellian Union*, Edinburgh, 1902.

Terry, CS, *The Scottish Parliament: Its Constitution and Procedure, 1603–1707*, Glasgow, 1905.

Wight, A, *Inquiry into the Rise and Progress of Parliament, chiefly in Scotland, and a complete System of Law concerning the Election of Representatives from Scotland to the Parliament of Great Britain*, Edinburgh, 1784.

3 The Reforms of 1832

There is no doubt that the parliamentary Reform Acts of 1832, designed to extend the franchise to 'Men of Property and Intelligence' (*P.G.Stat:* 1832, cap 65), occupy a critical place in British constitutional development. At the time they were recognised as marking a major change from the past, and from a modern perspective the point from which the democratisation of the House of Commons began. In Scotland, the psychological impact was such that a leading reformer, Henry Cockburn, following the first bill's publication wrote in his diary: 'it is impossible to exaggerate the ecstasy of Scotland, where to be sure it is like liberty given to slaves: we are to be brought out of the house of bondage, out of the land of Egypt' (Cockburn 1874a: 5).

The reforms, however, were also modest, so modest that Moore has chosen to regard the reform act in England and Wales more as a 'cure' to protect the landed interest rather than a 'concession' to the demands of new social forces (Moore, 1961; 1966; 1976); and Gash has argued that 'there was scarcely a feature of the old unreformed system that could not be found still in existence after 1832' (Gash: x). The new franchise enrolled barely 3 per cent of the population, many small constituencies still remained, and representatives of the traditional ruling classes continued to dominate the Commons.

The paradox applicable to Britain as a whole was no less true of Scotland, where Ferguson concluded both that 'The Scottish Reform Act... was more revolutionary than its English counterpart,' and that sloppy drafting of the bill 'introduced as many evils as it cured' (Ferguson: 106, 105). Proportionately fewer Scotsmen than Englishmen were enfranchised, and there was virtually no suppression of exiguous burghs north of the border. It was more a reflection on the old dispensation than the radical character of the new order that reform in Scotland could be be squared with Cockburn's Liberation Theology or regarded as revolutionary.

The shape of Scottish parliamentary reform was determined by three main factors: the indifference of the government, the hostility of Scottish MPs, and the more positive, (though not always consistent, decisive, or well thought through), contributions of Henry Cockburn, the Solicitor General, Francis Jeffrey, the Lord Advocate, and Thomas Kennedy of Dunure, MP for the Ayr Burghs.

With reform perceived at the time to be of fundamental constitutional importance, it was inevitable that it presented considerable problems to the government in terms of parliamentary management. Not only did England and Wales, Ireland and Scotland each require its own separate measure, but opposition in both houses necessitated the introduction of three bills for each country within the space of a year, precipitated a general election in the early summer of 1831, and a constitutional crisis in the spring of 1832. Consequently, the government was forced to concentrate on its basic priorities. Of central concern to the administration were the proposals for England and Wales, for their representation was not only by far the largest component in the Commons, but that most in need of change, and where redistribution, as necessitous as a new franchise, involved the suppression and creation of a large number of seats.[1] The shape of reform in Ireland, where the increasingly irreconcilable forces of nationalism and Protestant ascendancy both had somehow to be placated, also required much thought and skilful handling following Catholic emancipation (Gash: esp. Ch. 11).

The reform of Scottish representation, by contrast, was of least importance for the Whig administration. The 45 Scots MPs constituted less than 7 per cent of all members in the Commons, less than half those from Ireland, so that provided some changes could be made to Scotland's discredited franchise, the most arcane of the four nations, only minimal amendments were absolutely necessary to the constituency settlement of 1707. Consequently, Scottish members exercised considerable influence over redistribution north of the border. It was a measure of the low priority given to reform in Scotland, that while seven full days were devoted to the first reading of the first English and Welsh bill, that for Scotland was introduced and disposed of within an hour late at night.

Scottish MPs, largely due to the rigidity of the unreformed franchise, were more antagonistic to reform that the other national groups. In England, the expansion of the old freeholder franchise in urban areas was already undermining the landed interest in industrial counties. Consequently, agricultural proprietors were attracted to a reform which would separate the new manufacturing centres from their rural hinterlands (Moore, 1961, 1966). The exclusivity of the electorate in Scotland, however, meant there were no such pressures on her county members, so that reform for them had mostly negative aspects. As Sir George Clerk, the member for Midlothian, remarked:

> The Scotch Representation [was] not likely to be led away by popular influence as the members for the English counties, who were dependent for their seats upon the manufacturing interest. The body of Scotch Representatives...was most useful... as a check upon the increasing democratic influence (*Hansard* 7: 549).

The Scottish MPs returned to the parliament of 1830-31 emerged as the most implacable opponents of the government's reform legislation. On the second reading of the first English and Welsh bill they divided 13:16 against, or 17:28 against, taking into account pairings, tellers and absentees. The English and Welsh, by contrast, were only marginally disposed to reject the measure (238:241), while the Irish, by coming out 53:26 in favour, ensured it entered committee by a single vote. Even more telling, Scottish members voted 25:16 in favour of Colonel Gascoyne's amendment that the number of seats accorded to England and Wales be not reduced, thereby not only denying Scotland extra representation, but securing defeat for the bill and precipitating a general election. Burgh members, in dividing 4:11 against the English bill on second reading, and 10:5 in favour of Gascoyne's amendment, were even more hostile than their shire colleagues. Had the Scots divided evenly on the amendment, it would have fallen. Following the general election of 1831, however, government influence succeeded in securing an 11:4 majority in favour of reform amongst the burgh MPs, but even that was insufficient to produce a pro-ministerial contingent overall. On the three crucial votes relating to reform after the 1831 election,

Scots MPs broke either 17:13 or 18:12 against. Only on the second reading of the second Scottish bill would a full attendance of Scots members have produced a majority in favour of reform, and then merely by a single vote.

The most progressive influence on reform in higher political circles was Henry Cockburn, who was primarily responsible, in conjunction with a government committee comprising Lord John Russell, the Earl of Durham, Lord Duncannon and Sir James Graham, for preparing the Scottish bill. His main priority was to ensure that eligibility to vote was as extensive in Scotland as in England and Wales. He also favoured the institution of independent constituencies by breaking the domination of close corporations over burgh elections, the ending of nomination counties, and increased representation for the new industrial areas. Unfortunately for his allies, he was not a member of parliament, and had to watch the progress of the legislation from the isolation of Edinburgh. He was, however, assisted in Westminster by Kennedy, with whom he sustained a steady flow of correspondence (Cockburn, 1874: b).

The task of piloting the Scottish bills through parliament fell to Francis Jeffrey. He had had a distinguished career in the law, becoming Dean of the Faculty of Advocates, but it was as co-founder and later editor of the *Edinburgh Review* for more than 20 years that his reputation was acclaimed. He had no experience of Westminster before January 1831, when at the age of 57 he entered the Commons as Lord Advocate and member for the Perth Group. His election was overthrown in March, forcing him to repair to Malton, a Yorkshire burgh in the pocket of Lord Fitzwilliam. In the subsequent general election he was returned for both Malton and the Perth Group, appropriately choosing to represent the latter. Such problems were not assisted by illness, which for a time forced him to hand over his bill to Lord Althorp, primarily responsible for the English legislation. When in the House, Jeffrey discovered that neither he nor his cause was sufficiently distinguished to catch the Speaker's eye before the third day on the opening debate on the first English bill. There seems little doubt that the combination of inexperience, infirmity, election difficulties, the hostility of Scottish backbenchers, and ministerial indifference, rendered Jeffrey, mightily impressed by the difficulties which lay before him, vulnerable to compromise. Consequently, the progress of the Scottish measure was accompanied by an increasing political estrangement between Jeffrey and Cockburn.

For Cockburn, as he commenced his task of constructing the rudiments of a Scottish bill in the autumn of 1830, the reform of the franchise was of central importance. When he met the government coordinating committee in December 1830, he was elated to find that 'we had no difficulty whatever in adopting the £10 franchise, after which everything else resolved itself in mere detail and machinery,' (Cockburn, 1874 a: 1). Briefly, the bill which was to be finally passed in 1832 extended the vote to £10 householders in the burghs, and to £10 owners, 57-year £10 leaseholders, or 19-year £50 leaseholders in the shires. The changes emancipated the middle class in the burghs, and in the counties appeared not only to transfer the basis of the franchise from mere superiors to actual possessors of land, but also to rest considerable influence in village £10 owners, who could not be easily controlled by landed proprietors. It was not surprising, therefore, that Jeffrey should claim 'that no shred or rag, no jot or tittle of the old system was to be left' (Ferguson: 105).

Given the centrality of the franchise to Cockburn's objectives, remarkably scant attention was paid to the problem of translating provisions that derived from forms of landholding in England to the Scottish context, where patterns of tenure deriving from Scots feudal practice prevailed. As a result, terms were used in the legislation that were at times meaningless, obscure and mutually exclusive when applied to the Scottish situation. Considerable technical problems were faced by the registration courts, and the way was opened for serious abuse in the counties. Concluding that 'it is indeed the worst drafted of all the acts which deal with the representation of Scotland,' Ferguson places the principle blame on 'Jeffrey and Cockburn because the main defects of the bill derive...from actual ignorance of the law of Scotland... The authors were... talented men of letters and political theorists rather than practical lawyers or politicians' (Ferguson: 106, 113).

Although Scottish backbenchers were generally agreed that the electoral system in the burghs was beyond redemption, and were tactically receptive to urban claims for a wider franchise, there was a great fear that the £10 owners in the counties would swamp traditional landed interests. Sir William Rae, MP for Bute, and a flamboyant Lord Advocate in previous Tory administrations, 'regretted the extension of the franchise because it was well known that Scotchmen seldom came together in a multitude without causing bloodshed, or at least a riot.'[2] William Ramsay (Stirlingshire) bluntly described the Scottish bill as 'too sweeping and decidedly revolutionary' (*Hansard* 7: 540); while Colonel Lindsay (Fife) objected that 'by its provisions respecting the £10 householders it would throw all power into the hands of manufacturers' (*Hansard* 7: 551). It was, however, almost inconceivable that the English members would permit Scotland a more restrictive franchise than they had imposed upon themselves, or that the ministry would permit what they considered a central principle of the bill to be compromised. Consequently, although the new franchise was at the root of Scottish backbench opposition to the reform process, it ceased to be a matter for serious debate after the second reading. The major influence of Scottish members was to be exercised over redistribution.

Though it has been demonstrated that redistribution in England and Wales failed to remove many anomalies of the old system, at least it can be recognised as a serious attempt to redress the grotesque imbalance of representation between north and south. Furthermore, even if the government unwisely chose the 1821 census as its statistical guide, it indicated, nevertheless, a willingness to relate in some measure the location of seats to the distribution of the population. The early (and critical) development of the Scottish legislation, by contrast, suggests that the reformers' obsession with the franchise was such that they failed to recognise the significance of redistribution, which was vitally important to their aim of establishing independent constituencies and gaining proper recognition for the new urban centres. Consequently, they failed to press, (even if they had failed in the attempt), for an objective measure whereby weak burgh groupings could have been systematically suppressed and the smaller counties amalgamated. Such indifference was all the more remarkable in the context of late autumn 1831, when it was not at all certain that Scotland would have more members. In the absence of a clear policy, the approach of the reformers was characterised by prejudice and reaction rather than principle and initiative. Jeffrey failed in the Commons to offer any convincing rationale behind his proposed constituency settlement, (there was none), thereby exposing the measure more openly to the opponents of reform and the compromises of political accommodation.

The approach of the anti-reform Scottish MPs, if at times confusing, was relatively consistent. In the parliament of 1830-31 they were against any change to the constitution, even to the extent of getting more seats for Scotland. After the general election of 1831, recognising that radical change to the franchise was unavoidable, they sought to minimise its impact through the redistribution provisions. They attempted to protect the shires against the burghs and towns by preserving the existing burgh groupings, and by throwing the new manufacturing centres into them. At the same time, they upheld the principle of individual county representation, and advanced the claims of the eight largest shires for second members. Under their proposals Scotland would have had 61 rather than 53 MPs after 1832. The strength of this policy was that it had considerable attraction for the pro-government county Whigs, because they had no more cause than the Tories to promote the interests of industrial areas. Lack of clarity on the part of the government only served to enhance the credibility of their opponents' position.

The initial attitude of the reformers towards redistribution was expressed neither by Cockburn nor Jeffrey, but in a memorandum sent to Lord John Russell by Kennedy in November, 1830, which assumed that Scotland would still only have 45 seats. His most radical proposal was for the suppression of the Anstruther Group to find a separate seat for Dundee. For the rest, Kennedy wanted an end to alternating counties, suggesting the amalgamation of Caithness with Sutherland, Ross with Cromarty, Elgin with Nairn, and Bute with either Renfrew or Dunbarton. Such a settlement would have released a second seat, which he proposed to award to a joint constituency of Edinburgh/Leith (Cockburn, 1874b: 258-266).

Kennedy's proposals, however, hardly attempted to deal with the problem created by the growth of manufacturing centres in the west. In December 1830, Cockburn suggested an amendment whereby the Tain, Anstruther, Wigtown, Haddington and Ayr groupings would all be suppressed to enfranchise Paisley, Greenock, Leith, Kilmarnock and Glasgow (Cockburn, 1874b: 273). This was prompted not so much by first principles, but from the discovery that in several Royal Burghs there were fewer £10 householders than councillors! Cockburn's lack of consistency was revealed a few days later when he produced a solution worthy of the most dedicated Tory: 'I begin to suspect that the best way of removing the objection of the towns drowning the counties, will be by making a new allotment of burghs, and throwing most of the towns and large villages into these districts; e.g. let Kilmarnock vote with the Ayr Burghs' (Cockburn, 1874b: 278). By February, 1831, less than a month before the publication of the bill, the Solicitor General had come to the conclusion that the only solution was the creation of more seats in Scotland, and urged Kennedy to procure them, as well as ensuring the junction of Selkirkshire and Peeblesshire, and 'the sinking of Caithness in the belly of Stafford' (Cockburn, 1874b: 293). In such a manner the great enterprise of Scottish redistribution began its tortuous journey.

Although the bill presented to parliament in March 1831 reflected the caution of Jeffrey, the influence of Cockburn and Kennedy seemed evident in the five extra seats found to enfranchise the new urban centres without causing severe retrenchment elsewhere. Even so, the government proposed to amalgamate the counties of Peebles and Selkirk, Ross and Cromarty, Clackmannan and Kinross, and to throw the Anstruther burghs into Fife. Edinburgh was to gain a second member, and a new district conjured out of Leith, Portobello and Musselburgh. Glasgow was to be separated and given two representatives, Aberdeen and Dundee were to be detached from their existing groups, and Paisley and Greenock raised to parliamentary status for the first time as single member seats. Kilmarnock was to be added to the remnants of the Glasgow Group; 'the thriving port of Peterhead' was to replace Aberdeen in a reconstituted Montrose District; Falkirk was to be elevated to lead the old Linlithgow Group; and Cromarty was to be revived to strengthen the Wick Burghs. The most progressive aspects of these somewhat conservative proposals were the introduction of joint shire constituencies in the place of alternating counties, the granting of parliamentary status to non-Royal Burghs, and the rejection of the principle that royalty should confer automatic representation. Indeed, all the burgh constituencies were re-designated as Parliamentary Burghs, and their boundaries frequently extended beyond the jurisdictions of the Royal Burgh corporations. Cockburn, who at last was beginning to recognise the importance of redistribution wrote not a trifle disarmingly of this scheme:

> The main defect of the plan consists in not extinguishing more districts of towns, and throwing the burghs into counties, even though this had led to giving some counties two members. Every member should be member for one known and visible place; but this is one of the many sacrifices we have been obliged to make of principle to management. Every encroachment on vested right has produced formidable opposition, and we have been obliged to leave out, to bring in, and to classify towns, and to keep them off counties, merely to avoid shipwreck (Cockburn, 1874a: 12).

The anti-reformers, led by Sir William Rae, attacked Jeffrey for his failure to justify specific proposals, and impugned the integrity of his motives. Sir William suggested that no reason had been offered for the suppression of the Anstruther Group, and, while he agreed with the treatment of Glasgow and Edinburgh, felt Inverness had a better claim for separate representation than the Leith District, which in his opinion was part of the capital. He 'also objected to the union of Peebles and Selkirk' (*Hansard*, 1831: III, 323), and to the fusion of Bute with Dunbarton. Though he concurred that Clackmannan and Kinross did not justify individual representation, he felt there were historical precedents for the former being associated with Stirlingshire and the latter with Fife. He further suggested that the larger counties should each have a second member. Sir William's purpose, however, was not to offer constructive criticism, but to demonstrate the partisan nature of the proposals, for while the Tories would lose two seats through the union of Peebles with Selkirk and Bute with Dunbarton, the treatment of Kinross and Clackmannan was designed to present a Whig nomination seat to the Adams of Blair Adam and Baron Abercromby. The greatest weakness in the Lord Advocate's armour, however, was his failure to combine Sutherland with Caithness. Sir William stated that he personally had no objection to seats open to nomination by a peer, 'but those who brought in the bill did object...and it would be consistent with their principle to have weakened it by uniting Caithness to Sutherland' (*Hansard*, 1831: III, 323). A shortage of both principle and management would probably have threatened Jeffrey's proposals had the bill reached its committee stage.

In the period between the first and second Scottish bills, (March to September, 1831), the pressure to preserve the Anstruther Group and resistance to the union of Peebles and Selkirk counties increased. The intended amalgamation of the border counties was opposed not only by Tories, but by Whigs who were against a reduction in county representation. Furthermore, a powerful lobby was mounted in favour of an independent constituency for Perth, and another pressed for university seats. Cockburn was fearful that Jeffrey would sacrifice Leith and Greenock to these demands in order to secure votes in the Lords, because the Perth, Peebles-Selkirk and Anstruther lobbies had already suggested to the Solicitor General that Edinburgh and Leith could be married to placate their demands. Cockburn's conclusion was that 'there is but one course for avoiding confusion and obstruction arising from all this felonious concession, which is to concede nothing;' and regarded it the duty of the government to 'protect that part of the country which, from being most defenceless, has the strongest claim on its protection.' He pronounced himself *'utterly'* opposed to the proposed amendments regarding Leith, because the burgh was Edinburgh's 'natural foe' (Cockburn, 1874b: 327, 337). The Solicitor General, nevertheless, was not without his own refinements. He was anxious that parts of Perthshire sympathetic to the Whigs be annexed by Clackmannan and Kinross, that Port Glasgow be raised to support a weak Wigtown District, and that Rutherglen should fall into Glasgow, making way for Hamilton to enter the putative Kilmarnock District of Burghs.

The government sought to resolve the conflicting pressures by awarding Scotland three more seats. By restoring the number of county constituencies to 30 it proved possible to maintain the separation of Peebles and Selkirk, and to release Bute from the clutches of Dunbarton, although it was to be united to the Cowal district of Argyll.[3] In consequence, Rothesay, the county town of Bute, was to lose its parliamentary status, and the Royal Burghs of Peebles and Selkirk were also to be thrown into their respective counties, allowing room for Airdrie in the Linlithgow Group. The third additional seat was to establish an independent Perth, whose former associates, St Andrews and Cupar, were to gain the threatened Anstruther Group. Other changes were relatively minor. Peterhead was to be transferred to the new Elgin District, and be replaced in the putative Montrose Burghs by Forfar from the disbanded Perth Group. Port Glasgow was to be annexed by its neighbour, Greenock, to keep it out of Renfrewshire; parts of Stirlingshire and Perthshire were to be added to Kinross and Clackmannan, while the Nairnshire district of Ferintosh was to be pushed into Ross and Cromarty. The university claims were ignored.[4] Although the progressive elements in the first bill were preserved, the changes marked a major victory for conservative influences, because the three new seats had been won for the forces of county reaction and not for the new towns.

Despite the concession made by the ministry in the draft of the second bill, they failed to placate the opponents of reform, who took the gesture as a sign of weakness and pressed for more. Tory members objected quite fairly that the dismemberment of Perthshire and the addition of Cowal to Bute were no more than attempts to strengthen the Whig interest in Kinross and Clackmannan and to weaken theirs in Bute. Nor was the ministry comforted by the indisposition of Jeffrey, which forced Lord Althorp, custodian of the English measure, to assume responsibility for the Scottish bill. Mercifully, the Lord's rejection of the English bill in October 1831 curtailed further consideration of its Scottish counterpart.

The most instructive digression during the aborted progress of the second Scottish bill was an amendment presented by the anti-reformer, Sir George Murray, MP for Perthshire. It proposed that the eight Scottish counties with populations over 100,000 should each receive an additional member, so raising for the first time the fundamental question of how many seats Scotland ought to have, and, by implication, the basis of their internal allocation. Sir George claimed that because reform had broken the 1707 constitutional settlement, the size of Scotland's representation required fundamental reconsideration. He argued that his request for 61 seats was quite modest. Scotland was entitled to 59 on the basis of taxation, and 85 on account of her population, assuming an English and Welsh contingent of 500. More specifically, he observed that the claims of the large Scottish counties were hardly excessive when Rutland still retained two members. It was a skilful ploy. It enabled the opponents of reform to display cheap patriotism, and exposed the muddled approach of the government. Lord Althorp made no attempt to resort to arithmetic. As Scotland's representation had not been fixed by any firm principle in 1707, he held there was no reason to do so in 1831, and that the noble intentions of his critics would be more credible had they themselves shown some concern for the under-representation of the manufacturing interest. Their position, he countered, was no more consistent than his, because they had been vehemently hostile to any reform whatsoever. Certainly, the reluctance of the Scottish anti-reformers to discuss internal redistribution served to blunt the force of Sir George's attack and defeat his amendment.

The rejection of the English bill by the Lords failed to encourage a more rational discussion of Scottish redistribution in the light of the debate on Sir George Clerk's motion. Rather it weakened the will of the government to resist the more atavistic forces. Faced with demands from Bute to be rid of Cowal, for Elgin to be separated from Nairn, and the desire of the Orcadians and Shetlanders to be dissociated, Lord Althorp, by the end of November 1831, was giving serious thought to the revival of alternating counties by linking Bute with Shetland, Nairn with Cromarty, and Orkney with either Caithness or Sutherland. The news drove Cockburn near to despair. He urged Kennedy and Lord Abercromby to alert the convalescing Jeffrey that such amendments would create a host of nomination counties and imperil the structure of the whole scheme. Even the return of Jeffrey to the fray did little to revive the sagging spirits of the Scots reformers as the Lord Advocate increasingly eschewed contact with Cockburn. In a letter to Kennedy at Christmas, however, a more optimistic Lord Minto expressed his belief that the bill was still intact, but he would 'toss Jeffrey in a blanket' if the rumours of alternating counties proved true (Cockburn, 1874b: 369-70).

In the event, the only change from its predecessor in the third Scottish bill, presented in January 1832, was the severance of the connection between Greenock and Port Glasgow, the latter being return to Renfrewshire. Before the second reading, however, Jeffrey acquiesced in the return of Cowal to Argyll,[5] a *quid pro quo*, perhaps, for the continued dismemberment of Perthshire. Attempts in committee to renew the association of Greenock and Port Glasgow were rejected on the grounds it would give Glasgow's merchants too much influence in Greenock; but a motion to place Port Glasgow in the new Kilmarnock District was carried without a division. The only further changes accepted included the replacement of Rothesay by Oban in the Ayr District, and the addition of Hamilton to the Falkirk Burghs.

The most significant aspect of the closing stages of the bill was an amendment moved by the anti-reformer, Alexander Pringle, MP for Selkirkshire, 'That the classification of boroughs [sic] of Scotland be referred to a Select and Special Committee' (*Hansard*, 1831–2: XIII, 741), because it questioned for the first time since 1707 the basis on which burgh groupings were determined. Pringle thought, for example, that the continued presence of Campbeltown and Inverary in the Ayr Burghs was somewhat anomalous, as was the exclusion of Kirkcudbright from the Wigtown group.[6] He withdrew his proposition on the Lord Advocate showing no interest. As with the more lengthy debate on Sir George Murray's motion, it indicated a deep reluctance on the part of both ministers and backbenchers, reformers and anti-reformers, to discuss Scottish redistribution in any fundamental or systematic way.

If the opponents of reform in Scotland had been forced to concede much over the franchise, they and their more conservative allies amongst the reformers emerged as substantial victors on the question of redistribution (Figure 3a). They preserved all fourteen burgh groupings and 30 seats for the counties; lost only Rothesay, Peebles and Selkirk from the list of burghs; secured the removal of Kilmarnock, Port Glasgow, Falkirk, Airdrie, Hamilton, Cromarty, Oban and Peterhead from their counties without the creation of extra burgh constituencies to accommodate them; and ensured that the new seats required for Edinburgh, Leith District (whose burghs were removed from Midlothian), Aberdeen, Dundee, Glasgow, Greenock and Paisley, were found from England. Even the Perth burgh constituency, in effect a creation of the anti-reformers because it denied a burgh seat to more deserving cases, was provided by liberation south of the border. Despite the annexation of Nairn by Elgin and Cromarty by Ross, and the junction of Clackmannan and Kinross together with bits of Perthshire and Stirlingshire, the problem of small county constituencies remained essentially untouched. Not only did Selkirk, Peebles and Sutherland retain separate representation, but Bute and Caithness actually had theirs enhanced through the acquisition of permanent separate seats.

The System

The Burgh Franchise

It was in the burghs that the reformed franchise had its greatest impact, removing control over representation from self-appointing town councillors, and making the £10 Resident as True Owner or Occupant 'either as proprietor, Tenant or Life-renter of a House, Warehouse, Counting house, shop, or other building…of the Yearly Value of Ten Pounds' *(P.G.Stat:* 1832, cap 65) the basis of the new dispensation. Those claiming the vote as Occupants were to have paid any taxes due for settlement before 6 April, to have been in occupation for

Figure 3a: Summary of Scottish Constituency Distribution, 1832–1868

A. Burghs

(Between 1707 and 1832 when the Presiding Burgh in any group changed at each election, it was customary for the group to be named after the Presiding Burgh e.g. Aberdeen Group, then Montrose Group, Brechin Group etc.)

1. Remaining the same: Edinburgh, and the Districts of Dumfries, Kirkcaldy, Haddington, Inverness, Stirling, Wigtown.
2. Newly created: Greenock, Paisley and the Leith District (Leith, Portobello, Musselburgh).
3. Amended:

1707–1832	1832–1868	1707–1832	1832–1868
(a) Aberdeen	(a) Aberdeen	(e) Glasgow	(f) Glasgow
Montrose	(b) Montrose District	Dumbarton	(g) Kilmarnock Dist.
Brechin	Brechin	Renfrew	Dumbarton
Arbroath	Arbroath	Rutherglen	Renfrew
Inverbervie	Inverbervie		Rutherglen
	Forfar (ex-Perth)		Port Glasgow
(b) Ayr	(c) Ayr District	(f) Perth	(h) Perth
Irvine	Irvine	Dundee	(i) Dundee
Rothesay	(Rothesay	St Andrews	(j) St Andrews Dist.
Inverary	Suppressed)	Cupar	Cupar
Campbeltown	Inverary	Forfar	(Forfar to
	Campbeltown		Montrose Dist.)
	Oban		
(c) Elgin	(d) Elgin District	(g) Anstruther E.	Anstruther E.
Banff	Banff	Anstruther W.	Anstruther W.
Cullen	Cullen	Pittenweem	Pittenweem
Kintore	Kintore	Crail	Crail
Inverurie	Inverurie	Kilrenny	Kilrenny
	Peterhead		
(d) Linlithgow	(e) Falkirk District	(h) Wick	(k) Wick District
Selkirk	(Selkirk	Tain	Tain
Lanark	Suppressed)	Dornoch	Dornoch
Peebles	Lanark	Kirkwall	Kirkwall
	(Peebles	Dingwall	Dingwall
	Suppressed)		Cromarty
	Airdrie		
	Hamilton		

B. Counties

1. Remaining the same: Aberdeen, Ayr, Argyll, Banff, Berwick, Dumbarton, Dumfries, Edinburgh, Fife, Forfar, Haddington, Inverness, Kincardine, Kirkcudbright, Lanark, Linlithgow, Orkney and Shetland, Peebles, Renfrew, Roxburgh, Selkirk, Sutherland, Wigtown.
2. Amended: Bute ceased to have alternating representation with Caithness, Clackmannan with Kinross, and Nairn with Cromarty. As a result, Bute and Caithness remained separate constituencies but with permanent representation; and joint constituencies of Clackmannan and Kinross, Elgin and Nairn, and Ross and Cromarty were created.

The Perthshire parishes of Tulliallan, Culross, Muchart, Logie and Fossaway were annexed by Clackmannan and Kinross, as was the Alva parish of Stirlingshire.

twelve months or more of their property, to have been in residence for six months in the burgh prior to 31 July (not necessarily in the premises on which the vote was claimed), and not to have been in receipt of parochial relief at any time during the twelve months prior to the end of July. True owners were subject to the same restrictions and privileges as Occupants, except in their case the act did not stipulate the need for a twelve months' occupancy. Joint proprietors and joint tenants were also recognised provided their subjects were valued to the requisite multiples of £10. A husband could claim on his wife's property.

As with the county provisions, the courts were faced with the interpretation of an act which lacked precision. The legislation, for example, drew a distinction between the Occupant as Proprietor and a True Owner. Whereas to claim the franchise an occupant proprietor was required both to have been an occupier for twelve months and a resident for six months prior to 31 July, a true owner had only to fulfil the residential qualification in the year he sought registration. True owners, however, were a class unknown to Scots law, and the courts chose to define them as proprietors. (In Ayrshire the definition was extended to include leaseholders and life renters.) Consequently, occupancy ceased to apply to proprietors because they could claim as true owners, thereby removing a restriction on their right to enfranchisement seemingly intended by the act. Thus, in practice the occupation franchise only applied to tenants and life-renters (Cay: 529-42).

Occupancy was understood as 'such natural possession as excludes the use of the premises by any other party...so that no other party could...have excluded him' (Cay: 483). It important, however, to stress that occupancy had to be linked to tenancy or life-rentship, because it did not *per se* confer the right of enrolment. Dr Clark, Professor of Chemistry at Aberdeen University, for example, was denied his claim for a vote as the occupant of 'the chemical lecture room, practical class room, and laboratory in Marischal College' (Cay: 472).

The residence provision, which required a claimant and voter to live within seven miles as the crow flies of the burgh in which he intended to exercise the franchise, was regarded by Cay as particularly important because 'its object seems to have been to localise the constituency of burghs, and to limit the franchise to those likely to take an interest in their welfare' (Cay: 430). Residency was more personal than occupancy or true ownership because it involved regular eating and sleeping (Cay: 430-6). A place of business, therefore, was not sufficient alone to secure the franchise.

Problems arose when a claimant or voter was absent on business, as might have been the case with a jobbing mason, joiner, sailor, or even an MP. In such cases the courts employed the concept of constructive residence in which *'animus revertendi* is a most important essential element' (Cay: 431). Thus, for example, Major Cumming Bruce, MP for the Inverness Burghs, retained his vote in the constituency on account of property therein, because he claimed his parliamentary commitments prevented him fulfilling the residential qualification. (In fact he lived in London, where he was a director of the East India Company, and on relinquishing his seat lost his vote as well.) In some instances, interpretations of the residential provision appeared harsh and even corrupt. For example, a bank agent with a job in Whithorn was denied a vote in Wigtown, where he spent the week-ends with his father's family, because the court regarded him as permanently absent. At the same time, however, Colonel Agnew was permitted a vote in Wigtown despite the fact he wintered in London, only returning to his Scottish county home in March. Undoubtedly, the sheriff's partial treatment reflected deference towards an ancient county family that could be denied to a mere banker. Votes were also refused to those who could not return home without breaking the law – a ruling which fell harshly on soldiers and sailors. Any loss of residence was a ground for expunging from the roll.

The section regarding receipt of parochial relief was defined narrowly by the courts, who indicated such payments must involve the receipt of money, and did not include the waiving of local taxes or the receipt of other charitable support. The sheriffs were also biased towards generosity in their attitude towards the taxation requirements, when they ruled that because in this matter the provisions of the act referred to 'claimants' only and not to 'claimants and voters' (as with the other limiting restrictions), a person once enrolled could not be expunged for non-payment of taxes (Cay: 415-6). Equally noteworthy, the courts decided that the taxation requirements applied to national taxes only. By 1850, the Window Tax was regarded as the only relevant impost remaining, despite the introduction of income tax in 1843 (Cay: 425).

Burgh tenants, in contrast to those in the counties, were not required to possess tenancies for a specific duration before claiming the vote. Nor was the amount of rent paid a determining factor, although a lease was required to establish occupancy, and rent was used an an important indicator of annual value. It was also permissible for an owner and tenant to be enrolled on the same property because the proprietor as a true owner did not have to be an occupant. Most Scottish courts were further prepared to register sub-tenants and lodgers as joint-occupiers, but not both they and tenants on the same property, even when a sub-tenant held a 999-year lease. Lodgers could claim the ballot, despite the landlord retaining 'command of the outer door' (Cay: 628) so long as the lodger had exclusive access to his apartments. Tenants who occupied property as a result of official appointment (e.g. schoolmasters and teachers), could claim providing the terms of their employment 'excludes a power of removal at the displeasure of another.' Consequently, it was essential for such claimants to 'show that dismissal will not be necessarily attended by his immediate removal from the premises claimed on' (Cay: 618). Although tenancies could easily be created to make votes in the burghs, it is unlikely that the scale of abuse was as extensive as in the countryside, due to prohibitive costs and one-party dominance.

The initial preparation of the electoral roll fell upon the various town clerks, who received the names of new claimants, published their names on various church doors, and passed objections to them and those already on the register to the sheriff. The sheriff then determined which of the unopposed claims were valid. Where objections were made the onus of proof of ineligibility fell on the objector. Objections to existing voters were reduced because their names were not published annually, and anyone wishing to scrutinise the roll had to consult that in the hands of the town clerk. Thus, the yearly revision did not involve a complete redrafting of the register, so that errors developed as time passed by. Under the Burgh Registration Act, 1856, however, the town clerk was required to prepare a totally new register each year, in an effort to reduce anomalies.

The burgh electorate rose from 31,332, in 1832 to 55,515 in 1865, when for the first time it was greater than that of the counties. Over 70 per cent of that increase came in the four large cities, whose combined electorate more than doubled, to constitute just over three fifths of all burgh electors in 1865. Indeed, in that year, three in ten of all burgh electors were resident in one city, Glasgow.

There were numerous indications that the registers were systematically revised from time to time by assiduous town clerks. For example, despite unopposed returns in 1841, the Edinburgh electorate was reduced from 9,640 in 1837 to 5,346, and was largely responsible for producing the only inter-election period in which the aggregate of all burgh electors fell. Also between 1837 and 1841, the Paisley electorate declined by 18 per cent, and a further 20 per cent by 1847, although there was no major electoral confrontation between 1836 and 1852; and in St Andrews Burghs the register was reduced from 835 in 1841 (the last contested election before 1857) to 680 by 1852. Even Glasgow's burgeoning roll fell by 400 in the four years prior to 1841, although the largest cull was the net loss of almost 2,000 electors between 1859 and 1865. The impact of the 1856 legislation was most obvious in Aberdeen and Dundee, whose respective electorates dropped from 4,547 to 2,346 and 3,190 to 2,343 between 1852 and 1857. Nevertheless, the observation that there were more burgh electors in 1857 than before suggests that even prior to the Burgh Registration Act the lists were robustly accurate.

An 1844 survey amongst some 36,700 burgh electors classified 38.5 per cent as proprietors (true owners), 59.3 per cent as tenants, 0.8 per cent as life renters, and 1.4 per cent as husbands holding the vote on their wives' property (*PP*, II: xxxviii, 1844). Excluding Glasgow, the proportion of owners rose to 44.8 per cent and tenants fell to 52.6 per cent of the total. Proprietors were most dominant in the St Andrews and Montrose Burghs, where they respectively constituted 70.8 per cent and 62.4 per cent of the enrolled; and were more than half the electorate in the burgh districts of Falkirk, Kirkcaldy, Haddington, Kilmarnock, Stirling and Wigtown. Tenants, by contrast, accounted for 81.3 per cent of the enfranchised in Glasgow, over 70 per cent in Greenock, and all 39 of those registered in Cullen, a fiefdom of the the Earl of Seafield.

In contrast to the counties, however, the distinctions between the classes of voters were generally of next to no importance, for although there were opportunities for the manufacture of votes through joint-ownership and tenancies, the domination of proprietors over subordinate tenants was not a significant feature of burgh politics. Indeed, it was the independence of each elector that was the most innovative feature of the new franchise there. Whereas in the counties the reformed franchise favoured capital held in land by enabling the proprietors to to create faggot votes, the industrial capitalists of the burghs were unable to mobilise their wealth to make a client electorate out of their economic dependents, the work force. The owner of a large textile factory was not at much greater electoral advantage than a small grocer. The urban electorate tended to reflected the range of economic activity in any burgh rather than the relative importance of each industry measured in terms of either turnover or of numbers employed. Thus, electoral power in the burghs was invested in the hands of the petit bourgeoisie.

In Aberdeen, for example, more than 170 occupations were listed amongst the 1,340 who registered a vote in 1847 (*Poll Book*, 1847). Of those voters, 196 were from the established professions – 69 advocates, 37 doctors and surgeons, 25 druggists, 22 ministers, 13 school teachers and 10 service officers. They were reinforced by a further 48 associated with financial services, encompassing 3 bankers, 17 insurance agents, 15 brokers, and a couple of bank tellers. The drink trade included 161 electors, consisting of 102 grocers, 25 spirit dealers, 20 vintners, 13 brewers and distillers and a distillery clerk. The agricultural and fishery interest was represented by 149 voters, composed of 53 farmers, 37 gardeners, 17 stablers, 12 meal sellers, 5 crofters, 3 fleshers, 3 salmon fishermen, a couple of farm servants, and a fish curer. The other major group were the 134 voters connected in various ways with the textile industry. Amongst them the dominant group were 37 tailors, 24 clothiers, and 8 drapers. Those engaged in the processing side of the industry included 3 linen, 3 wool, 1 cotton, 1 thread and 4 unspecified textile manufacturers, 11 weavers, 7 dyers, 5 ropemakers, 5 managers, a mill overseer and 2 mill clerks. Of the rest, 75 were engaged in various forms of building and construction, amongst whom 29 masons and 17 slaters were the most numerous. 85 voters were employed in different forms of engineering and allied trades from 24 wrights to 14 watchmakers; 41 worked in or sold the products of foundries – 17 blacksmiths, 11 ironmongers and the like; and 54 voters were connected with shipping and the harbour, encompassing 17 shipmasters, 11 shipowners and 10 shipbuilders. Various forms of manufacturing, in addition to those already mentioned, claimed a further 72 voters, amongst whom were 5 candle-makers, 6 paper makers, 15 cabinet makers, 10 coopers, a soap boiler and a soda water maker. Foodsellers (in addition to grocers, fleshers and fish merchants), were represented by 57 voters, amongst whom 33 bakers and 16 confectioners were the most numerous. Remaining electors included, *inter alia,* 51 designated as residenters (presumably men of independent means), a couple of house servants, a beadle, the tacksman of a weighouse, and a billiard table keeper.

Table 3.1: Economic Activities of the Aberdeen and Inverness Voters of 1857 and 1859

	Aberdeen, 1857 (1,884)	Inverness, 1859 (411)
	%	%
Drink	13.0	16.8
Food Retail (except Grocers)	4.2	4.6
Textiles	8.9	6.6
Construction	5.5	3.4
Engineering & Allied Trades	4.9	4.4
Leather Trades	4.4	4.9
Foundry & Forge	2.9	3.2
Other Manufactures	3.5	6.8
Miscellaneous Sales	5.8	3.9
(All Manufacturing & Retail)	(53.1)	(54.6)
The Professions	15.1	11.2
Banking & Insurance	3.7	3.9
Shipping	3.9	4.1
Non-Maritime Transport	3.1	1.0
Miscellaneous Services	2.6	4.4
Agriculture & Fisheries	12.3	9.0
Residenters	6.2	11.8
All	**100.0**	**100.0**

Sources: Poll Book, Aberdeen, 1857; Poll Book, Inverness, 1859.

We can be confident that the same pattern was reflected in Dundee, and more extensively by the electors of Edinburgh and Glasgow. The smaller burghs were more restricted, because their numbers of professional men was significantly less and the variety of manufactures more circumscribed. In such cases, the natural bias of the franchise towards the shopocracy was even more accentuated. Even so, because the franchise discounted the electoral significance of industries employing large numbers, the differences between the range and balance of economic activities from one burgh to another represented by their respective electorates were minimised. Thus, for example, although only 98 self-designated occupations are found amongst the 411 Inverness voters of 1859, as against 254 amongst the 1,884 voters in Aberdeen two years earlier, the business interests they represented were remarkably similar (Table 3.1).

It was only in 1868, with the advent of the householder franchise, that the employment structure of a burgh began to be adequately reflected in the composition of the electorate.

The County Franchise

According to Cay, the object of the franchise reform was to remove the vote from its roots in Crown Vassalage, and attach it to 'actual property, to the *dominium utile* of the subjects affording the qualification, dispensing with the ancient requisite, viz. that the lands must be held of the Crown, abolishing (prospectively) all qualifications based on bare superiority' (Cay: 3). Consequently, in 1832, the vote in the counties was extended to adult males, subject to various limitations, in four main categories: (1) Freeholders, (2) £10 Owners, (3) Tenants and (4) Liferent Office Holders.

1. *Freeholders* under the old law were those already on the roll; those so entitled to be enrolled at the passing of the Reform Act; and those who became owners or superiors of lands affording the qualification before 1 March, 1831. No new names were to be added to this list after 1832.

2. *£10 owners* were owners and/or possessors of lands, houses, feu duties and other heritable subjects – whether they had made up their titles or were infeft or not, to the value of £10 or more having deducted feu duty, ground annual, or other considerations etc. as a condition of their right. Such claimants also had to have been owners (though not possessors) for six months prior to 31 July; and at the time of registration possessors by themselves, tenants, or vassals or others, and be either in actual occupation or in receipt of profits and issues to the extent of £10 per annum. Husbands were entitled to claim a vote in respect of property belonging to their wives; and co-proprietors or joint owners could also claim provided that the share or interest in the property of each owner was of the yearly value of £10 or more.

3. Various categories of *Tenants* who had held their tenancies for at least twelve months prior to 31 July, were eligible:

(i) Where (a) the Tenant had a 57 year or more lease and the yearly value of his interest was £10 or more; or (b) the Tenant had a 19-year lease and where the clear yearly personal value to him was not less than £50. Personal possession under this head was not a requirement.

(ii) Joint Tenants under 19- or 57-year leases or more provided that the share or interest of each tenant was £50 or £10 as the case may be.

(iii) Tenants who were also occupiers and whose yearly rent was not less than £50.

(iv) Joint Tenants and Occupants, provided the share of each was £50 or more.

(v) Sub-Tenants or Assignees to sub-leases of 19–57 years of £50 or £10 as the case may have been.

(vi) Tenants who had paid a price, grassum or consideration of not less than £300 for their interest in the subject.

4. *Life Rent Office Holders*. This qualification was extended to an unspecified group of persons 'when any property which would entitle the owner to be registered and to vote shall come to any person...by appointment to any place or office, such a person shall be entitled to be registered' (Cay: 94).

Commentators have pointed out that these provisions 'bristled with difficulties' (Ferguson: 108) because insufficient attention was given to the definition of terms, especially 'ownership', 'possession' and 'actual occupation'. The confusion arose because qualifications featuring in the English Act were applied to the Scottish legislation without due consideration to the legal differences between the two countries, particularly with respect to landholding. The requirement to establish both ownership, the equivalent of proprietorship, 'the right of using and disposing of a subject as our own' (Cay: 39), and 'actual occupation' caused particular difficulties, because in Scots law 'actual occupation' was defined as 'the appropriating to oneself things that have no owner' (Cay: 40-41). Thus, 'ownership' and 'actual occupation' were mutually incompatible provisions. Furthermore, the notion of possession had two distinct branches: (a) natural possession (which was not necessarily associated with ownership), defined as 'holding the thing possessed corporally or naturally; in the case of lands, by cultivating, sowing, and reaping the fruits; of houses by inhabiting them' (Cay: 40); and (b) civil possession, 'holding the subject by a sole act of mind, or by the hands of another, who holds it in the name of the party possessing *civiliter*' (Cay: 40). Cay resolved the problem by defining 'owners' as 'proprietors', 'possessors' as 'civil possessors', and 'actual occupiers' as 'natural possessors'.

Further problems arose from the need to establish ownership while at the same time waiving the requirement to have made up one's titles, because it was doubtful 'whether anything will suffice to support a claim short of formal and probative conveyancing' (Cay: 133). In some registration courts the entry of a claimant's name as a feuar in a superior's rental book was acceptable, whereas others were more strict, requiring the claimant to prove in writing that a transfer of property was sufficiently advanced as to prevent resiling. Difficulties also arose also when an elector, who had been enrolled as an owner of land over which he was also superior subsequently sold the land but retained the superiority. Sheriffs like Cay held that, in such circumstances the voter would lose his qualification as an owner of land, and could only be re-registered as the owner of feu-duties, (a category specifically indicated by the act), should they be £10 or more. Otherwise there might be two persons enrolled as owners (not joint proprietors) of the same property, and it may mislead an 'objector in his inquiries, and only direct his attention to the value of the land, which may be sufficient, while that of feu duties may not' (Cay: 42). Other sheriffs, however, holding the feudal view that the superior was 'not truly divested of the lands by grant to his vassal' (Cay: 41) did not require such a voter to seek re-registration.

The justifiable irritation of the fastidious Cay also extended to the somewhat cryptically defined class of Life Rent Office Holders. In the opinion of the Sheriff of Linlithgow, the act should have stated exactly which persons were meant to be enfranchised under this category, for while in feudal society it would have extended the vote to a whole variety of officials (e.g. governors of castles and keepers of royal parks) in the context of the 1830s it seemed only to apply to parochial ministers on account of their manses and glebes, and schoolteachers with respect to their houses and gardens. To qualify, provided the subjects were of the yearly value of £10 or more, ministers and schoolteachers, had only to 'show they had been duly appointed, and the right to the subjects follows as a matter of course' (Cay: 95). Schoolmasters, however, could not successfully claim on either a schoolhouse or playground, nor could they include extra salary payment to compensate for the absence of a garden. Dissenting ministers were also enrolled under this clause, but the courts needed to satisfy themselves that the manses and glebes on which the vote was claimed were such that the congregation had the right to convey a life rent interest, and had given them to their minister as part of his terms of appointment.

The major weakness of the act lay in its failure to protect the integrity of the franchise from the creation of faggot votes on a large scale, and open voting exposed the tenantry to coercion by politically active landlords. As Ferguson indicates, to create votes a proprietor had only to portion up an estate into as many life rent interests as would yield each part £10 of annual value, so that 'instead of property being regarded merely as a qualification, the vote...was now invested *in* property' (Ferguson: 111). The exploitation of the life rent qualification was particularly abused through a system of 'interposed trusts' (Brash: xliii-xliv). Under this method a proprietor established a large number of life renters, although none of them actually gave him money for the purchase of the life rent. Instead, each life renter executed a trust deed naming the proprietor's agent as the trustee, and assigning him rents due on the property.

Although the Midlothian Whigs were the first to employ interposed trusts, it was the Tories who used them more successfully to establish an ascendancy in the south east counties. In 1837, it was estimated that of the 700 voters in the county of Peebles more than 300 were nominal life renters. The pressure to make votes was so severe in some counties that as tenancies expired incumbents were forced to accept co-tenants, so that the 'Reform Act was often described not as a charter of enfranchisement but of slavery' (Ferguson: 112). For many tenants, to defy the political preferences of the landlord was to hazard eviction at the expiry of a lease, and there is hard 'evidence that such practices were used in Ross-shire' (Ferguson: 112).

Abuses of the system were also assisted by the reorganisation of registration, which unintentionally led to the quashing of former acts and associated case law that had done much to check the admission of nominal and fictitious votes. Prior to 1832, it had been the duty of freeholders (i.e. electors at election time) collectively to revise the register, enrolling new voters and expunging others. Any appeal went to the Court of Session. In 1832, however, a new system was introduced whereby parish ministers were responsible for compiling and publishing on their church doors the names of claimants. The sheriffs were empowered to admit or reject such claims, and an Appeal Court, consisting of three sheriffs, (including the original one), adjudicated on contested cases. This removed the Court of Session from the process and separated registration from the actual period of the election. Not only were the precedents of the Court of Session lost, but so was uniformity of interpretation and the admission of 'special interrogatories' designed to check abuses by establishing intention (Ferguson: 109). The procedure was not helped when sheriffs were related to interested parties, (as they frequently were), and Appeal Courts were not unknown to divide on political lines (Brash: xliii-xliv).

The number of county electors expanded more than tenfold in 1832, when just over 33,000 were registered, and rose to almost 48,000 in 1841, as the Tories sought to recover ground lost to the Whigs. It was not, however, until 1852 that more than 50,000 county residents were enfranchised. The onus on individuals and party managers to seek registration for themselves or their supporters not only had a clear influence on the size of the register, but also on its accuracy. As the number of contested elections declined after 1841 so did the number of challenges to those enrolled. Consequently, the registers became cluttered with names of the deceased, those whose names appeared more than once, and those whose qualifications had lapsed. At the same time, there were others qualified to be enfranchised who had not bothered to enter a claim. By 1859, for example, the Renfrewshire register had 'not been purged for many years, and...more than half [were] disqualified under the present law' (Brash: xxxix). The cost of revising the registers became a significant disincentive to anyone contemplating a contest. In 1861, however, the County Voters Registration Act made the county assessors, appointed under the Valuation Act of 1854, responsible for revising the register, taking it out of the hands of the parish ministers and objectors. Consequently, 'in 1862 of 57,788 names on the Scottish county rolls 21,294 were struck off, and 13,735 new voters were added' (Brash: xl). As a result, there were fewer than 50,000 county electors in 1865, and the electorate was apparently smaller than in the three elections of the 1850s.

The most important post-Reform electors were the £10 owners because they constituted a clearly independent class of voters. They were not, however, a socially homogeneous group, as they included both the modest shopkeepers of the towns and villages and the landed gentry. Nor were they politically equal, for whereas the independent shopkeeper had only one vote (his own), the landowner frequently influenced the preferences of his tenantry, effectively giving him many votes, even when he, himself, as a member of the House of Lords, had no vote of his own. The outcome of county elections tended to rest on the relative strengths of the urban smallholders, who leant towards the Liberals, and the landed magnates, who were more Tory than Whig.

In 1844, owners accounted for 37.2 per cent of some 49,000 county electors (Table 3.2). Regionally, they were most numerous on Clydeside (50 per cent), and weakest in the Highlands, where they accounted for barely a quarter of the enrolment. Clackmannan and Kinross (67.3 per cent) was the most proprietor-dominated constituency, closely followed by Orkney and Shetland (62.9 per cent), which differed radically in this respect from other seats in the northern region. Proprietors were also more than half the electorate in Bute, Fife, Dunbarton and Renfrew. At the other extreme, there were a mere five proprietors listed amongst the electorate of Sutherland, which, together with Inverness, Argyll, Wigtown, Elgin and Nairn and Aberdeen, had less than a fifth of its electorate registered as owners. The most numerous class of electors was the various sub-groups of tenants, who accounted for almost half of all the county franchise. In Argyll, Wigtown and Aberdeen they were more than seven out of ten of all electors, and more than six in ten of voters in Sutherland, Ross and Cromarty, Elgin and Nairn, Banff, Kincardine, Perth and Dumfries. Unlike the proprietors, however, they did not constitute an independent class of voters, and were certainly in no position to organise as an interest against the lairds.

Table 3.2: Structure of the Scottish County Electorate, circa 1844

	£10 Owners	Life- Renters	Various Tenants	Husbands on Account of Wives	Ministers & Teachers	Old Freeholders
	%	%	%	%	%	%
Highland	26.7	5.1	56.6	0.6	4.7	6.3
East	30.9	2.9	57.9	1.2	3.0	4.1
Clydeside	50.0	2.8	40.8	1.2	1.2	3.9
Central	43.6	8.3	41.0	2.0	1.6	3.5
Borders	34.0	8.9	48.5	1.1	2.4	5.1
All	**37.2**	**5.6**	**49.1**	**1.3**	**2.4**	**4.3**

Source: P.P. Vol. II: xxxviii, *Return of Registered Electors, 1844.*

Life renters (who could well be included as part of the tenantry) were significant, less for their overall distribution, than their concentration in certain constituencies. Although only 5.6 per cent of the total county electorate, they were 35.4 per cent of the enrolment in Peebles, 26.1 per cent in Midlothian, 16.1 per cent in Selkirk, 14.8 per cent in Linlithgow, and 13.0 per cent in Roxburgh, reflecting the efforts of the Duke of Buccleuch in reviving the Tory interest in a geographically contiguous group of counties. As indicated earlier, most of these electors were completely subordinate to proprietorial influence as faggot voters, rendering them even less vital than the tenantry. Just over 4 per cent of the electorate were those remaining from the pre-1832 registration, 2.4 per cent were ministers and teachers, and 1.3 per cent were husbands registered to vote on account of their wives' property.

The subordination of tenants to owners was well illustrated in Sutherland, where a non-elector, the Duke or dowager Duchess, nominated the MP without ever having to mobilise a tenant vote, which was politically impotent despite dominating the register numerically. The stage armies of tenants and liferenters were only required when the proprietors were evenly divided politically, or when the landowners needed to offset the influence of an increasing number of urban £10ers. Significantly, the probability of contested elections increased as the proportion of owners on the register grew. In the eleven counties where proprietors were in excess of 40 per cent of the enrolment, 45 per cent of all returns were opposed, as against only 22 per cent of in the 13 constituencies where owners were less than 30 per cent of the electorate. (In the remaining six seats, where proprietors were between 30 and 40 per cent of the electorate, a third of all possible elections were opposed.) Only where the landowners had little interest in an electoral outcome did the tenantry have much room to manoeuvre.

The most significant aspect of the Great Reform Act in the counties, therefore, was its failure to establish even the rudiments of a popular constitution. The county franchise did little more than consolidate and deepen the legitimacy of the narrow oligarchies that dominated the political and economic life of rural Scotland.

Seats and Electors

It was inevitable, given the nature of the redistribution process, that the relationship between the distribution of seats and electors in 1832 was weak, so that while there was an average of 1,216 electors per member, constituencies ranged in size from only 84 in Sutherland to 6,989 in Glasgow. Counting Edinburgh and Glasgow each as two separate constituencies for the purpose of these calculations, the coefficient of variation in electoral size across all constituencies was high: 0.75 across the counties and 0.71 across the burghs. Differences, however, were somewhat reduced when each sub-type of burgh are considered separately, because the single burghs (coefficient of variation 0.47), with an average electorate of 2,188 electors, had mostly larger electorates than the burgh districts (coefficient of variation 0.41), who averaged only 832 electors in the first reformed elections.

Perthshire, the largest county, (elect. 3,180), was more than ten times greater than Bute, Caithness, Orkney and Shetland, and Peebles and Selkirk, and 38 times the size of Sutherland. Aberdeen's modest enrolment of 2,024 was more than the combined burgh district electorates of Wick, Wigtown, Haddington and Kirkcaldy. Just over half the burgh members of 1832 represented constituencies with less than 1,000 electors, while thirteen of the counties had electorates in excess of that number. The average county electorate of 1,104 was not qualitatively smaller than a mean burgh electorate of 1,362. Thus, the overall variations could not be attributed to a franchise which was more generous to the burghs than counties.

In regional terms, apart from Glasgow and the Borders, there was a robust association between the distribution of seats and the dispersal of the population, but a significantly less coincidence between seats and electors (Table 3.4). The Borders, with an allocation of 9.4 seats, gained most from the constituency settlement, for on the basis of population it only merited 5.5 seats, or 6.2 based on its share of the electorate. The burghs of Peebles and Selkirk had lost parliamentary status, but that had been a small price to pay for the continued separation of their shires. Their sacrifice might also have served to sustain the Haddington District (elect. 545), which included the Border burghs of Jedburgh and Lauder. Particularly remarkable was the survival of the highly vulnerable Wigtown District (elect. 316).

Table 3.4: Regional Impact of the 1832 Reform Act

	Electorate	% Population Enfranchised	Seats	'Fair' Distribution of Seats by:	
				Population	Electors
Aberdeen	2,024	3.5	1.0	1.3	1.7
Dundee	1,622	3.6	1.0	1.0	1.3
Edinburgh/Leith	7,672	4.7	3.0	3.6	6.3
Glasgow	6,989	3.5	2.0	4.5	5.7
Highland	3,764	1.0	8.0	8.7	3.1
East	13,599	2.6	10.8	12.2	11.2
Clydeside	8,378	3.0	6.2	6.3	6.9
Central	12,871	3.0	11.6	9.9	10.6
Borders	7,528	2.9	9.4	5.5	6.2
All	**64,448**	**2.7**	**53.0**	**53.0**	**53.0**

In the Highlands and Islands, too, reapportionment erred on the side of generosity, for although its eight seats was rather less than deserved on the basis of population, the share was considerably in excess of the 3.1 constituencies justified by the level of enfranchisement. Sutherland had survived, Caithness no longer had to share its representation, there was no challenge to the survival of the Wick Burghs (elect. 366), and Inverness Burghs (elect. 715) not only remained intact but its head burgh almost became a constituency on its own. With the elevation of Oban, the region had an interest in eight seats, marginally more than before the act. The most distinctive feature of the Highlands, however, was its chronically low level of enfranchisement – barely 1 per cent overall. Only 0.5 per cent of Orcadians and Shetlanders were registered, but that was greater than 0.4 per cent in Sutherland; and out of more than 100,000 souls in Argyll, barely 1,000 were electors. Taking the Borders and Highland together, with less than a fifth of the total Scottish electorate and just over a quarter of the population, they determined almost a third of the nation's parliamentary representation.

Despite the four major cities and the Leith District benefiting most directly from the suppression of former English constituencies, their treatment by parliament was less than benign. Possessing almost one in five of the population and almost three out of every ten electors, they were awarded barely an eighth of the seats. With 62 per cent more electors than in the Borders and Highlands combined, they had only two fifths of their representation. The two metropolitan areas, each with more voters than in the whole of the Highlands, had the greatest cause for complaint. Edinburgh and Leith had a strong case for at least three more MPs on account of their registration, and Glasgow four more on account of both electorate and population. The prejudice against Glasgow remained a particular scandal throughout the century not only because it was offensive to notions of arithmetical fairness, but also in terms of the greater recognition afforded to cities like Liverpool and Manchester in 1885.

The treatment of Glasgow compares instructively with that meted out to her neighbouring Clydeside counties of Lanark, Renfrew and Dunbarton, where representation rose to agree closely with their share of the population and franchise. This coincidence had been achieved through the creation of Paisley and Greenock as separate constituencies, the addition of Airdrie and Hamilton to the former Linlithgow group (now the Falkirk District), and the inclusion of Port Glasgow in the Kilmarnock Burghs (constituted from the remnants of the Glasgow Group). Such 'fairness', however, was quite fortuitous. The desire of MPs to preserve a county or agricultural interest in the constituencies of Renfrew and Lanark had made them amenable to schemes designed to isolate the industrial burghs, even when it necessitated the creation of new urban seats. In short, the triumph of proportionality on Clydeside was no less a product of the anti-democratic influences which had dealt harshly with the Glaswegians.

In general, representation of the East and Central regions accorded with the principles of proportionality measured in terms of both population and voter registration, although the survival of Bute (elect. 279) was a cause of over-representation in Central. The particular, however, renders the generality somewhat misleading. In the East, for example, the county of Aberdeen, with an electorate of 2,271 in 1832, was flanked by Banffshire, which had fewer than 500 voters, and Kincardineshire (elect. 763), and three Aberdeenshire burghs (Peterhead, Inverurie and Kintore) formed part of the Elgin District, a constituency with only 776 electors. Further south, Perthshire was a constituency of more than 3,000 voters, whilst its county town had a roll of only 780. Fifeshire had 2,185 on its electoral roll, but the St Andrews Burghs had only 621, and Kirkcaldy District a meagre 507. Similarly, in Central, Ayrshire boasted 3,150 electors in the first reformed election, whilst Ayr Burghs mustered only 631 with the help of Inverary, Campbeltown and Oban from Argyll.

A major feature of the post-1832 system was the survival of burgh groupings based on the old Royal Burghs, although reinforced and reorganised with the addition of new members. In many ways they were fortunate to survive even in the context of the time. Some of the districts had very small electorates indeed, and represented no recognisable interest apart from their own decay. Only the Montrose Burghs and the newly created (atypical) Leith Burghs were larger than the average constituency; and the ten districts of Wigtown, Wick, Kirkcaldy, Haddington, St Andrews, Ayr, Inverness, Elgin, Stirling and Dumfries had a combined electorate smaller than the city of Glasgow. Individual components, naturally, bore even less scrutiny. New Galloway for example, in the Wigtown District, whose provost lived in London and had a town clerk resident in Kirkcudbright, had only 14 electors. A decade after reform there were only 13 voters in Anstruther Wester, fewer than 100 in five of the six Wick burghs, and 13 burghs had less than 50 electors. Only the Montrose, Leith, Kilmarnock, Falkirk, Stirling, and possibly the Dumfries Burghs could be defended on the grounds that a franchise which differentiated between county and burgh required such constituency arrangements, but there is no evidence of such an argument being advanced in 1832.

The burgh districts survived principally because they served the interests of the county members in three ways: (a) as a means of preventing county constituencies being swamped by independent voters; (b) as a means of minimising the number of seats awarded to the manufacturing interest; and (c) as an extension of proprietorial interests. (We shall consider the third point in the following chapter.)

The greatest immediate advantage of the burgh districts to the rural members was that they kept urban voters out of county constituencies. Not only, as we have seen, were industrial and commercial towns taken out of counties, but so, too, were the rural burghs of Peterhead, Oban and Cromarty. The refranchisement of Cromarty, whose 'manufacture and trade are trifling, and the herring industry, which for some time formed a considerable employment to its inhabitants has recently much declined' (*PP.* 1836: Vol XXIII, App. 17–79), which added only 50 or so votes to the Wick District, seems to have been particularly against the spirit of reform. At the same time, the extension of the new parliamentary boundaries beyond those of the royalty in many of the existing burghs, and in the case of Banff to incorporate Macduff on the opposite bank of the Deveron, further eased pressure on the counties.[7] Although it was quite logical to bring in suburbs and to strengthen weak groupings, one cannot conclude that technocratic rationality motivated the process. There can be little doubt that both Whig and Tory backbenchers defended the districts because any true rationalisation would have resulted in wholesale suppression and a consequent weakening of their political interests.

The retention of burgh districts also had the advantage of holding captive seats which ought to have gone elsewhere, for there was a serious maldistribution between them and the newly created single burgh constituencies. With barely half the number of voters to be found in the single burghs, the burgh districts accounted for three in five of all burghal constituencies. As a class, the burgh districts were a classic piece of gerrymandering against the interests of the larger towns.

Of similar importance to the survival of the burgh groupings was the continued rejection of proportionality in favour of independence as the basis of shire representation. In the final analysis, the members of the biggest shires were prepared to tolerate Sutherland, Caithness and Bute, and to fight for Peebles and Selkirk, rather than to challenge their anomalous positions. The anti-reformers and moderate supporters were well aware that to have pressed their claims for additional members in Aberdeenshire, Perthshire, Fifeshire, Ayrshire, Lanarkshire, Midlothian, Forfarshire and Renfrewshire, would have been to invite both the amalgamation of other counties and the wholesale suppression of burghs. Such a course of action was fraught with too many dangers for proprietors already fearful of the consequences for their power and status in the new franchise.

The Scottish constituency settlement, therefore, must be seen as the price paid by the ministry, (perhaps willingly so by some members), for the speedy settlement of reform in Scotland. The regional distribution of Scottish MPs remained substantially as it had been between 1707 and 1832, and seats won for the newer urban areas represented less a victory for the new social forces than a *cordon sanitaire* placed round them by the old.

Conclusion

At the conclusion of the reform process, Cockburn expressed a more sober sentiment than that with which he had greeted the promulgation of the first reform bill, when he wrote:

> No doubt with us the franchise is everything: but in arranging a prospective and permanent system, I cannot help, in spite of all my gratitude, feeling sorely the introduction of glaring blots, the bad working of which will hereafter be ascribed to the reform itself and not to any defect in it (Cockburn, 1874b: 400–1).

The issue in 1832 was not simply how many voters, but what it meant to be a voter. A mere increase in the size of the electorate neither proved nor guaranteed the triumph of reform. The creation of 65,000 electors where once there had been fewer than 3,000[8] did not indicate the number of those exercising free, unpressured decisions: the *sine qua non* for the establishment of the independent constituencies so keenly sought by the reformers. A high level of county enfranchisement, for example, frequently indicated the success of landowners in registering squadrons of faggot voters and compliant tenants to confirm their traditional powers rather than an excess of the democratic spirit. Indeed, a smaller electorate, which excluded tenants and liferenters, would have produced more radical change. Again, had all the burgh districts been thrown into their respective counties, a number of their tenant occupiers would have lost the ballot, but the surviving £10 owners would have critically weakened the influence of the county proprietors in constituencies such as Midlothian, where the Leith electors would have played a more decisive role than the Duke of Buccleuch. Furthermore, had the seats so released been redistributed to give more just representation to Glasgow, Edinburgh and the larger counties, then urban influence would have been strengthened even more: again with the same restricted electorate.

Not only might a smaller number of voters produced greater change, but so, too, might a smaller number of constituencies. The addition of eight extra seats might well have satisfied national pride, but it also weakened the case for redistribution within Scotland itself. Had only 45 seats been maintained, then more than serious consideration would have had to be given to the question of exiguous burgh districts and counties, unless the claims of the cities were to be ignored completely. Internal reapportionment would have assisted the reform process by abolishing seats more prone to nomination, relocating them in more populous areas where independent electors flourished. As it was, traditional rural interest lost nothing, and Bute and Caithness even gained permanent separate representation. It may well be, therefore, that the relative balance between the urban/manufacturing and rural/agricultural interests would have been more favourable to the former without the acquisition of liberated English seats.

To point to the deceptive features and shortcomings of the Reform Act, however, is not to deny that the system had changed. In both county and burgh constituencies, the increase in electorate broke the capacity of government agents to interfere with electoral outcomes in the intimately personal manner that had been previously possible. As a result, the determination of representation became much more locally based than hitherto in Scotland, making her MPs more independent of ministerial manipulation. The ground rules of burgh politics, in particular, had been transformed beyond recognition as the suzerainty of the corporation oligarches was broken with the enfranchisement of £10 occupiers and true owners, who became the new arbiters of power, especially in the larger urban settlements. In the countryside, the definition and size of the electorate was less indicative of the diffusion of political power than in the burghs, but the need to organise a wider number of voters, and the opportunities to manufacture additional electors, enhanced the importance of locally active proprietors.

In many respects, Cockburn's analogy between the liberation from Egypt and the impact of the Scottish Reform Act was more apt than he originally appreciated, because in Exodus the 'ecstasy' of 'liberty' was followed by 40 grievous years in the wilderness, and none of the 'slaves' entered the Promised Land. What Cockburn saw as fulfilment was but the starting point of a process to a destination known only to Providence. The Lord Advocate's disillusion rose from the recognition that his legislation was by no means the near-perfect instrument he originally thought it to be. It contained too many compromises and errors of his own making. Rather, he had fashioned a somewhat blunt hammer which had shattered the old system, but failed, (partly due to the uncertain objectives of the reformers themselves), to create an unblemished alternative. Perhaps the greatest contribution of the act was to establish the proposition that the electoral system was an institution amenable both to scrutiny and reform.

Notes

1 'The determination of voting rights was by no means the most important task attempted by the legislators in 1832...of equal or greater importance was the redistribution of seats,' (Seymour, 1916: 45).

2 The reformers also shared similar misgivings concerning the humours of their countrymen. (*Hansard,* (3rd Series), 1831, Vol. III, p. 324). 'But the Scots are bad mobbers. They are too serious at it; they never joke; and they throw stones... An English mob exhausts itself upon itself either in blows or in fun; a Scotch one acts because it hates its victim, and contains no corrective to its excesses in its own elements.' (Cockburn, 1874a: 16-17).

3 Cowal had a population of 7,943 as against 14,151 in Bute. This amalgamation was proposed with the purpose of weakening the Tory Marquis of Bute in the new constituency.

4 'In Scotland a Master of Arts is no high honour. It implies no pecuniary of permanent association with the college, and no importance is attached to it in the opinion of the country.' (Cockburn, 1874a: 12; see also 1874b: 295-9).

5 Cockburn's reaction on hearing of the concession, 'As to Bute, the blot for which posterity will blame us consists in the excessive preponderance we leave to our earthly aristocracy' (Cockburn 1874b: 401). It was not insignificant that on the very day these amendments were presented to the House, Jeffrey wrote to Cockburn's daughter, 'Tell your father...that I do not want any advice about the number of members generally, or of the county members to be allowed to Scotland' (Cockburn, 1852: III:247).

6 There was, however, a failed an attempt by the Lords, in the only amendment they proposed to the constituency settlement, to put Kirkcudbright in the Wigtown District.

7 Also Fortrose was extended to include Rosemarkie (*PP.* 1831-32: XLII).

8 Counting each Royal Burgh as having one elector apart from Edinburgh.

References

Aberdeen Poll Book, 1847 (MS. in Aberdeen Central Library).

Aberdeen Poll Book, 1857 (King's Collection, Aberdeen University).

Brash, JI, *Scottish Electoral Politics, 1832–1854*, Edinburgh, 1974.

Cay, J, *An Analysis of the Scottish Reform Act with the Decisions of the Courts of Appeal*, Edinburgh, 1850.

Cockburn, H, *Life of Jeffrey*, Edinburgh, 1852

Cockburn, H, (a), *Journal*, Edinburgh, 1874.

Cockburn, H, (b), *Letters Chiefly Connected with the Affairs of Scotland from Henry Cockburn to Thomas Francis Kennedy*, London, 1874.

Ferguson, W, 'The Reform Act (Scotland) of 1832: Intention and Effect', *Scottish Historical Review*, Vol. XIV, 1966.

Gash, N, *Politics in the Age of Peel*, London, 1952.

Hansard (3rd Series).

Inverness Poll Book, 1859 (King's Collection, Aberdeen University).

Moore, DC, 'The Other Face of Reform,' *Journal of Victorian Studies*, Vol. V, 1961.

Moore, DC, 'Concession of Cure: The Sociological Premises of the First Reform Act,' *The Historical Journal*, Vol. XI, 1966.

Moore, DC, *The Politics of Deference*, Hassocks, 1976.

Public General Statutes, 2 & 3 William IV, cap. 65 (Scottish Reform Act).

Seymour, C, *Electoral Reform in England and Wales*, New Haven, 1916.

Parliamentary Papers, *Reports Upon the Boundaries of the Several Cities, Burghs, and Towns of Scotland in respect to the Election of Members of Parliament, 1831–2,* XLII.

Parliamentary Papers, *Reports from Commissioners*, 1836, XXIII, appendix, pp. 17–79.

Parliamentary Papers, *Return of Registered Electors*, 1844, II, xxxviii.

4 The Operation of the System, 1832–1868

The politics of parliamentary representation after 1832 was the product of an electoral system in which the franchise continued to draw a distinction between shire and burgh, and a constituency settlement that divided urban representation between single burghs, with relatively large electorates, from burgh groupings, with mostly small enrolments. Such differences helped create four ideal types of electoral behaviour – the politics of nomination, registration, independence and influence.

The politics of nomination and registration were more characteristic of the counties than the burghs. The former was a survival of pre-reform politics, where a single proprietor retained the power to appoint the member. After 1832, the obvious examples of nomination counties were Bute and Sutherland, and there is evidence to suggest that Argyll and Aberdeenshire also fell into that category. By contrast, the politics of registration was a novel phenomenon resulting from loopholes in the reform legislation. According to Brash, although 'personal considerations were still important in determining how the individual elector cast his vote,' and 'support could still be obtained through the exercise of patronage and a little gentle blackmail,' the post-reform power brokers soon realised 'such influence was insufficient… [and that] it was the exploitation of property for the manufacture of votes' that enabled a party to establish its dominance. Consequently, 'it was increasingly understood that the path to electoral success lay through the registration court; [and] the politics of personal influence, patronage and deference yielded in effectiveness to the politics of registration' (Brash: xxxviii). Such developments, however, did little to extend the base of local political power, because 'county politics was still the preserve of a small group of interested gentlemen' (Brash: liv). This type of politics was probably the dominant mode in the counties between 1832 and 1868.

The politics of independence was the antithesis of the politics of nomination, and represented the ideal sought by the reformers. It was, however, mostly confined to single burgh constituencies, in which the newly enfranchised £10ers were sufficiently numerous as to be free from manipulation by elites, and voters could express their preferences as freely as any system of open voting can permit. The politics of influence, resting somewhere between the politics of independence and more traditional forms, was best exemplified in the burgh districts. It shared with the politics of independence a franchise dominated by urban £10ers, who expressed a general preference for Liberal candidates, but unlike the independent constituencies had a political leadership dominated by landed proprietors, thus tempering the consequences of reform with a leavening of personal influence, patronage, and deference.

Between 1832-68, the most distinctive feature common to all types of constituency was the localised focus of electoral politics, because reform had ended ministerial control over Scottish representation and the external discipline of nationally-based parties had yet to develop. Attempts to establish a Scottish

Conservative Association in 1835, for example, soon collapsed, because it was confined to a small group of Edinburgh lawyers and Border lairds, and there was resentment against outside interference in constituency affairs (Hutchison: 8). Even within individual constituencies party structures were weak and impermanent. Embryonic Conservative organisations in the burghs collapsed with the defeat of the Peelites (Hutchison: ch. 1 & 2); and while the various Liberal factions in Edinburgh and Glasgow established semi-permanent 'parties', in most burghs the politics of parliamentary representation was organised by *ad hoc* election committees centred on individual candidates. In the counties party interests rested more on social connection than organised political associations, and any formal structures were subordinate to the great families who created them. Consequently, when leading Conservative landowners drifted towards Palmerstonianism, their personal disinclination to challenge the Whigs occasioned a decline in Tory representation.

Despite the importance of local factors in determining electoral outcomes, there were three issues of national significance which dominated Scottish politics after 1832, and laid the foundations of Liberal dominance for most of the century.

Firstly, there was gratitude towards the Whigs for having introduced parliamentary reform in the teeth of Scottish Tory opposition, and a recognition that the Liberals were more likely than the Conservatives to pursue a continuing programme of legislation designed to liberate the urban middle classes from the secular and religious control exercised by traditional elites. While the popularity of reform was most evident in the burghs, approval of the 1832 Act in the counties was sufficiently strong for the Liberals to capture most of the rural constituencies in 1832 and 1835, though not subsequently.

The second important issue was the crisis in the Church of Scotland created by Evangelical Non-Intrusionists, mostly members of the new urban middle class, who were opposed to the rights of superiors to nominate ministers, granted under the Patronage Act of 1712. In party terms, the Non-Intrusionists' position was initially ambivalent, for while their desire for reform pushed them towards the Liberals, their support for the principle of establishment put them at odds with the voluntary Dissenters, who strongly influenced Whig policy making and favoured disestablishment and the secularisation of education and welfare (Hutchison: 18). Consequently, while the Non-Intrusionists were strongly biased towards the Liberals as the party of reform, they could be tempted by the Conservatives on the issue of establishment, as in 1837. In 1841, however, as the crisis in the Kirk moved towards schism, the Evangelicals shifted decisively towards the Liberals, and following the formation of the Free Church at the Disruption in 1843, seceders consolidated the Liberal coalition in burgh constituencies. In rural areas the Disruption had a lesser political impact, largely because its supporters there were mostly unenfranchised tenant farmers. That was particularly the case in the Highlands, where Free Presbyterianism had proved particularly popular with the crofters.

By far the most important issue, however, was tariff reform. Support for free trade in Scotland was so ubiquitous as to constitute a national cause. In the burghs, the rectitude of free trade could well have been the eleventh commandment. At 'a convention of dissenting ministers,' for example, the Edinburgh Radical voluntary, Duncan McLaren, declared the Corn Laws 'alike opposed to the principles of religion and morality' (Fry: 39). It was a measure of the cultural hegemony enjoyed by free trade sentiment, that its supporters included not only numerous urban Conservatives, but also leading Tory landowners such as Buccleuch, Aberdeen, Dalhousie, Wemyss and Queensbury (Hutchison: 85), whose Peelite sympathies fatally compromised their party's cause after 1846. The identification of the Liberal party with free trade, therefore, not only transcended the conflicting religious factions within its own coalition, but marked it as the custodian of a national consensus cutting across the formal party divide.

Elections

The Burghs

Between 1832 and 1868 the dominant feature of burgh politics was the almost unchallenged sway of Liberalism. Over nine general elections the Conservatives won only seven seats: Inverness Burghs (1832, 1835), Kilmarnock Burghs (1837), Haddington Burghs (1841), and Falkirk Burghs (1841, 1847, 1852); and the Liberals enjoyed a clean sweep in 1857, 1859 and 1865. In Scotland, therefore, as had been anticipated in the debates over the Reform Act, burgh constituencies were Liberal almost by definition.

The most obvious consequence of Liberal hegemony was that despite the reformation of burgh politics, through the creation of more popular constituencies, only half of all burgh elections were contested between 1832 and 1865. In eight seats scattered down the east coast – in which Kirkcaldy only once went to the polls at a general election, Montrose Burghs twice, Perth and Leith Burghs three times, and Dundee, together with the districts of Inverness, Elgin and St Andrews four times – the modal return was 'unopposed Liberal'. There were only five contests in Edinburgh and Aberdeen out of nine opportunities; and although Glasgow, with eight elections settled at the polls, experienced two more contests than any other constituency, on four of those occasions there were only three candidates for two seats.

Table 4.1: Number of Contested Seats in General Elections in the Scottish Burghs, 1832–1865

	Seats	1832	1835	1837	1841	1847	1852	1857	1859	1865	%
Aberdeen	1	-	1	-	1	1	1	1	-	-	56
Dundee	1	1	-	1	1	-	-	1	-	-	44
Edinburgh	2	1	2	-	-	2	2	-	-	2	50
Glasgow	2	2	1	2	2	2	2	1	-	1	72
Highland	2	1	1	1	1	1	1	2	1	-	44
East *	5	4	2	2	3	2	-	1	1	-	31
Clydeside	3	3	2	2	3	1	3	1	-	-	56
Central	5	3	2	3	3	2	5	2	1	2	61
Borders	2	2	1	1	2	1	1	1	1	1	67
All	23	17	12	12	16	12	15	10	4	6	104
% Contested		74	52	52	70	52	65	43	17	26	50

* Including Kirkcaldy Burghs

The most vigorously contested elections were in 1832, when seventeen of the 23 burgh returns were fought all the way, and in 1841 and 1852, when the Conservatives made an attempt to challenge Liberal hegemony. By 1859, however, only four returns were opposed, and only six in 1865. Thus, rather than reform stimulating the development of a competitive electoral system, either between or within parties, the trend was towards non-contestation, particularly where an incumbent was seeking re-election.

Turnout in elections is difficult to estimate due to the unsystematic revision of registers before 1856 (Craig: xiv). The data, nevertheless, provide some point of comparison between rates of participation in burgh and county constituencies, and between different sorts of party contests.

Between 1832 and 1865, turnout in the burghs (Table 4.2), which averaged some 69 per cent in each contested seat, seems to have been some 5 per cent less than in the counties (Table 4.4), and only in 1859 and 1865, on a small sample of seats, did the urban electorate display more apparent commitment to the electoral process than their rural counterparts. Within five years of the 84 per cent turnout in 1832, participation had fallen on average to 63 per cent in contested seats, and below 60 per cent in the doldrums of 1847 and 1852. Although that was in part a function of increasingly corrupt registers, the failure to revise them was itself a consequence of a declining interest on the part of the various political parties and factions in enrolling potential supporters, challenging the registration of rivals, and engaging in electoral conflict. Latterly there was a revival in turnout, especially in 1859, but that has to be set against an election in which only six constituencies were fought. Consequently, ordinary electors were significantly less engaged in the electoral process in the 1850s, than in the 1830s and 1840s.

Table 4.2: Average Turnout in Burgh Elections, 1832–1865

	1832 %	1835 %	1837 %	1841 %	1847 %	1852 %	1857 %	1859 %	1865 %	All %
Aberdeen	-	62	-	64	40	26	81	-	-	55
Dundee	89	-	46	50	-	-	83	-	-	67
Edinburgh	78	58	-	-	45	55	-	-	82	64
Glasgow	89	57	55	51	41	27	52	-	64	67
Highland	96	90	79	69	62	63	81	81	-	78
East *	87	80	70	69	77	-	77	78	-	77
Clydeside	67	76	59	50	71	64	87	-	-	65
Central	90	78	62	77	71	67	82	77	76	74
Borders	91	86	74	76	70	70	86	80	86	81
All	84	72	63	64	59	57	77	80	76	69

* Including Kirkcaldy Burghs

It is notable that turnout in elections where Conservatives intervened (66 per cent), was less than where only Liberals were standing (73 per cent). The critical variable in accounting for variations in participation, however, was size. Excluding Aberdeen, where participation was particularly low, turnout in the single burghs averaged 66 per cent, but rose to 77 per cent in the burgh districts, where the rate was higher than in the counties. These differences probably reflect the greater ease with which elections could be organised in the smaller burghs, from the revision of the register to the mobilisation of voters. It is, nevertheless, ironic to discover an inverse relationship between those places which had most demanded reform and the propensity of their electors to cast a ballot.

It followed from the weakness of urban Conservatism, that a major feature of burgh elections was the frequency with which Liberals opposed one another (Table 4.3). Over nine general elections, the Conservatives contested barely a quarter of the seats, and Liberals were just as likely to find themselves facing Liberal as Tory opponents.

The Tory challenge was particularly poor in eastern Scotland, where they failed to contest the 'hopeless' districts of Kirkcaldy and Montrose (Horne: 243, 268) before the passing of the Second Reform Act. Likewise, they avoided a challenge in the Stirling Burghs, in which a Conservative had 'no chance' (Horne: 232), and the electoral struggle, instead, focused on attempts by the Radicals to unseat the incumbent Whig, Lord Dalmeny (1832-47), who, in order to retain his seat, was forced to make concessions to the Dissenters (Horne: 232). Dundee's Liberalism was only tested once by the Tories, when in 1847, Gladstone of Fasque, William Ewart's elder brother, was well beaten by Sir Henry Parnell, who, although a 'very unpopular' Whig (Horne: 241), could rely on Liberal unity to resist a Tory. Similarly, Leith was only exposed to a Conservative in 1852, although the Tories had stood in a couple of by-elections. Radical Perth, where the vociferous Non-Intrusionist, Fox Maule, held sway from 1841-1852, was only contested twice by the Tories, as was Aberdeen. In the far north, James Loch (1832-1852), the Duke of Sutherland's auditor, who not only enjoyed the support of his patron but also of the local Radicals and the British Fishery Society (Horne: 272), easily fended off the one Conservative intervention in 1841 in the Wick District; and in the south west, Tory candidates only stood twice in the burghs of Ayr, Dumfries and Wigtown.

The most two-party contests were in the Falkirk and Inverness Burghs, both hotly disputed in five elections by the major parties. Significantly, the Conservative victors in Falkirk, the local Gartsherrie ironmasters William and George Baird, (1841-46, and 1851-57), and the Earl of Lincoln (1846-51), were all free traders (Hutchison: 87). Conservatives opposed the Liberals four times in Edinburgh, Glasgow, Elgin and Kilmarnock Burghs, where, in 1837, their candidate, John Colquhoun of Garscadden and Killermont, an Evangelical Anglican and former Liberal member for Dunbartonshire, carried the constituency as a supporter of the Presbyterian Evangelicals. He lost the seat in 1841, however, having failed to persuade his party leaders to support Non-Intrusionism (Hutchison: 17, 21, 24-5). The dominant characteristic of contested burgh elections, however, was less the inter-party rivalry, than the conflict between the various Liberal factions. There were 43 general election battles in which only Liberals took part, and a further seven occasions where the Liberal vote was split, but not fatally, in the face of Conservative intervention. Such contests were more characteristic of open primaries in American one party states than modern British elections. With national issues, particularly free trade, a largely uncontentious matter, policy differences between competing Liberals were easily confused by personality conflicts and local rivalries. Consequently, generalisations about electoral outcomes across constituencies are dangerous to make: a problem further compounded by the declining frequency of contested returns and low turnout.

Table 4.3: The Structure of Electoral Competition in Burgh Elections, 1832–1865

	1832	1835	1837	1841	1847	1852	1857	1859	1865	Total
Liberal *v* Conservative	2	4	8	9	1	7	3	2	1	37
2 Libs *v* Conservative	3	2	-	-	1	-	-	-	-	6
3+ Libs *v* Conservative	-	-	-	-	1	2	-	-	-	3
2 Libs *v* 2 Cons.	1	1	1	-	-	-	-	-	-	3
Lib. *v* Con. *v* Chartist	-	-	-	1	-	-	-	-	-	1
Liberal *v* Chartist	-	-	-	1	-	-	-	-	-	1
2 Liberals *v* Chartist	-	-	-	1	-	-	1	-	-	2
Liberal *v* Liberal	8	4	3	3	4	5	5	2	2	36
Liberal *v* 2+ Liberals	2	-	-	-	2	-	1	-	2	7
Unopposed Liberal	5	10	9	6	12	7	11	17	16	93
All Constituencies	**21**	**21**	**21**	**21**	**21**	**21**	**21**	**21**	**21**	**189**

Local factors aside, disputes between Liberal candidates reflected a broad struggle taking place between traditional Whig commercial, professional and landowning elites, and a newer class of urban-based Radicals, with similar business interests, seeking to establish their social and political credentials. The Radicals, however, were frequently divided over church-state relations, so that the Whig-Radical struggle was intersected with a complex and fluid matrix of ecclesiastical relationships involving the various competing brands of Presbyterianism, the Episcopalians, Roman Catholics, and Nonconformists.

In the early 1830s there was a close political association between voluntaristic Dissenters and Non-Intrusionists wanting reform in the Kirk, and in 1835 and 1837 their influence was sufficient to remove Whigs in Kilmarnock and Glasgow, though they were not so successful in the Ayr and Stirling Burghs (Hutchison: 36). Subsequent differences between the Dissenters and Non-Intrusionists over the principle of establishment were exploited by the Tories, whose overtures to the Evangelicals broke the Radical alliance of the mid-1830s. Consequently, in 1840, the provostships of both Edinburgh and Glasgow were captured by a coalition of Non-Intrusionist and Tory councillors, united by their Kirkmanship, against Dissenter nominees (Hutchison: 41). Although the Non-Intrusionist-Conservative accord was shattered before the 1841 general election, its consequences remained evident in some constituencies. In Dundee, for example, Councillor George Duncan, a Non-Intrusionist with establishmentarian backing, carried the city against a fellow Liberal, John Smith, a Unitarian leader of the local Anti-Corn Law League, who enjoyed the support of voluntaries and Whigs (Hutchison: 39–40). In Edinburgh, by contrast, the Radical Non-Intrusionist, Fox Maule, was forced to withdraw his nomination because the Dissenters refused to endorse a candidate who had plotted against them over the provostship the previous year (Mackie, Vol. I, 126).

By 1847, following the Distruption, the Dissenters and Free Churchmen, (former Non-Intrusionists), were re-united through their common opposition to the Maynooth College grant because it offended the voluntaristic sentiments of the former and the anti-Catholicism of both. The Whigs, however, endorsed the grant, thereby ending their electoral understanding with the Dissenters. As a result, Macaulay lost the allegiance of McLaren's Independent Liberals in Edinburgh, who were instrumental in his defeat, securing the return of Charles Cowan, an activist within the anti-Catholic Evangelical Alliance, at the top of the poll (Hutchison: 65; Mackie: Vol. I, 161). In the same year, two incumbent Whigs were defeated in Glasgow, a Free Churchman took Aberdeen from a Whig-Tory candidate, and Lord Dalmeny was finally forced to stand aside for the Dundee Unitarian, John Smith, in the Stirling Burghs (Hutchison: 65).

It was a measure of the growing political influence of the Free Presbyterians that in 1852 Viscount Melgund was forced to withdraw from Greenock in favour of Alexander Dunlop, the Free Churchman he had defeated in 1847; and in the Stirling Burghs, Free Presbyterians were instrumental in forcing the withdrawal of John Smith in favour of a more theologically acceptable voluntary, Sir James Anderson, who went on to defeat a Whig opponent (Hutchison: 66). The Maynooth question was still sufficiently potent in 1855 to secure the election of William Baxter, the Dundee textile Dissenter, in the Montrose Burghs, against Sir John Ogilvy, a landowning Whig churchman, (Hutchison: 80). In Perth, however, there was a reverse for the Dissenter-Free Church accord, when, at a by-election in 1852, their candidate was defeated by Arthur Kinnaird, a Whig nominee enjoying Conservative support (Hutchison: 80).

Even before the Montrose by-election, however, the Dissenters and Free Churchmen had become once again divided over legislation extending subsidies to Free Church schools, which had been opposed in 1854 and 1855 by Dissenter MPs (Hutchison: 80–1). The result was to create an alliance of Whigs and Free Churchmen against the voluntaries. Consequently, the Whigs captured both of Glasgow's seats in 1857, pushing Alexander Hastie, a voluntary who had headed the poll in 1852, into bottom place (Hutchison: 82). In Dundee, a similar constellation of forces enabled Sir John Ogilvy to defeat a voluntary, George Armitstead, Baxter's brother-in-law; and in Edinburgh, too, the Whigs outmanoeuvred the Dissenters with the aid of Free Churchmen (Hutchison: 81). It was, nevertheless, a sign of a growing voluntaristic sentiment amongst urban Free Churchmen, that James Anderson (Stirling Burghs) and Alexander Dunlop (Greenock) were both unopposed despite their votes against the education bills (Hutchison: 82). By 1857, however, much of the passion surrounding the Disruption and its consequences was spent, and burgh Liberalism became more consensual, as the significant drop in the number of contested seats indicates.

Chartists intervened four times. In 1841 they secured 30 votes in Aberdeen and 355 in Glasgow. In Paisley the Chartist polled no votes at all in 1841, and only four in 1857. Their impact, however, was somewhat greater than the bare statistics suggest, due to their practice of making nomination speeches but withdrawing before the poll. In 1841, for example, John Neilson, a nailor, nominated one John McCance at the hustings in Greenock, which provided an opportunity for him to make a speech criticising the Civil List. On a show of hands, the overwhelming majority favoured the Chartist, (evidence of participation by nonelectors), but the following day McCance withdrew his nomination for financial reasons, although claiming to be 'the true representative of Greenock' (Donald: 27). Neilson and McCrae repeated the performance again in an 1845 by-election, when the candidate criticised the introduction of income tax, which was 'supposed to be a step in the right direction; but...employers devised means to extract it from the working man' (Donald: 28).

As indicated in the introduction to this chapter, there was an important distinction between the character of political life in the larger single and two-member burghs than in most of the burgh districts. In the former, economic development had produced self-confident middle class electorates, who interacted with established and rising indigenous elites to produce vigorous and self-sufficient polities, and the politics of parliamentary representation tended to flow from the needs of these locally-based centres of power largely independent of external influences. Writing in the middle of the century Dod attests to the independence of Aberdeen, Edinburgh and Glasgow, by observing that in none of them 'personal influence prevails' (Dod: 105). Similarly, in Paisley, where power focused on the 'heads of the silk and cotton factories' (Dod: 243) and in Greenock, where the shipbuilding and shipowning families were a major force, outside pressures were exceptionally weak or non-existent. The position was essentially the same in the Leith Burghs, although the Duke of Buccleuch in Musselburgh and Sir John Gladstone in Leith might have exercised a little personal influence. In Ayr, Kennedy's warning as early as 1834 that the Radical sympathies of the electors were such that they were likely to reject any stranger regarded as a government placeman (Hutchison: 53), and Dod's observation that 'the late Marquis of Bute and the Earl of Eglington have usually divided *such influence as remains* here' (Dod: 13, my italics), indicate a continuing drift towards independence in those burghs. Similarly, in Stirling Burghs, where control exercised by the Earls of Hopetoun and Rosebery was passing 'chiefly [to the owners of] manufacturing firms in Stirling and Dunfermline' (Dod: 294), traditional external control was nearly at an end. It appears, too, that in the Kilmarnock Burghs, where influence was 'much divided' (Dod: 164), and the Tory Campbells of Blytheswood, (powerful in the Glasgow group before 1832), had been reduced to a minor role in Renfrew, that politics was becoming free of the old politics. The politics of independence, nevertheless, remained atypical of the constituencies created in 1832.

The dominant mode in the burghs was the politics of influence. Because the majority of burghs in the districts were small and lacked large-scale economic enterprises, they were unable to produce political leaderships comparable in stature to those of the bigger cities, and tended to look to local Whig and Tory landowners for assistance in the organisation of elections and the selection of suitable candidates. Consequently, their independence was compromised by county influences, extending from blatant attempts to manage their elections, to the adoption of candidates whose backgrounds fitted them to represent landed rather than urban interests.

In rural areas the landed interest had a particularly strong presence in burgh politics. The Dukes of Sutherland, for example, were so powerful in the Wick Burghs that influence bordered on nomination (Hanham: 412); while in the Wigtown District, the Earl of Stair dominated Wigtown, Mrs Gordon, (heiress of Viscount Kenmure), was prominent in New Galloway, Sir John McTaggart was 'powerful' in Stranraer, and the 'weight' of Sir Alexander Reid told in Whithorn

(Dod: 344). Dumfries Burghs were subject to 'some influence' (Dod: 98), from the Earl of Mansfield, the Marquis of Queensberry and the Duke of Buccleuch; whilst the Earls of Seafield, Fife and Kintore brought varying pressure onto the representation of the Elgin District. The Panmure's were not without support in Perth, where an heir to the family title, Fox Maule, held the constituency from 1846 to 1852. Even in an industrial seat such as the Kirkcaldy Burghs 'the predominating influence is that of the Ferguson family' (Dod: 167), long-established local landowners, who personally represented the seat for all but two years between 1832 and 1862. Even the Falkirk Burghs, in which the manufacturer Bairds of Gartsherrie represented indigenous influence, were exposed to the proprietorial influences of the Duke of Hamilton, Lord Dunmore, and 'the considerable weight' (Dod: 294) of the Earl of Zetland. Of course, the pattern of influence could vary over time, as in the Inverness Burghs. In 1840, for example, James Morrison, a London merchant and previous member for St Ives and Ipswich, carried the constituency for the Liberals due to his influence with the East India Company, through which he secured clerkships for the sons of electors (Hutchison: 52), displacing the influence of the Tory Baillies of Tarradale. By the middle of the century, however, power in Inverness had passed to Alexander Matheson, the member from 1847-68, whilst 'at Forres the Cumming-Bruces of Altyre, at Nairn the Brodies of Brodie with the Roses of Kilravock, &c., have some influence' (Dod: 152).

The politics of influence is well illustrated by Brash's account of politics in the Haddington Burghs, a district of 545 electors in 1832 (Brash: 1968). All the burghs were dependent for their economic prosperity on the surrounding countryside, and had close contact with local landowners, who frequently participated in burgh politics. Prior to 1832, lairds were often appointed as burgh parliamentary electors in contests where they, themselves, were the candidates. Most of the proprietors were Tory, including the Earl of Lauder, who lived in a castle overlooking Lauder and owned a house in Dunbar; the Marquis of Lothian, who bestowed various benefactions on Jedburgh, and with the assistance of Lord Douglas and the Duke of Buccleuch sought to secure its allegiance to the Tory cause; and the Marquis of Tweeddale, who, together with the Earls of Wemyss, Haddington and Hopetoun, and the Balfours of Whittingham, sustained an interest in Haddington itself. Brash supposes that the Earl of Minto must have exercised a countervailing influence in Jedburgh, aided by Whig landowners such as Robert Steuart, who in the last unreformed election registered a vote for himself as the elector for Haddington, and the Hamilton-Dalrymples had potential influence in North Berwick.

At the election of 1832, Robert Steuart was returned unopposed, when Lord Maitland, son of the Earl of Lauderdale, anticipating defeat, declined to test his popularity at the polls. The Tories again failed to intervene in 1835 because they were discouraged by the patronage exercised by Steuart as Lord of the Treasury. In 1837, however, Thomas Hepburn, who mother was a niece of the Earl of Lauderdale, came close to winning the seat in a contest largely determined by the 'local issue of supporting or opposing the nominee of the Conservative landowners' (Brash, 1968: 49). The Liberals prevailed in Haddington, where there were sufficient Whig landowners for the tradesmen not to fear the loss of Tory custom, but Hepburn carried Dunbar and Lauder, where the Earl of Lauderdale's influence was particularly strong (Table 4.4). None of the voters in

North Berwick supported the Conservatives, mostly because 'by the late 1830s all the chief landowners were absentees' (Brash, 1968: 42). In Jedburgh the strength of the two candidates was almost even.

Subsequently, both parties sought to improve their positions. On the Whig side, for example, two landowners, George Hope and his father, purchased property in Haddington to get themselves on the register.

More crucially, leading Tories, including Buccleuch and Lothian, spend £7,600 on the property market in Jedburgh, so that by 1841 their activites 'influenced...no less than 80 votes' (Brash, 1968: 53).

Table 4.4: General Election Results, 1837, 1841 and 1852 in the Haddington Burghs

	Haddington Votes	Dunbar Votes	Berwick Votes	Lauder Votes	Jedburgh Votes	All Votes
1837						
Steuart (L)	103	43	25	12	85	268
Hepburn (C)	69	62	0	24	82	237
1841						
Steuart (L)	97	44	26	15	82	264
Balfour (C)	66	60	6	29	112	273
1852						
Ferguson-Davie (L)	113	65	31	14	89	312
Swinton (C)	32	26	9	34	84	185

L: Liberal   C: Conservative

Additionally, they paid the taxes of impecunious Tory electors, and made net gains in the registration courts. Consequently, in 1841, James Maitland Balfour, grandson of the Earl of Lauderdale, defeated Steuart, though at a cost of more than £10,000 (Table 4.4). After 1841, however, the Conservative position declined to such an extent that Balfour failed to defend the seat in 1847. In the first place, the Conservatives suffered from the death of important leaders such as the Marquis of Lothian (1841), Lord Douglas (1844), and Sir Francis Drummond (1844), and the Marquis of Tweeddale had left to become the Governor of Madras. Secondly, a Whig counter-attack in the registration courts had significantly increased the electorate to the Liberals' advantage; and thirdly, the Disruption and repeal of the Corn Laws both strengthened the appeal of Liberalism and divided the Conservatives in a region where several leading Tories were Peelites. Consequently, the constituency fell into the lap of General Sir Henry Ferguson-Davie, 'the son of Robert Ferguson of Raith, a popular Liberal landowner who had represented East Lothian from 1835-37' (Brash, 1968: 61). He held the seat until 1878, and was opposed only once, in 1852, by Archibald Swinton, Professor of Civil Law at Edinburgh University. Enjoying only the lukewarm endorsement of the Duke of Buccleuch, Swinton lost by more than 100 votes (Table 4.4).

Haddington Burghs was not an untypical example of the politics of influence which characterised the small parliamentary burghs in this period. As in the expanding urban constituencies, such burghs had a clear bias towards Liberalism, but there remained a strong deferential element in their political culture, and Liberal townsmen welcomed the protection of Whig landowners. The influence of landowners was not only a function of their high social status and political connections, but their wealth enabled them to exert a direct influence over the electoral process through the purchase of property and in providing the resources to conduct costly registration battles. Candidate selection, too, was firmly controlled by Whig and Tory proprietorial interests. There were, nevertheless, greater limitations than in county constituencies to the power magnates could exercise. Influence had to go with the grain of public opinion. Less in tune with townsmen than the Whigs, the Tories carried Haddington in 1841 not without a considerable degree of effort and financial commitment, so that when Conservative landowners were withdrawn from the fray, their advantage rapidly eroded; and following the Disruption and the triumph of free trade the Conservatives could no longer mobilise a sufficient number of proprietors and wealth to offset their increasing disadvantage on the issues. The balance between organisational effort and substantive matters is well illustrated by Horne's remarks in 1840, apropos the Wick District: 'The registrations this year were in favour of the conservative party, and if there be no split on the church question amongst Conservatives... Dempster will carry the seat' (Horne: 272). There was a split, and Dempster was beaten 270:189 by James Loch, nominee of the Staffords. As in the Haddington and Wick Burghs, the Whigs rather than the Tories were generally the main beneficiaries of the politics of influence, because there was a more natural association between themselves and the urban £10ers, which even in the most favourable circumstances to themselves was expensive for the Conservatives to break.

The Counties

With only a third of all returns determined by recourse to a vote, elections settled at the polls were even less a feature of county politics than in the burghs (Table 4.5). In the East and Highlands threequarters of all returns were settled at the nomination stage, as were 70 per cent of elections in the seven Border constituencies. Clydeside was the only region in which the recording of votes was the norm, and Dunbartonshire (6), Refrewshire (5), Stirlingshire (5), and Haddingtonshire (5), were the only counties in which it was more common than not for an election to be contested to the finish. In Dumfriesshire and Sutherland not a single vote was recorded.

There was a dramatic collapse in the number of contested elections from the 1830s, when more than half the seats were fought, to only eight in 1841, and as few as four in 1857 and 1859 (Table 4.5). Only in 1865 was there some recovery, but there was no indication of a return to the intense struggles which characterised the first decade of reform. It would appear, therefore, that the elections of the 1830s were the product of exceptional circumstances – uncertainty as to the consequences of the new franchise, and attempts by the Tories to recover ground lost to the Whigs in 1832. Once the new equilibrium of power had been established and the features of the system understood, the parties had little incentive to pursue their rivalries beyond the registration courts. Indeed, the increasing costs of registration were themselves a disincentive to political activity.

Although one must be cautious in commenting on turnout before the intro-duction of regularly revised county registers after 1862, it appears that the level of participation declined even earlier than in the burghs. From an average turn-out of 84 per cent in each of the nineteen disputed counties in 1832, (exactly the same as in the burghs), and a 77 per cent level of participation in 1841, there was a slump to 62 per cent in 1847, which failed to improve until 1865 (Table 4.6). The main point, however, is that with so few returns being pressed to a poll, most of the time most county electors were passive by-standers in the de-termination of parliamentary representation.

Table 4.5: Number of Contested Seats in General Elections in the Scottish Counties, 1832–1865

	Seats	1832	1835	1837	1841	1847	1852	1857	1859	1865	% Contested
Highland	6	3	3	3	-	1	3	-	-	1	26
East	7	4	3	4	2	1	1	-	1	1	27
Clydeside	3	3	3	3	1	1	-	1	1	2	56
Central	7	6	4	5	2	1	1	1	1	4	40
Borders	7	3	4	4	3	1	-	2	1	1	30
All	30	19	17	19	8	5	5	4	4	9	90
% Contested		63	57	63	27	17	17	13	13	30	33

Table 4.6: Average Turnout in County Elections, 1832–1865

	1832 %	1835 %	1837 %	1841 %	1847 %	1852 %	1857 %	1859 %	1865 %	All %
Highland	79	71	74	-	66	55	-	-	-	70
East	87	74	69	77	63	77	-	48	86	76
Clydeside	83	69	77	81	64	-	78	70	75	75
Central	83	77	76	72	59	65	79	56	72	75
Borders	88	80	76	74	56	-	59	74	73	74
All	84	75	74	74	62	65	68	62	73	74

What most distinguished county from burgh constituencies was the two-party character of the electoral system in the counties, because the traditional Tory-Whig confrontation was sustained, if not stimulated, by the new franchise. With intra-party strife more potentially damaging than in urban constituencies there were only eight instances where Liberals opposed fellow Liberals – Dunbartonshire, Lanarkshire, Orkney and Shetland, Renfrewshire and Roxburghshire in 1832, Renfrewshire and Wigtownshire in 1835, and Orkney and Shetland in 1847. On five of those occasions the Liberal vote was divided in the face of Conservative opposition, but in none of them was a Liberal denied victory. The two-party confrontation, however, did not lead to an increasing number of elections fought all the way, so that from 1847 onwards Conservative-Liberal contests on polling day in the counties were no more likely than in the burghs (Table 4.7).

Although most changes of constituency partisan allegiance involved voting, 17 of the 43 transfers came in uncontested elections (Table 4.8), and partisan change after 1837 as the result of voting was the exception.

Cases of uncontested transfers frequently reflected changes in the political sympathies of landed magnates. That was particularly evident in Argyll. In 1837, the 6th Duke of Argyll, having held office in Whig administrations, ensured that the Liberal Walter Campbell of Islay and Shawfield heavily defeated an Evangelical Tory, Alexander Campbell of Monzie; but with the Duke's death in 1839, and the succession of his Conservative brother to the title, Islay was forced to allow Monzie an unopposed return in 1841 (Horne: 233, 247-8).[1]

Table 4.7: Number of Conservative v Liberal Contested Elections in the Counties, 1832–1865, compared to the Burghs

	1832–1841		1847–1865		1832–1865	
	Contests	Contests as % of all returns	Contests	Contests as % of all returns	Contests	Contests as % of all returns
Counties	61	51	25	17	82	32
Burghs	34	37	19	17	53	26
All	**95**	**45**	**44**	**17**	**139**	**29**

Table 4.8: Summary of Changes of Party Allegiances in County Constituencies, 1832–1865

	1835 1837	1841, 1847 1852, 1857	1859 1865	All
Partisan Changes through Contested Elections	15	3	8	26
Partisan Changes through Uncontested Elections	2	9	6	17
All	**17**	**12**	**14**	**43**

Sixteen years later, however, following his accession to the title, the 9th Duke, a Whig who disapproved of the incumbent Tory's opposition to Palmerston, presented the seat to a Liberal, Alexander Finlay of Toward Castle, without the need for recourse to the polls (Hutchison: 90). Similarly, in Sutherland, the Duchess Dowager '[who] will return whom she pleases' (Horne: 258), replaced her deceased husband's Liberal nominee, in 1837, with the Conservative, William Howard, second son of the Earl of Carlisle. On the death of the countess in 1839, her son, whose wife 'is a strong Whig and in office as Mistress of the Robes' (Horne: 258) forced Howard to retire in favour of a Liberal, David Dundas of Ochtertyre, in 1840.

As the Peelites drifted into non-partisanship they became less willing to support protectionist Tories. In 1847, for example, Francis Scott, fifth son of Lord

Polwarth, declined to defend Roxburgh because his opposition to free trade had lost him the wholehearted support of Buccleuch, without which he was unprepared to seek re-election, and left the field open to a Liberal, John Elliot, son of the Earl of Minto, who he had defeated in 1841 (Hutchison: 89). Aberdeenshire was lost to the Tories in 1854, when William Gordon, brother of the 4th Earl of Aberdeen, resigned his seat in favour of his nephew, George Haddo, a Liberal, who became the 5th Earl in 1860; and Bute became Liberal in 1857, because Hon. JA Wortley, brother of the Tory Marquis of Bute, switched parties to serve as Solicitor General under Palmerston.

Renfrewshire was yet another county where the preferences of individuals could have a decisive impact on the development of electoral competition. Between 1832 and 1841 elections in the county were hotly disputed, with the Liberals prevailing in 1832, 1835 and 1841, and the Conservatives at a by-election and general election in 1837. In 1846, however, the seat passed into Conservative hands at an unopposed by-election, and remained uncontested until the Liberals retook it in 1865. The change in the intensity of electoral competition was caused by a switch in the leanings of the Shaw-Stewarts of Blackhall. In 1832 and 1835 Renfrewshire had been retained by Sir Michael Shaw-Stewart, the 6th Baronet of Blackhall, who had first been returned in 1830. On his death the seat was carried by the deputy lieutenant of the county, George Houston, a Conservative, largely because the former member had paid little attention to organisation and registration (Hutchison: 51). In 1841 Houston retired, and the constituency was narrowly regained for the Liberals by Patrick Shaw-Stewart, brother of the former member. When he died in 1846, however, the seat passed to a Conservative, William Mure, without a fight. The emergence of the Tories as the undisputed representatives of Renfrewshire had arisen because the 7th Baronet of Blackhall, Michael Robert Shaw-Stewart, had deserted the Liberals, thereby tipping what had been a delicate partisan balance firmly towards the Conservatives. It took almost 20 years for the Liberals to regroup and increase their forces sufficiently to mount a challenge, when, in 1865, Archibald Spiers, a soldier/landowner, grandson of a former member and son-in-law of the 4th Earl of Radnor, defeated Michael Shaw-Stewart, first returned ten years previously.

Not all uncontested transfers reflected the foibles of individual landowners exercising their powers of nomination. Electoral battles were also avoided when parties accepted defeat following reverses in registration contests. In Caithness, for example, Sir George Sinclair of Ulbster, having deserted the Liberals, stood successfully as a Conservative against George Traill of Hobbister in 1837, but in 1840 the Liberals made an overall gain of 75 in the registration court, so that Sir George stood aside to allow his former opponent a free run the following year (Brash: 250 n). Again, in 1841, for similar reasons, the Conservatives took Dunbartonshire for the first time without opposition, and the Liberals surrendered Edinburghshire to William Ramsay, grandson of Lord Belhaven, without a fight, and failed to contest the seat again until the passing of the Second Reform Act (Brash: xxv, lxvi).

The increasing importance of the registration process had the effect of transferring the focus of elections away from polling day. Thus, unopposed returns did not necessarily indicate apathy regarding partisan outcomes, although that does seem to have been a consequence over time, because the costs involved in revising and manipulating the register discouraged opposition to incumbents.

Wigtownshire is a case in point. In 1832, the county was carried unopposed by the pre-reform member, Sir Andrew Agnew of Lochnaw, who retained the seat again in 1835, defeating both Liberal and Conservative opponents. By 1837, however, Sir Andrew had thrown his lot in with the Conservatives because he disliked the disestablishment tendencies within his party. The Earl of Galloway persuaded Lochnaw to remove himself (unsuccessfully) to the Wigtown District, making room for his own nominee, James Blair of Penninghame, to carry the county against a Liberal opponent (Brash: 225 n). In March 1840, Sir John Hamilton-Dalrymple, Liberal member for Midlothian (1832–34), became the new Earl of Stair, and made extensive purchases in the county, enabling the Liberals to make a net gain of 116 votes in the 1840 registration court, just sufficient for his nephew to defeat Blair in 1841 (Brash: 259 n). Subsequently, the Earl consolidated his control over the county, and the Conservatives failed to contest the seat again until after his death. Similarly, in Lanarkshire, the Conservatives, having taken the seat by a single vote in 1837, entrenched their position by registration gains, and were unopposed until their defeat in 1857.

The politics of registration was most developed and best exemplified in the Lothians and Borders, where, as Professor Brash has demonstrated, the Duke of Buccleuch had considerable success in organising the Conservative interest following a poor Tory performance in 1832 (Brash: xvii–lxiv).

In Midlothian, according to Brash, despite most landowners being Tories, the promotion of the Tory interest rested heavily on three peers – the 5th Duke of Buccleuch, the 7th Marquis of Lothian and the 2nd Viscount Melville, assisted by the convener of the county and constituency chairman, Sir John Hope, Dundas of Arniston, and Sir Francis Walker-Drummond, 'who may be described loosely as the executive officers of the Conservative interest' (Brash: xxxiv). Towards the end of the 1830s, they were joined by four others, including William Burn-Callander of Westerton and Prestonhall, who became the party chairman around 1850, and Richard Trotter of Mortonhall, convener of the county from 1851. Under the tutelage of the Duke of Buccleuch, James Hope WS, and, from 1836 to 1854, Harry Inglis WS, acted as agents. Buccleuch also had intelligence from Donald Horne of Langwell, who the Duke employed to encourage the Conservative interest in Scotland generally.

Although most of the tenant voters leased their farms from Tory lairds, the incumbent Conservative, Sir George Clerk, lost the election of 1832 to Sir John Hamilton-Dalrymple. His defeat was due in part to weak organisation, the Liberalism of town and village £10ers: 'a class of men who cannot be relied upon at any time,' and the 'absenteeism, inactivity and unpopularity of Conservative landowners' (Brash: xix, xxxvii). The latter problem was especially evident in the western parishes, where the Whigs, led by the Earl of Rosebery and Sir James Gibson-Craig, leader of the party in Edinburgh, were influential. It was recognised, however, that even were Conservative proprietors able to maximise their pressure on existing tentants, 'the exploitation of property for the manufacture of votes [would be] necessary for the Conservatives to regain control' (Brash: xxxviii).

Both parties recognised the centrality of the register to electoral success. Horne, for example, encouraged Conservatives to buy property held by Liberals in urban settlements, noting, for example, that while £150 purchased a house in Dalkeith yielding one vote, two votes could be conjured through joint proprietorship on a property costing £210–£230 (Horne: 7). The electorate also grew as tenant farmers who had not been enrolled in 1832 came onto the register. Consequently, in 1835, Sir George Clerk, with a majority of 31, reclaimed the seat from a new Liberal candidate, William Gibson-Craig, heir to the baronetcy of Riccarton.

Inevitably, the narrowness of the result increased the intensity of the registration battle, so that between 1835 and 1837 the electorate grew by just over a fifth, mostly through the artificial creation of joint proprietorships and life-rentships. Hope's obsession with the village £10ers, 'who should never, for their own sakes, have been entrusted with the Franchise' (Brash: xi), led him to establish a fund of £5,000 underwritten by the Dukes of Buccleuch and Lothian and Sir John Hope, for the systematic purchase of urban properties as they came onto the market. The procurement of estates burdened by debt was always a bargain, and in 1836 one such morsel, East Camps, was purchased for £600, on which the Conservatives made fourteen votes. Thus, whereas in 1832 there had been only 43 liferenters, (mostly ministers and schoolmasters), there were 235 by 1837, of whom more than 100 were on jointly held tenures. The Whigs, however, had made more votes than the Tories, so that in 1837 Gibson-Craig emerged as the victor with a majority of 42.

As the parties redoubled their efforts to maximise support, the Whigs introduced interposed trusts, which in 1838 formed the basis of their attempts to enrol 248 new electors. The Tory deputy-registering sheriff, however, dismissed 200 of the applications; but on appeal, two of the three sheriffs held interposed trusts to be admissable, and 122 of the claims were reinstated, affording the Whigs a net gain of 50 voters. Significantly, the dissenting sheriff, William Horne of East Lothian, was the brother of Buccleuch's political agent. The Conservatives replied in kind, and with more property at their disposal quickly outdistanced their opponents, making an overall gain of 314 in 1839, and a further 114 in 1840. So great was the Conservative advantage by 1841, that Gibson-Craig surrendered his seat to William Ramsay of Barnton without a fight. The Liberals were not to contest the constituency again until 1868.

The politics of registration sharply increased the cost of elections in Midlothian. Between 1832 and 1841, excluding activity in the property market, Brash estimates the Tories spent approximately £20,000 on the registration of electors, (as much as £985 in 1838), and on the conduct of contested elections. The party also found itself encumbered with a £1,839 debt incurred by its first agent, James Hope. No formally agreed procedure existed for dealing with these various expenses, although there was a rule of thumb amongst committee members that the candidate should meet half the cost of election outgoings. In the special circumstances of 1832 it was agreed that Sir George Clerk was only required to find a quarter of the amount, but in 1835 he appears to have been saddled not only with more than half the bill for the current election but also with the debt left over from 1832. Ramsay of Barnton, a committee member, considered the candidate also responsible for defraying registration costs – until he, himself, was adopted. Sir George cavilled over the committee's view that he was liable for James Hope's debts, and they were finally settled by Buccleuch and Lord Lothian. The root of these various problems was the reluctance of Conservative gentlemen to finance their interest. At election time, for example, they could not be relied upon to stump up much more than £1,000 between them.

The Conservative capture of Midlothian in 1841 was part of a general revival of Tory fortunes, as the party carried twenty county constituencies, against only nine in 1832 (Table 4.9). The achievement reflected favourably on the Duke of Buccleuch, whose direct efforts had not only secured the return of Edinburghshire, Roxburgh, Selkirk and Berwick to the fold, but had renewed the party throughout Scotland. Most importantly, the 1841 general election firmly established 15 years domination of county representation by the Tories. As Brash underlines: 'the significance of the 1841 election lay not in the number of seats gained but in the consolidation that had occurred. In 1837 when the Conservatives won eighteen counties they were unopposed in seven; of the twenty-one won in 1841 there was no opposition in sixteen' (Brash: lxii).[2] In short, the Conservatives had knocked out the Liberals following protracted registration battles in a number of constituencies. In 1841, they prevailed not only in the Borders, but held three Highland counties, (Argyll, Inverness, and Ross and Cromarty), and captured Dunbartonshire for the first time, holding it until 1892. Stirlingshire had been lost by the Liberals in 1835 for 30 years, Lanarkshire was Conservative for two decades from 1837, and Ayrshire rejected the Liberals between 1841 and 1857.

Table 4.9: Number of Seat Won by the Liberals in the Counties, 1832–1865

	1832	1835	1837	1841	1847	1852	1857	1859	1865	All
Liberals Elected	21	16	11	10	11	11	16	17	19	132

The Conservative grip did not weaken until 1857, when the loss of Bute, Ayrshire, Lanarkshire, Aberdeenshire and Argyll tilted county representation in Liberalism's favour for the first time since 1835 (Table 4.9). It has already been noted that Palmerstonian Tories had been responsible for the desertion of Bute, Aberdeenshire and Argyll, and similar forces were at work in the other two counties. In Ayrshire, the refusal of the incumbent Tory, Sir James Fergusson, to endorse Palmerston's foreign policy, lost him the crucial support of Alexander Oswald, the former Peelite member, and the Duke of Portland; and similar divisions amongst Lanarkshire Conservatives proved equally fatal (Hutchison: 90). Further Liberal gains in 1859 and 1865, arising from the continuing drift of Conservatives towards non-partisanship, and the growth of more independent voting amongst the tenantry, reduced the Scottish Tories to eleven county seats. Thus, over the period 1832-1865, with the Conservatives winning a total of 138 county seats to the Liberals 132, the two parties were evenly matched. Liberals dominated in 1832 and 1865, the Conservatives carried almost two thirds of the representation in 1837, 1841, 1857 and 1852, and the Liberals shaded their opponents in 1835, 1857 and 1859.

Regionally (Table 4.10), Liberal strength was at its greatest in the Highlands, where the party held 72 per cent of all the seats over the nine general elections, and only Inverness (Conservative 1837-1885) leaned heavily to the Tories. In other parts the Conservatives were the dominant party, epecially in the seven counties of Central Scotland, where burgh constituencies minimised the threat posed by urbanisation. Clackmannan and Kinross, controlled by the Adams of Blair Adam, which accounted for nine of the 24 Liberal successes in Central, and Ayrshire, recording five Liberal victories, were the only counties in the region to indicate an anti-Tory bias. The East was polarised between Elgin and Nairn, Aberdeen, Kincardine and Perthshire, in which Conservative candidates were elected on 31 out of a possible 36 occasions, and Banff, Forfar and Fife, where a single win in Banff constituted the only Conservative success. The Borders, too, were divided. To the west, in Galloway, Wigtown, and Kirkcudbright, an 1837 Conservative win in Wigtown constituted the only Tory success, and in Roxburgh the Liberals only failed in 1835 and 1841; but in Berwick, Selkirk, Peebles and Dumfries, Conservatives were returned in all but four instances. The Tories also had the better of the battle on Clydeside, where only Lanarkshire just favoured the Liberals, Renfrewshire returned Conservatives in five general elections, and Dunbartonshire turned decisively to the right from 1841.

Table 4.10: Regional Distribution of Liberal support in County Constituencies, 1832–1865

	Highland	East	Clydeside	Central	Borders	All
Liberals Returned	39	30	12	24	28	132
Liberal Returns as % of all	72	48	44	37	44	49

Party support, therefore, was more or less randomly distributed in regional terms, with the exception of the Whig-dominated Highlands. It was only when a more generous franchise increased the heterogeneity and interests of the county electorate, that the regional dimension in electoral behaviour became important.

Conclusion

The conflicting interests and compromises which had been a feature of the reform legislation were reflected in the operation of the 1832-68 electoral system. The objectives of the advanced reformers were realised in the independent burghs, but elsewhere the more conservative influences on the reform process prevailed. Landowners dominated county politics, and Whig proprietors exercised a great deal of influence in the smaller burgh districts. In partisan terms, the new burgh franchise virtually ensured the monopolisation of urban representation by Liberals and Whigs, whilst the county settlement was associated with an even division of influence between the Whigs and Tories.

A distinctive feature of the system was the high level of independence enjoyed by each of the 51 constituencies in the determination of their Westminster representation, because the new franchise made it impossible for ministerialists to control elections and national political parties had yet to introduce new forms of external political control. Consequently, electoral politics was less integrated at the national level than it had been in the eighteenth century. Indeed, the concept of 'general election' as a national phenomenon, whether considered in traditional terms as a question of management, or in the post-1880 context as a nationwide political struggle with local variants, was something of a misnomer. With Liberalism in the burghs such a ubiquitous sentiment, local autonomy discouraged the development of a two-party system with clearly defined ideological and organisational boundaries, so that general elections focused more on local rivalries between competing Liberal factions and individuals than on the national rivalries of the major parties. In the counties party remained largely coterminus with family interest; and in both burgh and county members were more reliant for their security on satisfying constituency opinion, (whether that of a single laird or an urban multitude), than on the favours of their party leaders. The absence of national political parties was the major factor in accounting for the high number of uncontested returns.

The extent and quality of the integration of the new electorate was clearly varied. Most of the electorate most of the time were passive by-standers in the electoral process. Excluding Glasgow and Edinburgh, the number participating in 1832 (31, 946), was never surpassed, although the highest county vote came in 1837 (Table 4.11). The 7,790 Scots who voted in 1857, nevertheless, were more than twice the entire enrolment before the Reform Act.

Table 4.11: Number of Votes Cast in Elections, 1832–1868

	1832	1835	1837	1841	1847	1852	1857	1859	1865
Counties	20,364	18,247	24,628	8,457	3,634	4,309	6,947	3,982	7,953
Burghs	11,582	8,382	6,263	9,851	6,540	7,622	10,243	3,808	3,094
Edinburgh & Glasgow*	21,809	18,541	9,724	8,275	13,227	15,259	18,869	0	36,774

* Each elector in Edinburgh and Glasgow had two votes. They could, however, use only one if they so wished.

The distinction between the county and burgh franchises, however, ensured that the county voters were far less independent than their burgh counterparts, and in most essentials county representation was determined by non-electors, the landed nobility. Only when the lairds showed little interest in the electoral process, (an increasingly significant tendency), was the enfranchised tenantry free to express its own preferences. By contrast, elections in the larger burghs reflected the independence and self-confidence of the new electorate, and even in the smallest burghs the results reflected public opinion in some measure. To that extent, the hopes of the reformers had been fulfilled.

Notes

1 Campbell of Monzie was distinguished as the only Tory Non-Intrusionist returned in 1841. He resigned his seat in 1843 following the Disruption. In 1852, he sought election in Edinburgh as a Liberal-Conservative, but failed miserably.

2   Brash's estimate of the number of Conservative wins is slightly at variance with mine in Table 4.9, derived from Craig.

References

Brash, JI, 'The Conservatives in the Haddington District of Burghs, 1832–1852,' *Transactions of the East Lothian Antiquarian and Field Naturalists' Society,* Vol. XI, 1968.
Brash, JI, *Papers on Scottish Electoral Politics, 1832–1854*, Edinburgh, 1974.
Craig, FWS, *British Parliamentary Election Results, 1832-1885,* London, 1977.
Dod, CH, *Electoral Facts Impartially State*, 1852.
Donald, J, *Past Elections in Greenock*, Greenock, 1933.
Fry, M, *Patronage and Principle*, Aberdeen, 1987.
Hanham, HJ, *Elections and Party Management*, Hassocks, 1978.
Horne, D, *Election Surveys,* edited by Brash (1974) pp. 220–278.
Hutchison, IG, *A Political History of Scotland*, Edinburgh, 1986.

5 *An Independent Scottish Constituency Aberdeen, 1832–1864*

Aberdeen was one of the few Scottish constituencies which could be described as independent. Not only were the constituency's political leaders independent of external control, but they themselves were subject to the critical scrutiny of an independent electorate. Indeed, a major theme of political behaviour in Aberdeen was the lack of deference shown by the voters to both old and new elites. The autonomy enjoyed by individual electors was reinforced by the factional character of political conflict, because each contest restructured electoral choice, requiring an elector to consider his vote anew.

Party organisations were virtually non-existent. Campaigns centred on the activities of leading families, groups of citizen and candidates, who formed *ad hoc* election committees serviced by a variety of law firms, to advance their respective causes. In order to demonstrate the popularity of their nominees, contending factions published lists of their election committees in the press, which in 1841 included almost half those who eventually voted. A vigorous political debate was sustained by public meetings, pamphleteering, and local newspapers, including the Tory *Aberdeen Journal,* the Whig *Aberdeen Herald,* the Non-Intrusionist *Aberdeen Banner,* and latterly, the Liberal *Aberdeen Free Press.*

Apart from free trade, the issues confronting the electorate, even when national in character, (such as municipal and ecclesiastical reform), had a distinctly local focus. That was particularly the case after the Conservatives ceased to contest the seat following the general election of 1841. Some matters, particularly the question of civic improvement, were purely local, and cut across conventional partisan and religious divisions. There were also geographical differences of interest within the constituency between those living in the old royalty, the new suburbs, and those outwith the municipality altogether, which were reflected in the shaping of electoral choice. Thus, the interpretation of elections involving competing Liberals cannot be reduced to a one-dimensional explanation based on religion or Whig versus Radical – to the extent those terms had any precise meaning. The selection of candidates deliberately to obfuscate the boundaries between competing social categories, in order the maximise support, only adds to the forensic problem. Indeed, as we shall see, the outcome was so confused in 1857 that the local press itself was at a loss to explain the outcome.[1]

The Constituency

In 1832, 2,024 £10 residents became the arbiters of representation in the new parliamentary burgh of Aberdeen. By 1852 their number had risen to 4,547, but following the Burgh Registration Act, (1856), fell away to 2,346 in 1857, and only rose to 3,996 in 1865.

The electors were distributed between five wards, four of them within the

Royal Burgh (Table 5.1). Wards 1-3, accounting for three fifths of the electorate, constituted what had been until the early nineteenth century the totality of the urban part of the royalty, confined on the east by the North Sea and narrowly to the west by the Denburn valley. Ward 1, centred on the harbour, was characterised by shipbuilding, commercial and trading interests, and latterly included the railway station. Ward 2 incorporated the Town House, the Sheriff Court and the North of Scotland Bank, virtually a single complex in the heart of the city, Marischal College (the younger of the two universities), and the 'Mither' Kirk of St Nicholas, to which the council paraded each Sunday. Ward 3 was dominated by manufacturing and retail interests, though not significantly more so than its neighbours.

Table 5.1: The Proportion of Voters in Contested Elections, 1835–1857 by Ward

	1835 %	1841 %	1847 %	1852 %	1857 %
Ward 1	20.7	18.6	21.4	17.9	21.6
Ward 2	17.1	16.9	17.5	15.5	14.7
Ward 3	22.1	22.4	21.0	22.6	21.1
(Wards 1-3)	(59.9)	(57.9)	(59.9)	(56.0)	(57.4)
Ward 4	20.8	23.7	23.5	27.2	26.2
Ward 5	19.3	18.3	16.6	16.8	16.3
All	100.0	99.9	100.0	100.0	99.9

Ward 4 was a new residential suburb immediately to the west of Wards 1–3, whose development had been made possible in the early years of the nineteenth century by the construction of a new major thoroughfare, Union Street, which bridged the Denburn. The separation of this new quarter from the old city was more than geographical, because it became the focus of the new middle class revolt against the traditional urban leadership, and an important location for the new Free Churches following the Disruption (MacLaren: 4–5, 61–2).

Ward 5 was outwith the municipal boundaries, and included Old Aberdeen, a Burgh of Barony with 64 inhabitants, huddled around King's College, (the older of the universities), and St Machar's Cathedral, *(P.P.,* 1835: vol. xxxix, 49). It also incorporated Woodside, an industrial village that later became a Small Burgh, an agricultural hinterland, and textile mills along the river Don, including that owned by the Haddens, the arbiters of Aberdeen politics in the years prior to reform.

Differences of character between the wards were predictably reflected in the occupational composition of their electorates (Table 5.2). In 1857, for example, against an overall 47.6 per cent of the electorate engaged in manufacturing and retail, those so employed accounted for around three fifths of the voters in Wards 1 and 3, and more than half in Ward 2, but less than a third in Wards 4 and 5. The drink interest (mostly grocers) and food retailers incorporated more than a fifth of the voters in Wards 1-3. In Ward 4 a quarter of the electors were associated with the professions; and three in ten voters in Ward 5 were engaged in agriculture. These occupational differences in some measure help to explain differences in voting behaviour between the various parts of the constituency.

Table 5.2: Aberdeen Voters in 1857 by Occupational Categories and Ward

	Ward 1 %	Ward 2 %	Ward 3 %	Ward 4 %	Ward 5 %	All %
Drink	16.5	14.8	15.8	8.1	10.7	13.0
Food Retail	6.6	5.4	5.5	2.4	1.3	4.2
Textiles	10.1	8.7	12.6	6.5	6.5	8.9
Leather	5.2	4.3	4.8	4.0	3.6	4.4
Engineering & Allied Trades	5.7	5.8	6.0	3.6	3.6	4.9
Foundry & Forge	2.7	2.9	5.5	1.6	1.6	2.9
Other Manufacturers	4,2	4.7	3.5	3.2	1.6	3.5
Miscellaneous Sales	7.6	7.2	7.8	3.2	3.6	5.8
(Manufacturers & Retail)	(58.6)	(53.8)	(61.5)	(32.6)	(32.5)	(47.6)
Service	3.2	3.2	2.5	2.0	2.3	2.6
Construction	4.4	3.6	4.5	7.9	5.8	5.5
Shipping/Harbour	9.3	3.6	1.3	3.4	1.3	3.9
Non-Maritime Transport	3.2	4.3	2.0	3.8	1.9	3.1
Banking/Insurance	4.7	6.1	2.5	4.5	0.3	3.7
The Professions	7.9	13.0	13.3	25.3	12.3	15.1
Gentlemen	4.7	3.2	3.0	6.5	10.1	5.5
Agriculture & Fishing	3.9	8.3	8.8	12.8	30.8	12.3
Other	0.2	0.7	0.5	1.0	2.6	1.0
Total	**100.1**	**99.8**	**99.9**	**99.9**	**99.9**	**100.3**

Elections

In Aberdeen between 1832 and 1865 elections fell into three phases: (1) The Whig-Liberal Ascendancy, 1832–1841, characterised by competition between Liberal and Conservative candidates; (2) The Free Church and New Middle Class Revolt, 1847–1852, characterised by a rejection of traditional elites; and (3) The Waning of Old Alignments, 1857–1865, characterised by a confusion of earlier alliances.

The Whig-Liberal Ascendancy was dominated by a conflict between two local families, the Haddens (Tories) and the Blaikies (Whigs), and their respective allies. The Haddens had been the incumbent power in the city for at least 30 years prior to reform. James Hadden of Persley, textile manufacturer and father of the modern city, was Lord Provost 1801–3, 1809–11, and 1832–33, and his brother, Gavin, Lord Provost 1820–22, 1824–26, and 1830–32. Their power rested on the control they exercised over the close corporation, and the patronage they exerted with respect to municipal improvements, harbour and kirk works, and the appointment of ministers and the professors of mathematics and divinity at Marischal College *(P.P., 1835: vol. xxxix, 20)*. They were largely responsible for bridging the Denburn, which had laid the foundations for Aberdeen's expansion and increased prosperity. The Haddens were also landowners, and had close connections with agricultural proprietors. They opposed burgh, parliamentary, and ecclesiastical reform, and supported protection. The *Journal,* whose editor, David Chalmers, was a member of the unreformed corporation, gave the Haddens its support.

As part of an inter-connected commercial aristocracy, the Blaikie Whigs were more like their opponents than the new £10ers, and like the Haddens were involved in textile manufacturing and the law. They also had interests in iron founding and shipbuilding. If there was a distinction between the Whigs and Tories it is that the former were more exclusively tied to the commercial activities of the burgh than their opponents (MacLaren: 19–22). The main conflict between them was a political struggle for the control of municipal affairs. The Blaikies were particularly concerned about the mismanagement of harbour improvements arising 'from the vast preponderance of self-selected magistrates'[2] on the board of trustees. Following burgh reform, the Blaikies assumed municipal leadership, the lord provostship being held by James Blaikie, 1833–1836, and Thomas Blaikie, 1839–1847 and 1853–1855.

Close allies of the Blaikies were the Bannermans. Alexander Bannerman, a wine importer, who became the Liberal candidate in 1832, had previously been appointed to the council by James Hadden, but in 1812 had been forced to leave the corporation over a dispute regarding the appointment of a minister. The mouthpiece of the Whigs was the *Herald,* whose editor, Adam, an anti-clerical in the European mode, disliked the enthusiasm of the Non-Intrusionist Evangelicals even more than the Moderate establishment.

Exclusion from political patronage led the Whigs to identify with the movement for reform. Bannerman blamed the bankruptcy of the council in 1818 on the incompetence of the Haddens, and suggested the improvements they had effected had been done for private rather than public gain. In 1830 he organised a reform petition signed by 121 members of the Seven Incorporated Trades and Burgesses of Guild, which was rejected by James Hadden. The strength of support for political change and free trade amongst even this conservative section of the trading and manufacturing community underlined the wide base of Bannerman's coalition. Bannerman also identified with Non-Intrusionist sentiment within the kirk, although the political significance of this issue was less central in 1832 than it was to become later in the decade. Given the antipathy towards the Tories for having opposed reform, it was not surprising that James Hadden withdrew his intention to contest the seat in 1832.

The wisdom of Hadden's retreat in 1832 was confirmed in 1833 when the Whig-Liberals carried every seat on the reconstituted burgh council. Despite a system that favoured plumping, (six candidates to be returned in each of three wards)[3], all former members of the corporation who stood were defeated. In Municipal Ward 3, James Blaikie topped the poll, with James Hadden 92 votes behind the candidate returned in sixth place. In a separate election for the Dean of Guild, Thomas Bannerman defeated David Chalmers, editor of the *Journal,* by 283 to 145, underlining the extent of business support for Whiggery. It was not until 1837 that the first Tory was returned to the reformed council.[4]

The Whig apotheosis came with the general election of 1835, when Bannerman received 71.6 per cent of the votes against a Tory, Admiral Sir Arthur Farquhar, a landowner with a town house in Aberdeen (Table 5.3). Although the committee lists are too limited to make a comprehensive analysis of party support, it is instructive to note that while no fewer than 49 of the signatories to the 1830 petition requesting burgh reform were members of Bannerman's election committee, only two declared themselves for Sir Arthur. It is noteworthy, too, that in the industrial and commercial Wards, 1-3, the sitting member received more than threequarters of the vote. Even in the fastnesses of Ward 5 the admiral failed to win 40 per cent of the poll. The lesser support for Bannerman in Wards 4 and 5, nevertheless, indicated a weakening of Whig influence away from the commercial and manufacturing heart of the Royal Burgh.

Table 5.3: The Results of the Aberdeen Elections 1835 and 1841 by Ward

	1835			1841*		
	Bannerman	Farquhar	Bannerman %	Bannerman	Innes	Bannerman %
Ward 1	200	70	74.1	150	91	60.2
Ward 2	170	53	76.2	137	81	61.2
Ward 3	228	61	78.9	181	109	60.5
Ward 4	184	87	67.9	183	124	59.2
Ward 5	156	96	61.9	129	108	53.3
All	938	367	71.9	780	513	59.0

* In 1841, a Chartist won 30 votes or 2.3 per cent of the poll. (8 votes in Ward 1; 6 votes in Ward 2; 9 votes in Ward 3; 2 votes in Ward 4; and 5 votes in Ward 5)

Given the outcome in 1835, it was no surprise there was an unopposed election again in 1837, but by 1841, as part of a general trend in Scotland towards the Conservatives, there was a significant diminution in Bannerman's popularity (Table 5.3). To a certain extent that reflected a weakening of gratitude towards the Liberals for the Reform Act, but more specifically it indicated strains within the Whig-Liberal coalition precipitated by the crisis in the kirk.

In many respects the reform alliance between the Whig elite and the new middle class had been one of convenience, for while the former had been prepared to ride the tiger of reform to replace the Tories as the arbiters of social control, they did not share the desires of the latter for a fundamental transformation of the political, social and ecclesiastical establishment. As long as the kirk remained unified, the Whigs could temporise with Non-Intrusionist sentiment, but as it became more insistent and drifted towards schism the alliance could not be sustained. Furthermore, whereas in 1832 the Non-Intrusionists had been politically unorganised, by the end of the decade they had established a network of connection outwith the traditional urban leadership, and had established their own newspaper, the *Banner*, to press their case.

In response, the *Herald*, formerly a bitter opponent of the Haddens, voicing the opinions of the Whig leadership, advocated a *rapprochement* between the Whigs and Tories to resist the putative Free Churchmen. By 1839, local government elections were being contested between Whig-Tory Moderates (Intrusionists), thereby effecting a political alliance between the Haddens and the Blaikies, and Non-Intrusionist opponents. The new local government alignment was particularly problematical for Bannerman because it opened a rift between his major backers and the majority of his voters, whose evangelical cause he could not ignore.

Bannerman was fortunate that he faced a Conservative, (Innes of Raemoir, a Kincardineshire landowner), rather than a fellow Liberal, at the general election of 1841, because it revived the reform coalition that had broken down at local government level. Although his election address made no mention of the crisis in the kirk, he could not ignore the 'very delicate' religious question. As a non-Presbyterian Dissenter he attempted to distance himself from the issue, and waffled his way between support for 'any new measure to give the people a substantial choice in the choice of their ministers,' and opposition to proposals 'intended to give the clergy more power' (*Banner:* 3.7.1841). Thus, he sought to satisfy the demand of the Non-Intrusionists for greater control by congregations over their own affairs, while at the same time, in order to placate the voluntaries, distancing himself from evangelicals seeking a significant secular role for the kirk in a spiritually reformed establishment. The fudge proved acceptable to the *Banner* and the *Herald*, but risked alienating traditional Kirkmen.

Although Bannerman won comfortably, a drop in overall support of 12.9 per cent on 1835 indicated a weakened alignment. While the parameters of support remained essentially the same as before, with the inner city wards most supportive, Bannerman's decline in Wards 1-3 of 15.9 per cent was almost twice as much as in Wards 4 and 5 (8.5 per cent). The greater movement of traditional Aberdeen towards the Conservatives suggested a greater affection for the Auld Kirk than was the case in the suburbs. As the *Banner* (10.7.1841) noted, 'A number of Whig-Moderates refused to vote, notwithstanding the editor of the Herald's "satisfaction" with Mr Bannerman.'

In occupational terms, electors engaged in manufacturing and retail were strongly behind Bannerman (Table 5.4). Collectively, they constituted 59 per cent of his election committee and 71.3 per cent of all manufacturers and retailers who declared their affiliation. Food retailers (72.3 per cent) and the drink trade (75.0 per cent) were particularly supportive. It was, however, a reflection of the Hadden influence that those connected with textiles were hardly more Liberal than the constituency as a whole. By contrast, Innes had the overwhelming backing of those associated with banking and insurance (66.7 per cent) and the professions (59.8 per cent); enjoyed a clear lead among those engaged in agriculture (53.4 per cent); and had an almost equal share (48.7 per cent) of the residenter vote. Consequently, there was a clear distinction between the profiles of Liberal and Conservative support in respect of economic interest. Whereas three fifths of all Liberals were associated with manufacturing and retail, as against 49.2 per cent of all voters, only 36 per cent of Conservatives were so engaged; and although only 37.8 per cent of those declaring their voting intentions were classified as residenters or connected with the professions, banking, insurance, and agriculture, they accounted for 52.8 per cent of all Conservatives as against 26.6 per cent of Liberals.

The Free Church and New Middle Class Revolt Whig-Tory co-operation in local politics reflected a mutual commitment to civic improvement and commercial development, in which the principals drew little distinction between their own private ambitions and the public interest. (The Blaikie's, for example, made sewage pipes.) Those efforts were stimulated by the North of Scotland Bank, the creation of Anderson, a Tory, but whose fellow directors, including

Provost Blaikie, were predominantly Whig. The bank, appealing to local patriotism, attracted investors from the new middle class, and advanced cheap loans to its friends, notably Thomas Bannerman & Co., Hadden & Sons, and Masson & Co., and advanced a substantial loan to Adam & Anderson to assist the promotion of a railway bill (Keith: 49–51). There was also a masonic link, Alexander Hadden and Thomas Blaikie being quondam master and deputy master of the Provincial Grand Lodge. The apotheosis of the Whig-Tory alliance came with the formation of the Aberdeen Marketing company in 1839 under the chairmanship of James Hadden, with James Blaikie as a co-director. It was a measure of their accord that at the opening of the covered Market in 1842, which included the building of new streets, Blaikie said of Hadden that, 'No man has ever done so much for the improvement of the city' (*Herald*, 30.4.1842).

Table 5.4: Profiles of Liberal and Conservative Support at the General Election of 1841 by Occupation based on the Composition of the Election Committees

	Bannerman Share of Poll	Above/ Below Overall Share	Profile of Bannerman Support	Profile of Innes Support
	%	%	%	%
Drink	75.0	+14.8	12.7	6.4
Food Retail	72.7	+12.5	4.5	2.6
Textiles	62.2	+2.0	13.6	9.9
Leather	76.0	+15.8	5.4	2.6
Engineering & Allied Trades	68.6	+8.4	6.8	4.7
Foundry & Forge	69.2	+9.0	2.5	1.7
	75.0	+14.8	4.2	2.1
Miscellaneous Sales	70.2	+10.0	9.3	6.0
(Manufactures & Retail)	(71.3)	(+10.1)	(59.0)	(36.0)
Service	66.7	+6.5	0.6	0.4
Construction	70.6	+10.4	6.8	4.3
Shipping/Harbour	65.2	+5.0	4.2	3.4
Non-Maritime Transport	50.0	-10.2	0.6	0.9
Banking/Insurance	33.3	-26.9	1.1	3.4
The Professions	39.8	-20.4	12.2	27.9
Residenters.	51.3	-8.9	5.7	8.2
Agriculture & Fishing	46.6	-13.6	7.6	13.3
Other	58.3	-1.9	2.0	2.1
(Non Manufacturers & Retail)	(49.4)	(-10.8)		
All	60.2		99.8	99.9

The Hadden-Blaikie accord, which sustained the Provostship of Thomas Blaikie, 1840–47, was based on a dynamic civic leadership, which established a coalition that extended across the religious spectrum from Tory Episcopalians to Liberal voluntaries, leaving the Free Churchmen isolated. In 1840, for example, the Non-Intrusionists attributed their poor performance in the local elections to 'worldly-minded Churchmen, Episcopalians, and revilers of scriptural principles' *(Banner*: 7.11.1840); and in the first post-Disruption municipal election in 1843: 'Not a single candidate of Moderate views in Church matters [took] the field but his starting is forthwith traced to the intrigues of the Market Company' *(Herald*, 21.10.1843), and 'of the three candidates started by the Non-Intrusionists...not one [was] returned' *(Herald*: 11.11.1843).

In the latter half of the 1840s, however, an economic recession weakened confidence in the traditional leadership, and in 1847 the initiatives of the Haddens and Blaikies were brought to an end when a meeting of citizens rejected an improvement plan that involved, *inter alia*, the municipalisation of the gas company. This event was the first in a chain of crises which was to undermine the foundations on which the old civic leadership had been secured.

A leading opponent of improvement had been Alexander Dingwall Fordyce of Brucklay, a landowner and former naval captain living in Ward 4, who between 1842 and 1844 had been a city councillor. He was also an ordained elder of the Free Kirk (MacLaren, 233). From 1845 he began to canvass support of not only Liberals but also of Conservatives opposed to improvement, including David Chalmers of the *Journal,* who disagreed with the Haddens in this matter. With his electoral coalition divided, the Blaikies having lost the confidence of their municipal supporters, and Fordyce strategically placed to win the Free Church vote (the largest tranche of the electorate), Bannerman, on the eve of the dissolution, decided to retire from parliament rather than face a contest. As a riposte to Fordyce, the Blaikies and Haddens, with the backing of the *Herald*, jointly put forward an Anglican Englishman, Colonel Sykes, a director of the East India Company, as a Liberal. By choosing a candidate removed from direct involvement in the complexities of Scottish Presbyterian factionalism, his selection was designed to appeal to the commercial instincts of the electorate, and to minimise the importance of the religious question. Thus, local and national political alliances, which had differed in 1841, were once again reconciled.

The strength of Fordyce's candidature was that not only did he identify with the Free Churchmen, but as a landowner he could appeal to Tories of a similar social (though not religious) background in the countryside, and as an anti-improver could attract lower middle class Conservative electors who had lost confidence in the Haddens. On his committee, the *Herald* identified 'Roman Catholics and Unitarians, ultra-Moderates and Ultra Frees, Puseyites, Presbyterians, Dissenters, Congregationalists and Baptists, Free Episcopalians, and Episcopalians free and easy' *(Herald* 17.7.1847). Consequently, he attracted a level of support only marginally less than that of Bannerman in 1835, and won more votes across all wards than had his predecessor in 1841 (see Table 5.5, and compare with Table 5.3). It is, however, significant that Fordyce did best in Wards 4 and 5, covering the area outwith the commercial heart of the city, where Bannerman had been weakest. Explaining the outcome, the *Herald* concluded:

> Captain Fordyce had the ultimate support of three or four distinct parties... First, the Free Churchmen...bound to him hand and foot... Then came the Dissenters, who continued to bore a hole in Captain Fordyce's endowment principle, and then shrank from their own Voluntarism... After the Disestablishers came the Anti-Improvement faction – the most vicious, the most influential, but the least numerous of Captain Fordyce's supporters... Lastly came the Chartists, or rather,

perhaps a few of them, with Mr. John MacPherson at their head (*Herald*, 7.8.1847).

Table 5.5: The Results of the Aberdeen Elections 1847 and 1852 by Ward

	1847			1852		
	Fordyce	Sykes	Fordyce %	Thomson	Hay	Thomson %
Ward 1	200	87	69.7	138	70	66.3
Ward 2	139	95	59.4	90	90	50.0
Ward 3	193	89	68.4	142	120	54.2
Ward 4	222	93	70.5	205	110	65.1
Ward 5	164	58	73.9	107	88	54.9
All	918	422	68.5	682	478	58.8

In occupational terms, the voters were significantly less polarised than in 1841, so that the profile of support for each of the candidates was remarkably similar (Table 5.6). Nevertheless, reflecting his appeal to Conservatives, Fordyce performed substantially better than had Bannerman amongst residenters, landowner-farmers, and the professions, although the latter, dominated by lawyers who split 34:33 in favour of Sykes, were significantly less favourable to the landowner than members of other professions.

Table 5.6: Profiles of Support for Fordyce and Sykes at the General Election of 1847 by Occupation based on the Poll Book

	Fordyce Share of Poll %	Above/Below Overall Share %	Profile of Fordyce %	Profile of Sykes %
Drink	70.0	+1.5	12.2	11.6
Food Retail	75.4	+6.9	4.7	3.3
Textiles	68.5	0.0	10.2	10.2
Leather	65.1	-3.4	4.5	5.2
Engineering & Allied Trades	75.3	+6.8	7.0	5.0
Foundry & Forge	63.4	-5.1	2.8	3.6
Other Manufacturers	75.0	+6.5	5.9	4.3
Miscellaneous Sales	75.9	+7.4	7.2	5.0
(Manufactures & Retail)	(71.1)	(+2.6)	(54.5)	(48.2)
Service	26.7	-41.8	0.4	2.6
Construction	70.1	+1.6	6.0	5.5
Shipping/Harbour	66.7	-1.8	3.9	4.3
Non-Maritime Transport	89.5	+21.0	1.9	0.5
Banking/Insurance	68.1	-0.4	3.5	3.6
The Professions	58.2	-10.3	12.4	19.4
Residenters.	70.6	+2.1	3.9	3.6
Agriculture & Fishing	67.9	-0.6	11.5	11.8
Other	85.7	+17.2	2.0	0.7
(Non Manufacturers and Retail)	(65.6)	(-2.9)	(45.5)	(52.0)
All	68.5		100.0	100.2

The break-up of the 1841 alignments is well illustrated by the behaviour of individual electors between 1841 and 1847. A notable feature of the behaviour of 1841 voters in 1847 was that a third of those who had voted for Bannerman and almost two fifths of those who had supported Innes failed to register a vote for either Sykes or Fordyce (Table 5.7). Of those that did, resoundingly rejecting their former Whig leaders, less than one in five of Bannerman's former coalition backed the colonel. Similarly, the Haddens were only able to influence 54.5 per cent of the former Innes voters who expressed a preference. Consequently, while Sykes had an estimated[5] majority of 29 amongst former Innes supporters, Fordyce led by more than 300 amongst those who had voted for Bannerman, and more than 70 per cent of new electors expressed a preference for Fordyce (Table 5.8).

Table 5.7: Behaviour of Bannerman and Innes Election Committee Members at the 1841 General Election in the General Election of 1847

	Bannerman			Innes		
	(1841)	%	%	(1841)	%	%
Fordyce	187	53.0	80.3	66	28.3	45.5
Sykes	46	13.0	19.7	79	33.9	54.5
No Vote	120	34.0		88	37.8	
Total	**353**	**100.0**	**100.0**	**233**	**100.0**	**100.0**

Assuming that the new voters had similar political orientations as the old voters, four factions can be identified: (i) The Hadden Tories (Innes voters for Sykes), an estimated 19 per cent of the electorate; (ii) The New Conservatives (Innes voters for Fordyce), an estimated 17.8 per cent of the electorate; (iii) the Blaikie Whigs, (Bannerman voters for Sykes), an estimated 12.6 per cent of the electorate; and (iv) the New Liberals (Bannerman voters for Fordyce), an estimated 50.7 per cent of the electorate.

The rout of the traditional elite in 1847 over improvement, and their failure to secure the return of Skyes, was completed by the decision of Thomas Blaikie to retire from the council, and his replacement as Lord Provost by George Thomson junior, a Free Church shipowner and anti-improver, who had nominated Fordyce in the general election. The defeat of the old order was underlined a month later when the voluntaristic majority on the council reduced the status of the Auld Kirk, 'resolving that Magistrates attending church be dispensed with in future,' (Ross: 1889, 101). More traumatic for the commercial and manufacturing establishment was the collapse of the textile industry in 1848, whose unsecured loans (especially those of Leys, Masson and Hadden & Sons), almost brought down the North of Scotland Bank with it (Keith, 48-60).

Although the reconstituted board included most of the former directors, (including Lord Provost Thomson and Thomas Blaikie), greater concern for the interests of investors in its practices completed a shift in power towards the new middle class that had already taken place in the kirk and politics. The new social synthesis was typified by Lord Provost Thomson, who combined his close commercial contacts with the Whig-Tory establishment, with a cautious approach to municipal expenditure and strong commitment to the Free Kirk.

Table 5.8: Derivation of Support for Fordyce and Sykes in the General Election of 1847

	Fordyce		Sykes		Fordyce	Majority
		%		%	%	Fordyce
Bannerman*	413	45.0	102	24.2	80.2	+311
Innes*	145	15.8	174	41.2	45.5	- 29
New	360	39.2	146	34.6	71.1	+214
All	**918**	**100.0**	**422**	**100.0**	**68.5**	**+496**

* Figures adjusted from Election Committee numbers.

When Fordyce announced his intention to retire from parliament in February 1852, a meeting of his election committee, consisting of around 50 people, met to discuss the matter. After expressing their regret at the MP's decision, several members proposed that ex-Lord Provost Thomson be adopted in his stead. Thomson initially declined, but agreed to reconsider. Councillor Torrie (a Churchman), however, who was in correspondence with Colonel Sykes, demurred:

> Why if a candidate was to be fixed upon, not call all the electors... Captain Fordyce's election committee had been composed of all parties – Whigs, Tories, Conservatives, Liberals, Radicals and Chartists – why not allow all these parties a voice... It was an easy way of making Liberals assume, as several gentlemen had done, that this was a Liberal committee. He (Mr Torrie) used to be called a Conservative, and there were other Conservatives present... He had been present at many meetings and words failed him to characterise the manoeuvre attempted to be palmed upon the independent electors of Aberdeen (*Herald*, 21.2.1852).

Others expressed the view that the supporters of Hay, (a Liberal already in the field), should also be given an opportunity to participate. Consequently, although the Fordyce committee was to form the core of Thomson's committee, after he had agreed to stand, it had to be reconstituted on a somewhat narrower base. A major gain for Thomson, however, was the endorsement of the *Herald*, (which had deserted the Blaikies in this matter), for his 'steadfastness in the cause of Free Trade' (*Herald*, 3.4.1852), and although not approving of his Sabbatarianism, noted his backing for voluntarism and a national system of education, and 'forgave him his leanings towards the Pharisees, and the Puritanical nomenclature of his ships' (*Herald*, 28.2.1852).

Thomson's opponent, Sir Andrew Leith Hay, a soldier/landowner, was Governor of Bermuda (1838–41), and a former member for the Elgin Burghs, who had only supported free trade with qualifications. Although he was backed by the Blaikies, the Haddens took no interest in the contest, (none of them even bothered to vote). A meeting of Conservative electors failed to take a collective decision on which candidate they preferred, although of the 65 present 29 eventually voted for Hay and only five for Thomson.[6]

Given the hostility of the press, the indifference of the Haddens, and the reduced influence of the Blaikies, it was somewhat remarkable that Hay polled 56 more votes than had Sykes in 1847, whilst Thomson ran 236 votes behind Fordyce (Table 5.5).

As in 1847, a notable feature of electoral behaviour was the substantial turn-over of electors. In 1847, 49 per cent of participants failed to register a prefer-ence in 1852, and 35.6 per cent were new voters. Of those who had supported Fordyce, 40.8 per cent went to Thomson and 12.6 per cent to Hay, whereas only 11.1 per cent of former Sykes voters backed the ex-Provost and 34.4 per cent moved to Sir Andrew (Table 5.9). Of the Conservative electors who had backed Innes in 1841 and voted in 1852, (64.4 per cent did not), 55.4 per cent voted for Hay – virtually the same proportion as had declared for Sykes in 1847. On the other hand, while the 45.5 per cent of remaining 1841 Bannerman voters fa-voured Thomson with 68.6 per cent of their preferences, it was significantly less than the 80.3 per cent that had endorsed Fordyce. New voters broke 55.6 per cent in favour of Thomson. Thus, while the basic parameters of the Fordyce coalition had been sustained, it was not without amendment.

Thomson was clearly less popular than Fordyce in all wards. Only in Free-Church Ward 4 did he almost match his predecessor (Table 5.5). Hay, by con-trast, had a more variable performance. Despite an overall improvement on Sykes' performance, he ran behind the colonel in Wards 1 and 2, which covered the harbour and administrative centre of Aberdeen, but significantly outpolled him in Wards 3 and 5. Sir Andrew even polled better than Sykes in Ward 4, de-spite Thomson's strength there. In relative terms, Thomson performed much better in Wards 1 (66.3 per cent) and 4 (65.1 per cent), than in 5 (54.9 per cent), 3 (54.2 per cent) and 2 (50.0 per cent).

The significantly greater strength of Thomson in Wards 1 and 4 reflected his shipping interests and religious convictions. Thomson's success in the harbour ward, however, was somewhat ambiguous, for although he retained the bulk of continuing Fordyce voters, and attracted 43.6 per cent of continuing Sykes elec-tors, (as against less than a quarter of former Sykes voters across the constitu-ency), under half the 1847 electorate participated in the 1852 contest (Table 5.9). Significantly, Ward 1 contributed a smaller share of the total vote than in any election of the period (Table 5.1). It would appear, therefore, that while Thomson commanded the favours of harbour-based electors because of his shipping interests, his Free Churchmanship was a liability. Rather than vote for him or his opponent, a significant number of electors abstained. Elsewhere in the Old City (Wards 2 and 3), however, antipathy towards the Free Church can-didate remained as pronounced as in 1847.

Thomson's clearest strength came from the Free Churchmen. Fully 18 per cent of all his votes came from Free Kirk elders and deacons, who split 135:15 in his favour. Significantly, Ward 4, which contributed its highest proportion of the electorate in any election of the period, included three in ten of all Thomson voters. It was a reflection of the importance of Free Churchmanship in this sub-urb that a higher proportion of former Fordyce voters turned out for Thomson that in any other ward, (Table 5.9). Conversely, a smaller proportion of ex-Sykes voters in Ward 4 switched to the ex-Lord Provost than in other wards, suggesting that in this ward religious polarities, established in 1847, were par-ticularly important.

The contrast with 1847, therefore, reflected differences in the social charac-teristics of the candidates representing the two coalitions, and the ending of the improvement issue that had enabled Fordyce to establish a broad-based coalition that cut across the religio-political divide. Unable to combine the radicalism of the new urban middle class with a traditional rural interest, as had his predecessor, Thomson's 'great victory over a combination of city and county magnates' (*Herald,* 10.7.1852), was heavily dependent on his Free Churchmanship.

Table 5.9: Behaviour of 1847 Voters at the General Election of 1852

	Fordyce to Thomson %	Fordyce to Hay %	Fordyce* to Thomson %	Sykes to Thomson %	Sykes to Hay %	Sykes* to Thomson %
Ward 1	37.5	9.5	79.8	19.5	25.3	43.6
Ward 2	42.4	10.8	79.7	9.5	34.7	21.4
Ward 3	40.4	13.5	75.0	9.0	38.2	19.0
Ward 4	47.3	9.9	82.7	3.2	36.6	8.1
Ward 5	35.4	20.7	63.0	17.2	37.9	31.3
All	**40.8**	**12.6**	**76.4**	**11.1**	**34.4**	**24.5**

* Excluding abstainers in 1852 from the calculation.

The Waning of Past Alignments

Thomson had been a reluctant candidate in 1852, and announced his retirement on the eve of the 1857 general election. His retiral led to the most confused election of the period, mainly due to a split in the Free Church vote.

The two candidates in 1857 were John Farley Leith and Colonel Sykes, making a second attempt to capture the constituency. Leith was the son of a military officer and son-in-law of an Aberdeen doctor. Five years after graduating from Aberdeen University in 1825, Leith was called to the bar at the Middle Temple, and lived on an estate in Essex. Colonel Sykes had maintained his connections with Aberdeen after 1847, becoming University Rector in 1854, and by 1857 was chairman of the East India Company. Thus, for the first time since 1832 there was no local candidate.

Thomson claimed he left parliament due in part to his opposition (expressed in the lobbies) to the Opium War, described by the *Free Press* (6.3.1857), the voice of progressive mid-century Liberalism in the region, as 'one of the darkest chapters in our national history.' Leith was the obvious successor to the former Lord Provost in that he, too, opposed the opium trade. He also identified with growing disestablishment sentiment amongst both Free Church as well as Dissenting Presbyterians, and approved of Thomson's parliamentary votes against the state subsidy of religion in Ireland, which involved not only a grant to the Roman Catholic college at Maynooth, but also financial assistance to Irish Presbyterians and (particularly) the Episcopal Church of Ireland. Sykes, by contrast, was deeply implicated in the Indian poppy industry, and as a member of the Church of England supported the claims of the Church of Ireland.

Leith, however, failed to command the support of Thomson and his allies, ostensibly because he had been canvassing before the ex-provost had indicated his decision to retire. Consequently, having nominated Fordyce in 1847, Thomson declared for the colonel in the current contest. At the same time, Sykes rejected his formerly profitless alliance with the Blaikies and Haddens, and created a base amongst Free Churchmen through his commercial contacts, (including Thomson), so that both his proposer and seconder were Free Churchmen who had previously voted for Fordyce and Thomson.

As a result of these various manoeuvrings, Leith found himself representing a motley coalition that included the conflicting leaderships of the previous three decades. His principled stand on the issues attracted the support of Free Church ministers and John MacPherson, a leading Chartist, whilst Sykes' desertion of his 1847 backers also brought Leith the endorsement of the spurned Blaikies and Haddens. Sykes, however, had secured the Free Church secular leadership through Thomson, and commanded the favours of the Conservative *Journal*. He also enjoyed the support of the *Free Press,* which ignored its own opposition to the opium trade and the Maynooth Grant, and insinuated (without evidence) that Leith was a government nominee, whereas Sykes was free from sectional interest (*Free Press*, 20.3.1857). The new alignment of forces brought the comment that:

> Not only do the ties of political party seem fairly dissolved, but even the stronger bands of ecclesiastical connection and sympathy. It is not now the old antago-nism of Tory and Whig, or the more recent conflict between Conservative and Liberal – it is not even that of Churchman and Dissenter – of Voluntary and Anti-Voluntary, no, not even that of Old Church and Free. All the recognised, inveterate ambitions are at an end in Aberdeen, and out of the clouds two new ones are extemporised. For on the one side you see at the foot of Market Street, all those elements in happy (if but temporary) harmony, and coalescence, yet bristling all over with antagonisms to a like strange conglomerate at the top! (*Aberdeen Free Press,* 27.3.1857)

The result of the election, in which Sykes won 54.9 per cent of the votes, was the closest of the period, and attracted the most voters, 1,884, 81 per cent of the recently purged register. Almost three fifths of those participating (1,126) had not voted in 1852, and 45.9 per cent (865) voted in an Aberdeen parliamentary election for the first time. The overall geographical pattern of the result was less reminiscent of the outcome in the two previous contests than those of 1835 and 1841, in which the victor, basing his appeal on business interests, ran best in the old city and was at his weakest outwith the royalty (Table 5.10).

Despite a smaller overall share of the poll than Thomson, Sykes won a larger proportion of the poll than the ex-Provost in Wards 1–3, running best in Ward 1 (63.2 per cent) and Ward 2 (59.2 per cent), where non-1852 voters broke par-ticularly strongly in his favour. By contrast, Sykes was at his weakest in Ward 5 (41.9 per cent), where he became the first winning candidate not to carry all the wards. It was notable that whereas 55.7 per cent of continuing Thomson voters across all wards backed the colonel, in Ward 5 only 35.4 per cent did so (Table 5.12).

Sykes proved especially popular with those engaged in commerce and trade. The shipbuilding and harbour interest gave him 85.1 per cent of their votes (Table 4.11), and he carried the support of 70 per cent of those engaged in food retailing, and 62.9 per cent of the drink vote, which formed the basis of his success in Wards 1 and 2. Amongst most other categories, however, Sykes ran below the overall distribution of the vote. Leith's association with the Blaikies and Haddens helps to explain his strength amongst manufacturers, particularly foundrymen (57.4 per cent), and those engaged in the construction industry (58.3 per cent), which was reflected by the outcome in Ward 3. The growing rivalry between the new railway companies and establishing shipping lines brought Leith the backing of 58.6 per cent of those employed in non-maritime transport; and agriculturalists, almost a third of the voters in Ward 5, favoured him with 64.2 per cent of their registrations.

A critical dimension to the election was the behaviour of the Free Church vote. Leith, with his principled stand on foreign policy, opposition to Maynooth and leanings towards voluntarism, (increasingly popular with urban Free Churchmen), was the Free Church choice in religious terms.

Table 5.10: Result of the General Election of 1857 by Ward Comparing Voters in 1852 with Other Voters

		% of All Voters	Sykes	Leith	Sykes %
Ward 1	1852 Voters	40.8	98	68	59.0
	Others	59.2	161	80	66.8
	All	100.0	259	148	63.6
Ward 2	1852 Voters	54.0	64	58	52.5
	Other	56.0	100	55	64.5
	All	100.0	164	113	59.2
Ward 3	1852 Voters	40.0	89	70	56.0
	Others	60.0	131	108	54.8
	All	100.0	220	178	55.3
Ward 4	1852 Voters	39.3	105	89	54.1
	Others	60.7	158	142	52.7
	All	100.0	263	231	53.2
Ward 5	1852 Voters	38.0	48	69	41.0
	Others	62.0	81	110	42.4
	All	100.0	129	179	41.9
All Voters	1852 Voters	40.2	404	354	53.3
	Others	59.8	631	495	56.0
	All	100.0	1035	849	54.9

Indeed, all eleven Free Church ministers along with Dissenting ministers, (the Wesleyan Methodist being the exception), voted for Leith. By contrast, as would be expected, ministers of the Auld Kirk and Episcopalians supported Sykes. Elders and deacons of the Free Church, however, split only 83:70 in Leith's favour. It would seem reasonable to assume that ordinary members of the Free congregations with the vote were more likely to reflect the halted division of their elders than the unanimity of their ministers. Indeed, with Thomson's continuing voters giving Sykes 55.7 per cent of their vote, there is strong *prima facie* evidence to support that proposition (Table 5.12).

Table 5.11: Support for Fordyce and Sykes at the General Election of 1847 by Occupation

	Sykes Share of Poll %	Above/ Below Overall Share %	Profile of Sykes %	Profile of Leith %
Drink	63.9	+9.0	15.1	10.4
Food Retail	70.0	+15.1	5.4	2.8
Textiles	54.9	0.0	11.3	5.9
Leather	47.0	-7.9	3.8	5.2
Engineering & Allied Trades	48.9	-6.0	4.3	5.5
Foundry & Forge	42.6	-12.3	2.2	3.7
Other Manufacturers	58.5	+3.6	3.7	3.2
Miscellaneous Sales	57.8	+2.9	6.1	5.4
(Manufactures & Retail)	(60.1)	(+5.2)	(51.9)	(42.1)
Service	53.1	-1.8	2.5	2.7
Construction	41.7	-13.2	4.2	7.1
Shipping/Harbour	85.1	+30.2	6.1	1.3
Non-Maritime Transport	41.4	-13.5	2.3	4.0
Banking/Insurance	52.2	-2.7	3.5	3.9
The Professions	54.6	-0.3	15.0	15.2
Residenters.	56.3	+1.4	5.6	5.3
Agriculture & Fishing	35.8	-19.1	8.0	17.6
Other	55.6	+0.7	1.0	0.9
(Non Manufacturers and Retail)	(52.5)	(-2.0)	(48.2)	(58.0)
All	54.9		100.1	100.1

Source: Poll Book

Table 5.12: Behaviour of 1852 Voters at the General Election of 1857

	Thomson to Sykes %	Thomson to Leith %	Thomson to Sykes* %	Hay to Sykes %	Hay to Leith %	Hay to Sykes* %
Ward 1	47.1	31.2	60.2	47.1	35.7	56.9
Ward 2	41.1	30.0	57.8	30.0	34.4	46.6
Ward 3	38.0	25.4	60.0	29.2	28.3	50.7
Ward 4	35.1	25.4	58.1	30.0	33.6	47.1
Ward 5	21.5	39.3	35.4	28.4	30.7	48.1
All	36.8	29.3	55.7	32.0	32.2	49.8

* Excluding Non-Voters.

The probable behaviour of the Free Church vote is well illustrated by the outcome in Ward 4, the most religiously polarised ward in its voting behaviour. In 1852, Thomson had inherited 82.7 per cent of the continuing Fordyce vote, and Hay had carried 91.9 per cent of the continuing Sykes (1847) vote (Table 5.9). In 1857, however, although Leith shaded Sykes amongst former Hay electors, with 52.9 per cent of their continuing vote in Ward 4, he carried only 41.9 per cent of the continuing Thomson electorate (Table 5.12). It is, therefore, quite probable that ordinary members of Free Kirk preferred Sykes on balance. Had Leith won the same share of the poll in Ward 4 as had Thomson, and the results in the other wards been as they were, Leith would have come within six votes of Sykes (939:945). One is tempted to the conclusion that many Free Churchmen preferred, (as did Thomson), their commercial and economic interests, as represented by Sykes, to their religious scruples as represented by Leith.

The most instructive feature of this election was its underlining of the rapidity with which the political influence of elites and their alliance changed in the short 25 years after 1832. Leith's supporters included the Haddens, who had controlled politics in pre-reform days, the Blaikies, who had defeated them in the 1830s, the Free Church ministers who had led their flocks against both Tories and Whigs, all now lacking the combined ability to see their preferred candidate home, even with the help of John MacPherson, the leading local Chartist. On the other hand, the combined efforts of the *Journal* and *Free Press* and some leading lay Free Churchmen helped produced only the narrowest of victories.

Table 5.13: Behaviour of Earlier Alignments and New Voters at the General Election of 1857

| Alignment | | Sykes | | Leith | | % Voting in 1857 |
		Votes	Votes %	Votes	Votes %	
Bannerman	(1841)	165	58.1	119	41.9	36.5
Innes	(1841)	68	46.3	79	53.7	28.8
Fordyce	(1847)	215	53.6	186	46.4	43.7
Sykes	(1847)	105	55.6	84	44.4	44.8
Thomson	(1852)	251	55.7	200	44.3	66.1
Hay	(1852)	153	49.8	154	50.2	64.2
New Voters	(1857)	496	57.3	370	42.7	100.0

The fluidity of electoral alliances between 1841 and 1857 is well illustrated in Table 5.13, where it is found that the alignment of 1857 bore little relationship to those of previous elections. Even those who had supported Sykes in 1847 were no more disposed to back him in 1857 that were those of Fordyce, his previous opponent. The most polarised previous alignment in 1857 were the previous supporters of the Conservative, Innes, who on balance preferred Leith (53.7

per cent), and were 8.6 per cent less favourable to Sykes than the electorate as a whole. Syke's best performance was amongst the Bannerman coalition of 1841, where he ran 3.2 per cent ahead of the general distribution – a hardly significant deviation.

In the final analysis, the selection of Sykes rather than Leith was not of great importance, because it indicated the waning of old conflicts rather than the emergence of any significant new divisions. The *Free Press*, for example, chose to explain the outcome more in terms of Leith's tactical failure than as the triumph of any particular political principle:

> Should he [Leith] seriously regard the history of Colonel Sykes' relations to the electors of Aberdeen as affording a 'precedent' applicable to his own case, he may find, that he has failed to bring some elements into the probationary contests, which, in the gallant Colonel's case, have contributed not a little to his ultimate victory (*Free Press*, 3.4.1857).

Despite the narrowness of his victory, Sykes was returned unopposed until his death in 1872, the doubling of the electorate in 1868 notwithstanding. Having seemingly taken the advice of the *Free Press*, Leith returned to take the seat at the consequent by-election against Liberal and Conservative opposition.[7]

To a large extent the ambitions of the reformers to create independent constituencies were realised in Aberdeen. The city had a strong locally-based economic elite which had the skills and financial resources sufficient to provide political leadership in local government, (very important at this time), and to arrange for national representation to accord with constituency values and interests. At the same time the establishment, whose composition was changing as the city expanded, was often divided on the definition of those values and interests, and was forced to seek adjudication from an electorate capable of making up its own mind free from pressure. If necessary, the voters, were prepared to reject long-standing social leaders in favour of new ones whose aims were more compatible with their own needs and wishes. Political debate was sustained by a lively, informative, and diverse press, though with such a small electorate its influence was perhaps subordinate to less formal conversations conducted in board rooms and between leading members of the various religious congregations. Although in its particulars the politics of Aberdeen was *sui generis*, it was that very quality which characterised the politics of independence.

Notes

1 The examination of voting behaviour in Aberdeen is based principally on the membership listings of the *Conservative and Liberal Election Committees of 1841* (the equivalent of 45 per cent of the actual vote received by the candidates in both cases. Occupations of committee members were included); the *Poll Book, 1847*, the *Poll Book, 1852* (this book does not include the occupations of electors) and the *Poll Book, 1857*. For details of religious affiliation a major source was the *Post Office Directory*.

2 Statement as to the Harbour of Aberdeen transmitted to the Commission by James Blaikie, Esq., Provost of the City, in which he also pointed out that until 1829 all the

trustees had been magistrates. At the passing of the Act in 1810, Telford, the engineer, had informed the committee the work would be completed within five years. *(P.P., 1835, p 46).*

3 The Municipal Wards were not the same as the Parliamentary Wards.

4 Though local elections were not fought under national party labels.

5 Using the election committees as if a random sample.

6 The preference of this faction, however, were not representative of former Innes voters as a whole, who split more evenly.

7 The electorate, of course, had been much changed by the Second Reform Act. The result was JF Leith (Liberal) 4392, JW Barclay (Liberal) 2615, J Shaw (Conservative) 704.

References

Aberdeen Banner.

Aberdeen Free Press.

Aberdeen Herald.

Aberdeen Journal.

Aberdeen Poll Book, 1847. (Manuscript in Aberdeen Central Library.)

Aberdeen Poll Book, 1852. (King's Collection, Aberdeen University.)

Aberdeen Poll Book, 1857. (King's Collection, Aberdeen University.)

Aberdeen Post Office Directories.

Keith, A, *The History of the North of Scotland bank, 1836-1936,* Aberdeen, 1936.

MacLaren, AA, *Religion and Social Class: The Disruption in Aberdeen,* London, 1974.

Parliamentary Papers: *Report Upon the Boundaries of the Several Cities, Burghs, and Towns in Scotland in respect to The Election of Members to Serve in Parliament,* pp. 1831–32, XLII, 408; and *Municipal Corporations (Scotland), Local Reports of Commissioners, Part I, From Aberbrothwick to Fortrose,* Vol. XXIX, 1835.

Ross, JA, *Record of Municipal Affairs in Aberdeen Since the Passing of the Burgh Reform Act in 1833,* Aberdeen, 1889.

6 The Members 1832 and 1865

Probably the most negative feature of the 1832 reforms was the marginal impact they had on the sources of MP recruitment (Adyelotte, 1954; Woolley, 1938). Despite the addition of new constituencies and a radically expanded franchise, twelve of the 23 members elected in the Scottish burghs in 1832 had sat in the unreformed House of Commons, and in the counties, where the electoral system was less changed, only nine out of 30 members were new to Westminster. Of the ten successful Conservatives in 1832, all but one had been seeking re-election. Furthermore, virtually all of those entering parliament for the first time were indistinguishable in social background from those who preceded them. Thus, while the political elite could not ignore the opinions and wishes of the new voters, especially in the burghs,[1] it was likely that any changes in national policy would be negotiated with the minimum of inconvenience to the old order.

In the counties the strength of continuity was always likely to be great because the electoral system placed considerable power in the hands of landed magnates, who used their control over nomination to advance members of their immediate families, sons-in-law, (as if a parliamentary seat were part of the marriage dowry), kinsmen and ciphers. The influence of landowners also penetrated into the burghs, especially the burgh districts, so that traditional county interests, far from being undermined in the shires by village £10ers, critically inhibited the development of a distinctive burgh representation.[2]

Landowners virtually monopolised county seats in 1832. Any diversity of background there was came from those with military and legal experience, but that was hardly independent of the landed interest. A proprietor himself may well have completed his education with a short commission in the armed services, (an imperative during the Napoleonic Wars), and a period of service in the army or navy followed by a seat in parliament provided an ideal career for a younger son. Service officers, therefore, became MPs not because they had been in the forces, but because of their landed connections. Similarly, rural lawyers were not merely agents of landowners, but frequently landed proprietors themselves, and formed an essential support to an oligarchic power structure centred on proprietorial control over the commissions of supply, (precursors of the county councils), the sheriff court, and kirk and school through the appointment of ministers and schoolteachers.

New types of MPs were slow to emerge. Even in the big cities of Aberdeen and Dundee, landowners continued to hold seats, while in Edinburgh, MPs with a traditional legal background frequently secured election. Businessmen who came to the fore were much more biased towards commerce and trade than manufacturing, whose representatives were distinctly sparse.[3] Amongst businessmen MPs, colonial ties seemed especially prominent, with directors of the East India Company notably in evidence.

Not only were there few changes to the profile of Scottish MPs in the decade after reform, but there was precious little evidence to suggest that the base of recruitment had significantly widened 30 years later (Tables 6.1 and 6.2). The major break on the pace of change, however, was less the influence of the Tories, whose representation, though almost exclusively traditional, was small, (particularly in 1832 and 1865), than the dominance of the Whigs over the selection of Liberal candidates.

The Liberals

The Burghs

The dominance of landowners in burgh constituencies in 1832 was largely a function of their influence in the diminutive burgh districts, where they held nine of the fourteen seats. Robert Ferguson of Raith, married to the divorced wife of the Earl of Elgin, not only represented the Kirkcaldy Burghs from 1831, but as a landed proprietor had been returned for Fife county in 1806. Whig influence was particularly evident in Stirling Burghs, where Lord Dalmeny, heir to the Earldom of Roseberry, was returned, despite the opposition of Dunfermline Radicals to his Conservative Whiggery (Brash: 244n); and in Kilmarnock Burghs, where Dalmeny's future brother-in-law, John Dunlop, a 'Whig Radical' (Horne: 226) and husband of Lady Harriet Primrose from 1835 to his death fourteen years later, had become the member in 1832. Dunlop's father, a landowner/soldier, General James Dunlop, had sat for Kirkcudbright between 1812 and 1826. The Radical reformer, William Gillon, with property in Linlithgow and Sussex, was chosen to promote the interests of the Falkirk District; and the Borders' proprietor, Robert Steuart, returned for the Haddington Burghs, also had a Radical tinge in wanting the removal of the bench of bishops from the House of Lords. Soldier/landowners were popular in the Montrose Burghs, where Horatio Ross, the pre-reform member and notable deer-stalker, continued his association with the reorganised constituency, although his Conservative sympathies forced him to vacate the seat in 1835 in favour of a Radical, Patrick Chalmers (Horne: 227). In the Elgin District, Lieutenant-Colonel Andrew Leith-Hay combined landowning with a directorship of the National Bank of England; and the Dumfries District, was held in 1832 by Matthew Sharpe, an East India merchant and former lieutenant-general in the 28th Dragoons.

Proprietors in single burghs included Laurence Oliphant, a local landowner, who represented Perth; Sir John Maxwell, 7th Baronet of Pollok and master of the Renfrewshire and Lanarkshire Foxhounds, whose selection as the member for Paisley appears somewhat eccentric; and George Kinloch, a Radical returned in Dundee, whose espousal of reform in 1819 had led to him being declared an outlaw at the Cross in Edinburgh.

Lawyers held sway in Edinburgh/Leith and in the burgh districts of Ayr, Wick and Wigtown. In Edinburgh, Francis Jeffrey entered on a deserved, if brief, inheritance before becoming Lord of Session in 1834, and together with James Abercromby, a bencher at Lincolns Inn and land steward to the Duke of Devonshire, (who had sat for the Whig borough, Calne (1812–1830), becoming the last Chief Baron of the Exchequer in Scotland before his elevation to the Speakership of the Commons), easily outpolled a Conservative opponent. In Leith, John Murray, an advocate since 1799, was returned to become Lord

Advocate in 1834 and Clerk to the Pipe in the Exchequer Court. The Harrow and Edinburgh University-trained landowner/lawyer, Kennedy of Dunure, (related through his mother to the Adams of Blair Adam), had sat for the Ayr District from 1820, and for his important role in the reform process was appointed a lord of the treasury following the 1832 election.

Table 6.1: Backgrounds of Scottish Members of Parliament Returned in 1832

	Counties	Burghs	All Libs	Conservatives	All
Landowners	11	8	19	2	21
Landowner/Soldiers	1	1	2	2	4
Landowner/Sailors	1	-	1	2	3
Landowner/Lawyers	1	1	2	-	2
Landowner/Lawyers/Businessmen	-	2	2	-	2
Landowner/Businessmen	4	-	4	1	5
(All Landowners)	(18)	(12)	(30)	(7)	(37)
Soldiers	1	-	1	2	3
Sailors	2	-	2	-	2
Soldier/Businessmen	-	-	-	1	1
(All Soldiers and Sailors)	(5)	(3)	(8)	(7)	(15)
Lawyers	-	3	3	-	3
Lawyer/Businessmen	-	2	2	-	2
(All Lawyers)	(1)	(6)	(7)	(-)	(7)
Businessmen	-	5	5	-	5
(All Businessmen)	(4)	(9)	(13)	(2)	(15)
All	**21**	**22**	**43**	**10**	**53**

A second relative of the Adams', James Loch, admitted to the Faculty of Advocates in 1801 and called to the bar at Lincolns Inn five years later, sat for the northern burghs. As auditor for the Duke of Sutherland, the Earls of Carnarvon and Ellesmere, and for the trust estates of the Earl of Dudley and Viscount Keith, Loch cultivated Whig connections that had installed him as the member for St Germeins, 1827–30, and for more than twenty years from 1830 in the Wick District. Connection also played a vital role in the selection of Edward Stewart to sit for the Wigtown Burghs from 1831, for although still a student at Lincolns Inn, his credentials as a nephew of the 9th Earl of Galloway were sufficient to offset any personal inexperience.

Table 6.2: Backgrounds of Scottish Members of Parliament Returned in 1865

	Counties	Burghs	All Libs	Conservatives	All
Landowners	8	3	11	6	17
Landowner/Soldiers	3	1	4	1	5
Landowner/Sailors	1	-	1	-	1
Landowner/Lawyers	3	2	5	1	6
Landowner/Businessmen	2	4	6	1	7
(All Landowners)	(17)	(10)	(27)	(9)	(36)
Soldiers	1	-	1	-	1
Sailors	1	-	1	-	1
Soldier/Businessmen	-	1	1	1	2
(All Soldiers and Sailors)	(6)	(2)	(8)	(2)	(10)
Lawyers	-	5	5	-	5
(All Lawyers)	(3)	(7)	(10)	(1)	(11)
Businessmen	-	7	7	1	8
(All Businessmen)	(2)	(12)	(14)	(3)	(17)
All	19	23	42	11	53

The small band of businessmen were predictably to the fore in Glasgow, which in 1832 elected two merchants: Lord Provost James Ewing, 'a kind of Conservative,' who in 1830 had been returned as MP for Wareham, and a 'Whig Radical,' James Oswald, cousin of the member for Ayrshire (Horne: 226). Greenock chose a local merchant and West India proprietor, Robert Wallace, linked by marriage to the 12th Lord Semphill, who was opposed by the unreformed council, as was Alexander Bannerman, a wine merchant, unopposed in Aberdeen. The remaining merchant was Andrew Johnston, an English Churchman from Sussex, with wide interests in South America through his directorships in the Real de Monte and Balonas companies, who held St Andrews Burghs until 1837.

In socio-economic terms, the representation of the burghs changed little overall between 1832 and 1865, although there was a small net gain by the business interest at the expense of landowners. For example, the Falkirk Burghs, which had been in the hands of a landowner in 1832, was subsequently contested between Tory and Whig landed proprietors and manufacturers, and in 1865 was held by James Merry, a Glasgow merchant and local ironmaster; and the Montrose Burghs, which had elected a county proprietor in 1832, was represented for 30 years from 1855 by William Baxter, a Radical and 'member...of the Dundee millionaire family of flax and linen manufacturers' (Walker, 53). In

Paisley, however, where in 1836 the constituency had passed from a landowner to Archibald Hastie, a London East India merchant, and on his death to Humphrey Crum-Ewing, a Glasgow merchant with landowning interests in Dunbartonshire, (where he was lord lieutenant of the county), a synthesis between proprietorial and business interests had been effected.

Comparing 1832 to 1865, businessmen pushed aside lawyers through the election of William Miller, a local merchant in Leith, Duncan McLaren, a draper, in Edinburgh, and Samuel Laing, a landowner with railway interests, who defeated James Loch in the Wick Burghs. The legal profession, however, were compensated in the Stirling Burghs, where following a succession of MPs, the seat was held for three years from 1865 by Laurence Oliphant, a Lincolns Inn barrister, and in Greenock, where the Free Church lawyer, Alexander Dunlop, architect of the 1842 Claim of Right, temporarily broke the tradition of businessmen holding the constituency. The law also gained the Dumfries District, in which a landowner, Sharpe, was replaced on his retiral in 1841 by a Wiltshire-based Old Etonian, William Ewart, (a Middle Temple barrister and son of a Liverpool merchant), who in the peripatetic Whig tradition had previously sat for Bletchingley, Liverpool and Wigan, and had been defeated in Marylebone and Kilkenny.

The 1832 preference for merchants was sustained in Aberdeen, where an Englishman, Colonel Sykes, the last chairman of the East India Company, was MP from 1857 to 1874; and St Andrews, where a second Englishman, Edward Ellice, (whose mother was a sister to the 2nd Earl Grey, and his father a former MP for Coventry), took over from Johnston in 1837, following a brief spell as MP for Huddersfield. Local merchants continued to dominate in Glasgow through the calico printer, Robert Dalglish, and a fellow businessman, William Graham, who were elected in 1865. Similarly, the Tory landowner/soldier/ businessman, who had represented the Inverness Burghs in 1832, was replaced from 1837 to 1868 by a Liberal landowner/businessman, Alexander Matheson, a director of the Bank of England, whose family had owned property in Ross and Cromarty for six centuries.

Tradition, however, still remained influential. Replacing a proprietor elected in 1832, the Honourable Edward Bouverie, a landowner/lawyer and second son of the Earl of Radnor, sat for the Kilmarnock Burghs from 1844 until his defeat in 1874. Similarly, the Haddington District continued its tradition of harbouring landed MPs with the election of Ferguson-Davie, a soldier/landowner and son of the afore-mentioned Ferguson of Raith; and in Perth, the Whig tradition was also sustained by the Non-Intrusionist Old Etonian landowner/banker, the Honourable A F Kinnaird, who held the constituency from 1852 to 1878. In the Kirkcaldy Burghs, the Fergusons of Raith were followed in 1862 by another local landowner, Roger Aytoun of Inchdairnie, until he retired in 1874; and Sir John Ogilvy, landowner, lieutenant colonel of the Dundee Rifle Volunteers, and son-in-law of the 16th Earl of Sussex, was preferred by the electors of Dundee to a local merchant in 1857, and was unopposed in the two subsequent contests. Mountstuart Elphinstone Duff, the landowner/lawyer, who represented the Elgin Burghs sustained an established proprietorial interest in the constituency; and another landowner/lawyer, Edward Crauford, repeated the precedent set by Kennedy in the Ayr Burghs. As in 1832, representatives of the legal profession in 1865 were evident in the Wigtown District, where George Young, sometime sheriff of Inverness and a barrister at the Middle Temple, was the member from 1865 until appointed as a judge of the Court of Session in 1874, and in Edinburgh, where James Moncreiff, a former MP for the Leith Burghs and Dean of the Faculty of Advocates, and Lord Advocate between 1865 and 1868, balanced the return of McLaren.

The Counties

County Liberals elected in 1832 were little different from their predecessors, as they were mostly connected with the land and frequently the aristocracy.

Aristocratic connection was particularly evident in the cases of Sir John Dalrymple, returned for Midlothian in 1832, as he became the Earl of Stair in 1840; and the Earl of Ormelie (Perthshire), a former MP for Okehampton, who became the 2nd Marquis and 5th Earl of Breadalbane in 1834. Almost as elevated were the Honourable George Elliot, a naval officer and second son of the Earl of Minto, who sat for Roxburgh from 1832-1835; the Honourable Charles Fleming, another naval officer, second son of Lord Elphinstone, and a 'decided Whig' (Horne: 225), who represented Stirlingshire from 1802 to 1835; and the Honourable Douglas Hallyburton, the member for Forfarshire, second son of the 4th Earl of Aboyne and half brother of the Marquis of Huntly. Similarly, the MP for Berwickshire, Charles Marjoribanks, was the brother of a peer.

Others were associated with the aristocracy through marriage. The member for Lanarkshire, John Maxwell of Pollock, 'an ultra Whig [with] command of the county' (Horne: 224), and son of the member for Paisley, was married to a daughter of the Earl of Elgin and Kincardine. Somewhat surprisingly, he had preceded his father into parliament as the MP for his native Renfrewshire, 1818-1830, where he was a lieutenant colonel in the local militia. James Callander, who sat for Argyll, was the son-in-law of Lord Erskine; and the member for Ayr, Richard Oswald of Auchencruive, was married to a daughter of the 12th Earl of Eglington. Likewise, Sir Andrew Agnew of Lochnaw, whose family had sat in various parliaments since 1628, and who was himself first returned for Wigtownshire in 1830, was the son-in-law of the 26th Lord Kingsale; and 'a strong supporter of the Church' (Horne: 223), John Colquhoun, MP for Dunbartonshire, (and the Kilmarnock Burghs from 1847), was married to a daughter of the 2nd Lord Lilford. Ross and Cromarty was represented by James Stewart-Mackenzie of Seaforth, a grandson of the 7th Earl of Galloway, first returned for Ross in 1831. He resigned his seat in 1837 to become governor of Ceylon. His cousin, Edward Stewart, was the MP for the Wigtown Burghs from 1831–4, a constituency held by his father in 1762.

The pedigrees of the remaining county Liberals were hardly less well-established. Following his grandfather and father, Rear-Admiral Sir Charles Adam, having carried the family seat of Kinross in 1831, easily beat his Conservative opponent the next year, following the amalgamation with Clackmannan. Robert Cutlar Fergusson of Craigdarroch, who sat for Kirkcudbright from 1826 to his death twelve years later, was a lawyer/landowner/businessman, who, following his call to the Bar at Lincolns Inn in 1797, had mostly practised in Calcutta, and later became a director of the East India Company. He had achieved some notoriety by being imprisoned for twelve months, (1798–9), for attempting to 'assist O'Connor in his escape during his trial for high treason in Maidstone' (Forster:

135). Orkney and Shetland from 1830–5 was also represented by a law-yer/landowner, George Traill of Hobbister, who owned property in Orkney and Caithness. Following his defeat in 1835, he became MP for Caithness from 1841 until he retired in 1869. The remaining 1832 county Liberals, both landowners, were MacLeod of Cadboll, a former member for Cromarty, who was appointed by the Leveson-Gowers to represent Sutherland in 1831, until forced to repair to the Inverness Burghs by the Tory Duchess in 1837; and a 'not very popular' (Horne: 222) Charles Grant, sometime chairman of the court of directors of the East India Company, who having sat for the Inverness Burghs, 1811-1818, represented the county gentlemen from 1818 until his elevation to the peerage as Lord Glenelg in 1835, when he was appointed Secretary of State for War and the Colonies.

Dominated by members from well-established landowning families, the social characteristics of county Liberal MPs in 1865 had changed even less in the course of the previous three decades than those of their burgh colleagues.

In the Highlands and Islands, Orkney and Shetland returned Frederick Dundas, brother of the 1st Earl of Zetland and lord lieutenant of Orkney, who held the constituency, except for a small break between 1847 and 1852, from 1837 to his death in 1873. To the south, Caithness was retained by George Traill of Hobbister, the former MP for Orkney and Shetland (1830–4); and a fellow landowner/lawyer, David Dundas of Ochtertyre (Perthshire), an Inner Temple QC and former Solicitor General, kept Sutherland warm for the Staffords. From 1847 to 1868, Ross and Cromarty elected the son-in-law of the 7th Lord Beaumont and former member for Ashburton (1843–7), Sir Alexander Matheson of Ardross and Attadale, a highland landowner and director of the Bank of England. It was a measure of his local status that in addition to being a deputy lieutenant for Sutherland, Matheson was to become lord lieutenant of Ross in 1866. The member for Argyll, Alexander Finlay of Toward Castle and Deputy Lieutenant of Bute, was linked to the unreformed House of Commons through his father, a former Lord Provost of Glasgow, who sat for the Glasgow group of burghs between 1812 and 1818.

The Liberals held four Eastern county seats in 1865, one more than in 1832. In 1837 Banffshire had been taken from the Tories by James Duff, the future 5th Earl of Fife, whose family had held various seats in the north east since the late seventeenth century. In 1861, a relative, Robert Duff of Fetteresso (Kincardineshire), a landowner and former lieutenant in the Royal Navy, inher-ited the constituency, holding it until 1892, when he was appointed Governor of New South Wales. Similarly well connected was the Honourable Charles Carnegie, MP for Forfarshire, brother of the 9th Earl of Southesk, and son of a former member for the Aberdeen group (1830–1), whose family had sat in nu-merous parliaments since the sixteenth century. Carnegie sat for his native county from 1860 until 1872, when he left parliament to become Inspector of Constabulary in Scotland. In Fife representation continued to be drawn from the gentry, and in 1865 the incumbent was Sir Robert Anstruther, a former officer in the Grenadier Guards and local landowner; and although the new member for Kincardineshire, James Nicol, had not quite the elevated social status of Hugh Arbuthnott, the Tory member he replaced, he was, nevertheless, an Aberdeenshire landowner, Bombay merchant, and son-in-law of Edward Lloyd, the London banker.

The strong element of family continuity in Liberal representation was particularly evident in the Borders. In Wigtownshire, for example, the landowning-MP in 1865, Sir Andrew Agnew of Lochnaw, a former captain in the 4th Light Dragoons and married to the eldest daughter of the 1st Earl of Gainsborough, was the son of the member returned in 1832. Likewise, his fellow Gallowingian colleague, James Mackie of Ernespie, a landowner/advocate, whose property had been originally granted by Robert the Bruce, had inherited Kirkcudbright on the retiral of his father in 1857. Mackie's great grandson was to represent Galloway as a Unionist from 1931 until his death in 1959. Similarly, Berwickshire was held for the Liberals by David Robertson of Ladykirk, and cousin of Lord Tweedmouth. Both Robertson's father (1818–26) and second brother (1832–4) had represented the seat before him, and shortly after his own accession to the Marjoribanks peerage, the seat passed to another family member, Edward Marjoribanks, the eldest son of Lord Tweedmouth. In Roxburgh, however, where between 1812 and 1857 the Whig/Liberal interest had been represented in parliament by three sons of the 1st Earl of Minto, the task had passed to the sixth in a line of local baronets, Sir William Scott of Ancrum, MP for Carlisle (1829–30). Nevertheless, as if to demonstrate that deference was no less potent than in the rest of the Borders, Roxburgh was to elect an heir to the Earldom of Minto in 1880.

Amongst the Liberals returned in the central lowlands, the picture was similar. In Renfrewshire, for example, Archibald Speirs, a former captain in the Scots Fusilier Guards and landowner, was a grandson of the 1st Lord Dundas, son-in-law of the 4th Earl of Radnor, and son of the MP for the constituency between 1810 and 1818. In 1865, Stirlingshire elected Admiral John Erskine, ADC to the Queen, the grandson of a former MP (boasting an ancestor who sat for Culross, 1687–97) and led a company of foot in the cause of William of Orange. Clackmannan was represented by William Adam, formerly private secretary to the Governor of Bombay, 1853–8, and the latest in a family line of prominent Whig politicians to have held the seat, his father having been MP, 1831-1841. He later left parliament in 1880 to become the Governor of Madras. Bute returned the landowner James Lamont of Knockdow, a deputy lieutenant of Argyll and Bute. It was a measure of the influence of traditional forces that even in the growing industrial county of Lanarkshire, the MP, Sir Thomas Colebrooke, son of an East Indian merchant and member of the council at Calcutta, had a typically Whig background. Raised in England, and living at Ottershawe Park, Surrey, he had few Scottish connections, and from 1842 until his defeat in 1857 had been MP for Taunton. His uncle, however, the 4th baronet of Crawford, had died without issue in 1838, and Thomas inherited the title along with his Lanarkshire property. In 1857 he consolidated his Scottish interests by marrying into the Roxburghshire gentry, and captured Lanarkshire for the Liberals for the first time since 1835. By 1870 he had become lord lieutenant for Lanarkshire and undisputed member for the north division of the county.

The Conservatives

Ten Conservatives were elected in 1832, and all but one represented county constituencies. They were, perhaps, drawn from an even narrower base than the county Liberals in that they included no lawyers, so that the combination of a military and aristocratic background was much in evidence.

In the north east, where there was a small coterie of Conservative members in 1832, the newly combined counties of Elgin and Nairn were held by Francis Grant, whose family had exercised strong personal control over local parliamentary representation since the late eighteenth century. Both Francis' father and brother had sat for Elginshire in the unreformed parliament, whilst he had been returned for the Elgin group (1802–6) and the county from 1807 to 1832. In 1840, however, following the death of his brother, he was forced to resign his seat on becoming the 6th Earl of Seafield. Similarly, the 4th Earl of Aberdeen secured the return of his brother, the Honourable William Gordon, a captain in the Royal Navy, in Aberdeenshire; and the 7th Viscount Arbuthnott inserted his second son, Major-General Hugh Arbuthnott, a veteran of Corunna and the Peninsular War, in Kincardineshire, which he represented from 1826 to his retiral in 1865 at the age of eighty five. Amongst others 'reckoned as decided friends of the Wellington Administration' (Horne: 220) was the naval captain, George Ferguson of Pitfour, a deputy lieutenant in both Banffshire and Aberdeenshire, and connected with the aristocracy through his marriage to the eldest daughter of the 1st Lord Langford, who sat for his native Banffshire from 1832 until his death five years later.

Aristocratic and military connections were no less evident in the south. On becoming the 4th Earl of Hopetoun in 1800, John Hope passed his Linlithgowshire seat to his second son, General Sir Alexander Hope, an active soldier, who had lost an arm at the battle of Buren in 1795. Alexander held the constituency until he retired in 1835, when, in conformity with a family interest in the constituency dating back to the seventeenth century, he was replaced by his younger brother Charles. Family influence was also critical in the selection of Charles Stuart, a young captain in the Grenadier Guards and nephew of the Earl of Rothesay, as the member for Bute in 1832; and in the choice of James Balfour of Whittinghame, MP for the unreformed St Andrews group (1826–31), husband of Lady Elinor Maitland, daughter of the 8th Earl of Lauderdale, in Haddingtonshire. It was almost *laise majeste* that Peebles was held by a mere 6th baronet, Sir John Hay of Smithfield and Haystoun.

The remaining county Conservative, John Hope-Johnstone of Annandale and Raehills, keeper of Lochmaben, inherited Dumfries from his father, MP from 1804 to 1830. His mother, Lady Anne, was the eldest daughter of the 3rd Earl of Hopetoun. Johnstone's Tory credentials had been in doubt because of his support for the Reform Bill, but by 1837 his Conservatism was fully recognised (Brash: n 224). In 1847 he vacated the seat in favour of Viscount Drumlanrig, but returned to parliament in 1857 when the latter became the 7th Marquis of Queensberry. Undoubtedly, the most versatile Conservative member, (if not of all Scottish MPs returned in 1832), was the single Tory burgh MP, John Baillie, who sat for the Inverness Burghs from 1830–33. Belonging to a highland landed family, he was a director of the East India Company, a former colonel in the Bengal Establishment, and a professor of Arabic, Persian languages and Mohammedan law in the college at Fort William.

The Conservatives of 1865 (all eleven sitting for county constituencies), predictably continued to sustain MPs of the highest social status, although representatives of the gentry were somewhat more prominent than in 1832.

In the south east, the Duke of Buccleuch gifted Midlothian to his heir, the

Earl of Dalkeith, lord lieutenant of Dumfries and a lieutenant-general in the Royal Company of Archers. Unopposed when initially returned in 1853, he was defeated in his first contested election in 1868, and, having won back the seat in 1874, was again beaten, this time by Gladstone, in 1880. Dalkeith's younger brother, Lord Henry Scott, also benefited from his father's influence by inheriting Selkirkshire from the Tory, Alexander Lockhart, in 1861. Neighbouring Peebles was held in 1865 by the third in a line of baronets, Sir George Montgomery, lord lieutenant of Kinross and a brigadier in the Royal Company of Archers, whose uncle and father had represented the constituency before him. From 1847, Haddingtonshire returned Francis Charteris (Lord Elcho), ADC to the Queen, ensign-general in the Royal Company of Archers, and eldest son of the 8th Earl of Wemyss and March. When he assumed the title in 1883, the seat passed to his son. In the south west, George Walker of Crawfordton, (Dumfries), lieutenant colonel of the Scottish Borderers' militia, was first elected in his native county in 1865; whilst a landowner/soldier, James Fergusson, who had been wounded at the battle of Inkerman, currently held Ayrshire, which he had won and lost on previous occasions. On Clydeside, a local deputy lieutenant and governor general's agent in Vizagatapam, Patrick Smollett, inherited Dunbartonshire in 1859, following the retiral of his brother, Alexander, a convener of the county from 1847 to 1880, and MP from 1841.

Three of the remaining four Tory seats were in the East. The member for Elgin and Nairn, Charles Cumming-Bruce, former MP for the Inverness Burghs (1833-37), who had sat for the two counties from 1840, probably owed the seat to his mother being aunt to the 5th and 6th Earls of Seafield, who controlled the Tory interest in this constituency. Aberdeenshire was held by William Leslie, a partner in China-based Dent and Company, from a by-election in 1861 caused by the elevation of the sitting member, Lord Haddo, to the Earldom of Aberdeen. In Perthshire, the MP from 1852, Sir William Maxwell of Keir, was the ninth of a line of baronets, and son-in-law of the Earl of Leven and Melville. An ancestor, Sir John Stirling, had represented the burgh of Stirling in the Scots parliament of 1524. The family also owned property in Pollok, from which the baronetcy derived. His grandfather had been Liberal MP for Paisley from 1832 to 1834, and his father, Liberal MP for Lanarkshire from 1832 to 1837. Lastly, Henry Baillie of Tarradale and Redcastle and son-in-law of the 6th Viscount Strangford, who sat for Inverness from 1840 to 1868, came from a prominent highland landowning family, and was himself lord lieutenant of Ross. From 1858-9 he was Under Secretary of State for India.

Conclusions

Overall there is little evidence to suggest that in socio-economic terms the sources of MP recruitment in Scotland changed significantly as a consequence of the First Reform Act. Indeed, strong family links with parliaments prior to 1832 and before the Union were still evident amongst members elected in 1865.

The high degree of social continuity in Scottish representation was remarkable in that there had been an important political change north of the border after 1832, with the supplanting of a Tory-controlled polity by Liberals, whose alignment was most associated with the new social forces, and whose MPs largely determined the character of Scottish representation. Nevertheless,

Scottish Liberal MPs belonged almost exclusively to a proprietorial class of landowners in the counties, and in the burghs not a few of those with predominantly business backgrounds had enjoyed the patronage of Whig magnates both before and after 1832. Burgh Liberal MPs had a far greater involvement in Indian and other imperial commercial interests than in Scottish manufacturing, and as late as 1865 gentry continued to hold almost half the Liberals' urban seats. Thus, most Scottish Liberal MPs of this period had more in common with the rural Tory members than the middle classes of the industrial towns and cities. Indeed, the observation that the 'Conservatives tended more to be related to the peerage, baronetage and gentry' (Ayelotte: 258), was not applicable to Scotland, where an examination of all MPs between 1832 and 1868 suggests the reverse may have been true (Dyer). It was, therefore, no accident that the Radical Edinburgh linen draper, McLaren, looked to English members for support and political leadership (Hanham, 157). On the other hand, because Scottish Conservatives remained so heavily reliant on landed families as a source of candidates, and were so electorally weak in the burghs, Ayelotte's observations that in the parliament of 1841–47 'a businessman…was almost as likely to be a Conservative as he was to be on the other side' (Ayelotte: 258–9), was even more inapplicable to the Scottish situation. Thus, the social spectrum of Scottish representation seems to have been several degrees more traditional than in England.

The dominance of MPs with a landed proprietorial background in the counties, where party allegiance was not a significant variable, reflected an electoral system that enhanced the importance of local elites in the recruitment of candidates and the financing of campaigns, a franchise which placed a premium on the ownership of land, an electorate which was proportionately less extensive than in England, and a distribution of seats which favoured the counties. The strength of the Whig gentry in burgh constituencies was the function of a redistribution which granted only eight members to single burghs, and left numerous burgh district Liberal shopkeepers reliant on county Whig landowners to organise their interest. Thus, the probability of a major break-through by urban-based businessmen and manufacturers as Scottish burgh MPs had largely been precluded by the terms of the legislation.

Notes

1 It has already been noted, for example, that Lord Dalmeny had to make concessions to Dissenters to resist Radical pressure in Stirling Burghs; and in Perth, Fox Maule needed to be a strong supporter of Non-Intrusionism.

2 Woolley (1938: 252) noted: 'The aristocratic influence was strong in the counties and in those small burghs where voters were few and therefore more easily affected by local landowners.' That comment, though mostly relating to England, was particularly relevant to situation in most Scottish burgh districts.

3 Woolley (1938: 247), quotes from a pamphlet *The Assembled House of Commons* (1838), in which only 14 manufacturers were identified.

References

Adyelotte, WO, 'The House of Commons in the 1840s,' *History*, Vol. 39, October 1954.

Brash, JI, *Papers on Scottish Electoral Politics, 1832-1854*, Edinburgh, 1974.

Dyer, M, 'Mere Detail and Machinery: The Great Reform Act and the Effects on Redistribution on Scottish Representation, 1832-68' *Scottish Historical Review*, Vol. 62, 1983.

Forster, J, *Members of Parliament, Scotland, 1357-1882*, London, 1882.

Hanham, HJ, *Elections and Party Management*, Hassocks, 1978.

Horne, D, *Election Surveys*, edited by Brash (1974).

Walker, WM, *Juteopolis,* Edinburgh, 1979.

Woolley, SF, 'The Personnel of the Parliament of 1833,' *The English Historical Review,* April 1938.

7 *The Reforms of 1868*

From a conservative perspective, the success of the first Reform Act had been its incorporation of the urban middle class into the political system at minimal cost to traditional authority, emphasised latterly by the premiership of Lord Palmerston, whose administration, consensual in composition and approach, had weakened party divisions to such an extent that some commentators believed they were on the point of extinction (Smith: 46).

It was, nevertheless, soon evident that however felicitous were the consequences of the 1832 legislation, the new dispensation was more a Pandora's Box than a permanent settlement. The distinction between the county and burgh franchise was an obvious focus for complaint, especially among the residents of the industrialising counties, whose rights compared unfavourably with those of similar social status in nearby burghs. Criticisms also focused on the distribution of constituencies, which was inordinately biased towards rural interests in a society that by 1860 had become predominantly industrial and urban. The issue of the ballot, raised by men such as Cockburn immediately following the 1832 general election, also constituted another unresolved question, (Cockburn: 35). Additionally, there was the increasingly pressing matter as to whether the £10 qualification could be sustained in the burghs or whether it ought to be reduced. Various attempts were made to tackle some of these problems from the 1850s, but the Whig-Peelite coalition effectively thwarted any progress. Only with the passing of Palmerston in 1866 did further reform become unavoidable.

Although the factional character of the parties in 1866 makes it difficult to summarise their respective approaches to reform at that time, one can, perhaps, indicate the broad perspectives. Excepting the Whigs, the Liberals were most united in their attempts to broaden the franchise in the counties and on the need for further redistribution, because it would extend their political influence at the expense of the rural Whigs and Tories. They were, however, divided over franchise extension in the burghs between the Radicals, who wanted the qualifications significantly lowered, (but not too much), and the more moderate Liberals, who feared their constituency would be undermined by the infusion of working class voters. The Conservatives, Whigs and Tories were united in their desire to defend the landed interest, which made them particularly hostile to redistribution and the imposition of a burgh franchise in the counties. Although temperamentally suspicious of any lowering of any franchise qualification, the Tories and Conservatives, however, were less bothered than the Liberals about the probable consequences of a wider franchise in the burghs, where they were weak. Some Tories convinced themselves that working class deference might work to their advantage. Thus, while an alliance of Whigs, Tories and Conservatives could be mobilised to restrict the scope of redistribution and a lowering of the county franchise qualifications, an understanding between progressive Liberals, Conservatives and Tories could be assembled for a substantial extension of the burgh electorate. In the end, that is what took place, and accounts for the rather lopsided nature of the Second Reform Act.

The parliamentary management of the reform process, 1866–8, was similar to that of 1832, with different bills being introduced for England and Wales, Scotland, and Ireland; and the settlement of the franchise in Scotland was again basically determined by the English provisions. It followed that there was virtually no debate on the Scottish franchise, and the more detailed consideration of Scottish reform focussed on the redistribution proposals. As the development of the new franchise provisions have been considered in great detail elsewhere (Smith) those aspects will be summarised briefly, and greater attention given to the Scottish constituency settlement, which has been less comprehensively analysed. As in 1832, Scottish members had more influence over redistribution than the franchise.

The issue which most dominated parliamentary reform in the middle of the nineteenth century was the constitutional status of the working class. Should its members be incorporated into the new electorate despite their lack of wealth and relative poverty? Or should they be required to show their worth by demonstrating their intelligence through the acquisition of property? Many MPs were fearful of demos, and only the Radicals leaned towards household suffrage pure and simple. The Liberal, Lowe, expressing a Platonic view of society, regarded the working class as 'impulsive, unreflecting and violent people,' and held that state institutions should endorse 'the order of Providence that men should be unequal' (Smith: 80–1). There were others, such as Bright, who could see the danger of violence and revolution if no gesture was made to the lower orders; while Gladstone, ever sensitive to social change, was convinced by the close of the 1850s that certain of the unenfranchised were entitled to vote on account of their moral development, and identified himself with the social aspirations of the respectable working class. In the event, it was the question of working class enfranchisement in the burghs which was most comprehensively dealt with in 1867/8.

The resolution of franchise reform proved particularly tortuous, partly because there was no majority for any clear line of policy, and partly because uncertainty as to the political consequences of various proposed reductions in the voting qualifications confused ideological cleavages. An even greater complicating factor was that both Gladstone and Disraeli were anxious to exploit the issue not only for advantage over each other, but also as a means of establishing an ascendancy within their own parties. Consequently, reform was frequently subordinated to a wider Byzantine political struggle, which in the end led to the adoption of a burgh franchise far wider than had been intended by the leaderships of either party.

Scottish members reflected the conflicting interests. For example Samuel Laing (Wick Burghs), a 'shrewd and cantankerous Palmerstonian' (Smith: 69), wanted to retain the prevailing burgh arrangements and extend them to the counties; while Baxter, the Radical from Montrose, arguing from de Tocqueville 'that the strength and variety of American government derived from the participation of the whole people' (Smith: 231), supported household suffrage, (although with a two years residence qualification for the sub-£10ers). Other Radicals, such as Crum-Ewing (Paisley), Dalglish (Glasgow), and McLaren (Edinburgh), also supported household suffrage, partly out of conviction and partly because they came to realise that anything less might precipitate such a lowering as would 'sweep the adjustment of power beyond the point of supremacy of the commercial middle class' (Smith: 175). Amongst county members, views ranged from those of Sir Edward Colebrooke (Lanarkshire), a moderate Liberal, who was anxious to limit the opportunities for faggot voting, to those of Lord Elcho, a Conservative Palmerstonian, and Whig landowners such as Alexander Finlay (Argyll) and Robert Duff (Banffshire), who were in favour of the status quo and ill-disposed towards Russell's administration.

The introduction of an English franchise bill by Gladstone in 1866 underlined the diffidence with which most MPs approached the precarious and potentially dangerous matter of franchise extension. Gladstone's indication that the bill's initial proposal to reduce the the borough qualification to a £6 annual rental level was, on second thoughts, to be £7, hardly enhanced parliamentary confidence in the measure. It suggested the government itself was ignorant of the impact their own proposals would have on the size of the electorate, and the tenor of Gladstone's speech, which emphasised the restrictive rather than progressive features of the legislation, did little to cheer its supporters. In the counties, Gladstone proposed to reduce the £50 occupation qualification to £14, and permit holders of county property, but resident in burghs, to claim a county vote. Additionally, there were to be a couple of fancy franchises, £10 borough lodgers, (new to England but not to Scotland), were to qualify for the first time, as were £50 Savings Bank deposit holders in the counties. The lack of conviction with which these amendments were advanced, a fear the government had not properly estimated their probable consequences, divisions within the rapidly fragmenting Palmerstonian coalition, and the publication of unpopular redistribution proposals, forced out of the administration by the opposition, led to the collapse of the bill, the government, and the formation of a minority Conservative ministry under Lord Derby.

The Tory response to the reform question was uncertain, and the failure of an early initiative by Disraeli encouraged those who would have preferred to see the whole matter dropped. Pressure from the Queen, however, in part a response to popular agitation, which in Glasgow included an open air meeting attended by some 130,000 people, and Lord Cranborne, who wanted 'to forestall demands for wider distribution' (Smith: 134), convinced Derby that some measure had to be passed.

As with the Liberal legislation, the Conservative approach was bedevilled by internal party conflicts, some of which were principled, but most were dictated by opposition to the ambitions of Disraeli, who spent half his time plotting to outflank Gladstone and the rest to confusing his own supporters, (and sometimes himself), as to his intentions. Nevertheless, it was Disraeli who eventually piloted the rudderless ship of reform to its unchartered harbour. Initially, Disraeli favoured household suffrage in the burghs, but limited by a three years residential qualification, the payment of rates and taxes over that period, and a scheme to give certain electors as many as four votes each. These proposals, however, did not find immediate favour, as Tories such as Lord Cranborne, who had a particularly low opinion of the working class, felt there should in principle be a lower rental limit of about £5. After several false starts, and a cabinet crisis which led to the resignation of Cranborne, General Peel and Carnarvon, Disraeli moved the second reading of a bill on 18 March 1867, that formed the basis of the final legislation. It 'provided for household suffrage in the burghs, hedged by personal payment of taxes and two years residence. There were also dual votes for property, and fancy franchises for those with educational qualifications, those who had £50 in the funds of the Savings Bank, or who paid 20s in direct taxation. The county occupation level was reduced from £50 to £15, and redistribution remained at 15 seats' (Smith: 167).

In reply, Gladstone attacked the bill on a number of counts, including the introduction of plural voting and fancy franchises, the absence of a lodger franchise, and the two years residential qualification. He was, nevertheless, unable to unite his party to force a division on the second reading, and was defeated on a proposal to introduce an instruction to the committee which would have paved the way for a residential franchise based on a rating level to be determined. His isolation was caused by the unwillingness of the Radicals to defeat a measure based on household suffrage, the hostility of the Whigs who wanted him humiliated, and the reluctance of many Liberals to provoke a dissolution before some measure of reform was on the statute book.

The price Disraeli had paid for outmanoeuvring Gladstone was his undertaking to consider seriously amendments in committee, especially if they did not come from the Liberal front bench. Consequently, in the face of outside agitation against some of the restrictive features of his burgh franchise, the insuperable administrative difficulties in implementing some of the proposals, and Radical pressure in parliament, Disraeli lost effective control over the burgh franchise, and the various limitations on household suffrage were whittled away. At the end of the process, a measure which had been intended to add 237,000 new voters plus 305,000 fancy franchises to the 1866 burgh roll throughout the United Kingdom, finally added 818,000 new voters based on household occupation of twelve months and the payment of rates (Smith: 236). It was an outcome that few members of parliament had intended. Changes to the county franchise were less dramatic, and were a measure of 'the general success of the landed interest in their rearguard action' (Smith: 206). The proposed £15 annual rental occupation level was reduced to £12, and the leasehold qualification fell from £10, (as under the 1832 legislation), to £5, on amendment.

The Scottish legislation followed the English and Welsh provisions, with the introduction of household suffrage and confirmation of the lodger franchise. The county proprietorship qualification fell from £10 to £5, in conformity with similar persons in England, but tenants of lands and heritages had to occupy property valued at £14, as they were considered the equivalent of the £12 English leaseholders.

Three broad approaches are detectable in the prelude to redistribution in 1868. Firstly, the official Whig/Liberal line, which sought to balance the various interests within its coalition, from the protection of Whig nomination burghs to the claims of the burgeoning urban centres for greater political influence. Secondly, the aim of the Conservatives to mitigate through redistribution any negative consequences of an extended franchise. Thirdly, there was the dominant Scottish Liberal position, laced with a streak of Radicalism, which held Scotland to be substantially under-represented, and that new seats should be given to the larger urban constituencies (including the industrialising counties) through the suppression of small English boroughs. Although there were strong nationalist overtones to the demands of Scottish Liberals, they were prompted principally by a desire for equality of treatment throughout the United Kingdom, and Radical opposition to separate legislation for each country.

The official Liberal strategy was to consolidate and incrementally advance the settlement of 1832, rather than to challenge its anomalies. A bill presented by Palmerston's administration in 1860, for example, merely proposed an extra seat for Glasgow, and the creation of a constituency for the universities, following their reform in 1858. The extreme caution of 1860, however, was followed in 1866 by a somewhat more adventurous proposal to award an additional member each to Dundee, Edinburgh, Glasgow, Ayrshire, Lanarkshire and Aberdeenshire, together with a member elected jointly by the four universities. The extra seats were to be found through suppression in England. Although the Scottish measure explicitly recognised the claims of the more populous constituencies, it attempted neither to reconstruct existing ones nor to divide those receiving an extra member. Its results would have been to entrench Liberal strength through enhanced urban/industrial representation, while at the same time ignoring such glaring Tory and Whig anomalies as Bute and Sutherland. In a parliament of weak parties by modern standards and independent-minded members, it was a redistribution most likely by its compromises to maximise support.

The Scottish Conservative view was expressed by Sir James Fergusson, the member for Ayrshire. He claimed that the 1832 Act had been designed by the Whigs to fit their interests, and had been pushed through the Commons while English members were 'too much occupied to give their attention to the framing of a good Bill for Scotland' (*Hansard* 183: 523). Consequently, a 'great anomaly and great injustice' had existed, in which the counties had been 'swamped...by urban influences.' He therefore suggested that the burgh grouping system should be 'greatly extended', otherwise there was a danger that the system would 'give too great a preponderance to a particular class [which]...could not be right'. Thus, unlike the Liberals, he sought a more meddling approach to redistribution to protect agricultural landowning interests, especially in constituencies like his own, through the removal of industrial towns and villages from the counties to the burgh districts, and to recover for his party ground lost since 1832.

Speaking for the Radicals, McLaren, while grudgingly expressing gratitude for the extra members offered to Scotland, held that on a population basis the nation was entitled to twenty more seats. He also claimed that the counties of Ayr and Lanark were large enough to merit three members each, while the burgh districts of Leith, Montrose, and Stirling were entitled to a second member. His interest in proportionality, however, did not prompt him to dwell on the need for redistribution within Scotland, although admitting that 'too much credit had...been given to the system of burgh grouping' (*Hansard* 183: 526). Clearly, his recognition that any fundamental critique of the constituency system within Scotland would have challenged the interests of too many of his colleagues, led him to blunt any preferences he might have had for equal electoral districts. Nevertheless, a fellow large-city member, Colonel Sykes, aggrieved that his Aberdeen burgh constituency was not to gain extra representation, questioned the continued independence of Bute, Caithness and Sutherland. As the bill, however, failed to progress beyond its short debate on first reading, the position of the Scottish Liberals had no opportunity to mature into a set of coherent proposals.

The first bill introduced by the minority Conservative administration in May, 1867, sought to give shape to the views of Conservative critics of the previous Liberal offering. In accordance with the earlier proposals, there were to be seven new constituencies, but in in contrast to the Liberal scheme they were not to be found by suppression, nor were they to be distributed as under the 1866 schedules. In the first place, two seats were to go to the universities – one to Edinburgh and St Andrews, and the other to Aberdeen and Glasgow. Secondly, while Ayrshire, Aberdeenshire and Lanarkshire were each to get an extra representative, they were to be divided on the bogus grounds that hitherto no Scottish county had had more than one member. (In fact most counties had been plurally represented in the Scottish parliament.) Thirdly, although Glasgow was to receive an extra seat, it was to become a divided city. Glasgow North would be a two-member seat, and Glasgow South, a single-member constituency that would also include the Lanarkshire suburbs of Govan and Partick. The remaining seat was to be allocated to a new burgh district located in Renfrewshire. The major losers under these new distribution proposals were Edinburgh and Dundee, whose claims were ignored.

The second aspect of the Conservative scheme was the decision to raise a dozen or so towns with populations in excess of 6,000 to the status of Parliamentary Burghs. Alloa was to be removed from Clackmannan; Coatbridge, Govan, Partick, and Wishaw from Lanarkshire; Barrhead, Johnstone and Pollokshaws from Renfrewshire; Ardrossan, (together with Saltcoats), from Ayr; Kirkintilloch and Helensburgh from Dunbarton; Hawick from Roxburgh, and Galashiels from Selkirkshire. The new Parliamentary Burghs, with the noted exceptions of Partick and Govan, were to be accommodated through a redistribution of the Falkirk and Kilmarnock Burghs, the creation of an extra burgh district, and the expansion of existing groupings (Table 7.1).

Table 7.1: Burgh District Groupings Proposed in the 1867 Bill*

1. Falkirk Burghs: Falkirk, Linlithgow, Dumbarton, Kirkintilloch, *Helensburgh*.
2. Hamilton Burghs: Hamilton, Airdrie, *Coatbridge*, Lanark, Rutherglen, *Wishaw*.
3. Kilmarnock Burghs: Kilmarnock, Port Glasgow, Renfrew, *Johnstone Barrhead, Pollokshaws*.
4. Stirling Burghs: Stirling, Dunfermline, Queensferry, Culross, *Alloa*.
5. Haddington Burghs: Haddington, Dunbar, North Berwick, Lauder, Jedburgh, *Hawick, Galashiels*.
6. Ayr Burghs: Ayr, Irvine, Campbeltown, Inverary, Oban, *Saltcoats/Ardrossan*.
    Burghs Districts remaining the same: Wick, Inverness, Elgin, Montrose, St Andrews, Kirkcaldy, Leith, Dumfries, Wigtown.

*New Parliamentary Burghs in italics.

The proposals were clearly designed to help the Conservatives, because they removed fourteen burghs currently influencing county representation at the expense of only one extra seat in an expanded Glasgow, and one more burgh district. Secondly, by dividing three counties, they introduced the possibility of the Conservatives winning seats that would not win were they to remain united counties. Thirdly, there was even the possibility of Conservative success in

South Glasgow. The Conservatives also expected to benefit from the introduction of university representation. This redistribution scheme offers no better example of the crucial link between the franchise and the allocation of seats, for had they been adopted a substantial extension of the franchise in the burghs would have been accompanied by a reduction of urban influence in parliament. It was no surprise that in presenting this bill to the House, the Chancellor of the Exchequer concluded his remarks with the observation that he could 'hardly hope that every arrangement which we propose will pass unquestioned' (*Hansard* 187: 407).

Initial reaction to the bill was fairly predictable. Sir James Fergusson held that 'by the system of grouping and distribution...many of the irregularities and inconsistencies of the Reform Bill of 1832 had been remedied' (*Hansard* 187: 414). For the Liberals, McLaren indicated that while he imputed no base motives behind the scheme, it 'would increase the power and representation of the landlords [and was] therefore unjust and ought to be resisted' (*Hansard* 187: 427). Even more bluntly, Crum-Ewing stated that 'while giving a Liberal franchise it tended to make the representation more Conservative...Scotland was a Liberal country, but the present [redistribution] plan would destroy it;' and Bouverie, who objected to the reconstitution of his Kilmarnock Burghs, held that 'the House was not prepared to support a proposition...that the counties be purely rural' (*Hansard* 187: 441, 422). Other Liberal critics objected variously to the neglect of Aberdeen and Dundee, the division of the counties and Glasgow, and the failure to consider the grouping of counties such as Peebles and Selkirk and Sutherland and Caithness. On the other hand, the university settlement was welcomed, and Liberals such as Kinnaird (Perth), suggested that 'with a few amendments the Bill would be very acceptable to Scotland' (*Hansard* 187: 441). As with the previous Bill, however, the general strength of these various sentiments was never tested beyond its first reading.

The legislation presented in February 1868 was a modified version of the 1867 Bill. The proposals for the universities and the counties of Ayr, Lanark and Aberdeen remained unchanged. Glasgow was to gain its third seat. This time, however, the metropolis was to remain undivided, but in order to favour minority representation, each elector would still have only two votes. Changes to the burgh groupings were to be less complicated than hitherto, although all the burghs previously marked for removal from the counties were still to be raised to parliamentary status. In the west, a new district of Clyde Burghs was to be created out of Coatbridge, Wishaw, Helensburgh, Kirkintilloch, Johnstone, Barrhead and Pollokshaws; while Partick, Govan, Ardrossan and Saltcoats, Alloa, Hawick and Galashiels were to be treated as under the 1867 Bill, on the principle that 'unless the distinction between urban and county districts is to be totally ignored...these propositions are founded in reason and good sense' (*Hansard* 190: 819).

On the first and second reading, the attack on the redistribution proposals was left by the Liberal front bench to the Scottish backbenchers led by Baxter and McLaren. The former, claiming that 'the scheme was far worse than could have been anticipated' (*Hansard* 190: 820), criticised the institution of the Clyde District at the expense of 'important manufacturing towns like Dundee' (Baxter was a Dundee merchant), opposed the addition of seats to Scotland without suppression in England, and argued that on the basis of both taxation and population Scotland should have 25 extra seats. McLaren held that the electoral system proposed for Glasgow would make the city 'worse off than she is now' (*Hansard* 190: 832), because he feared it would secure the return of a Conservative, and held it would be preferable to divide the burgh into three 'wards'. He further suggested that one of the university seats should be given either to Dundee or Aberdeen, and pointed out that the removal of Hawick, Galashiels and Selkirk from their counties would swamp the Haddington District, and reduce the parliamentary county of Selkirk from 7,000 to 3,000 in population. Suggesting that Scotland would settle for an extra fifteen members, he felt that Kilmarnock, Arbroath, and Dumfries should be separated from their groups to form single burgh constituencies; that Dundee, Aberdeen, Leith Burghs, and an extended Greenock to include Port Glasgow, should have two members each; and that Edinburgh should get a third MP, as a central feature of a redistribution scheme. The second Edinburgh member, Moncrieff, challenged the fundamental principle upon which the Clyde District had been constructed: 'Renfrew and Lanark are interested in minerals – that was the interest of the county – and those large populous places...were therefore properly represented by the county member' (*Hansard* 190: 827). Strong support for all these sorts of opinions were echoed by members from Aberdeen, Dundee, and Glasgow.

Other Liberals tended to be more cautious, perhaps out of self interest, but also for fear that too strong an opposition would wreck the whole reform enterprise. McLagan (Linlithgowshire) for example, would have preferred to see the seven additional members for Scotland found at the expense of England, but was inclined to accept the scheme as an 'instalment' so as not to 'stultify' progress on the bill (*Hansard* 190: 1254). Laing (Wick Burghs) had the temerity to suggest that the Radicals were more interested in re-opening the general question of redistribution throughout Britain than in the intrinsic merits of the Scottish bill, and that the 'regular old party Whigs' were content to support any moves that might embarrass the government, whereas among 'the really moderate independent Liberals of Scotland, there was a great disposition to accept the present Bill' (*Hansard* 190: 1261). Although criticised by other Liberals for his frankness in suggesting that Scottish Liberalism could be so easily satisfied, they essentially endorsed his position by supporting the bill on second reading, reserving their criticism for the committee stage.

The government spokesmen appealed to moderate Liberal support. Replying to the first reading debate, the Chancellor of the Exchequer emphasised that 'the great principle of the Bill is the extension of the franchise' (*Hansard* 190: 1261). That was indisputable, and being more radical than the proposals of 1866, made it difficult for advanced Liberals to reject. The only other principle involved was 'that the representation of Scotland should be increased' (*Hansard* 190: 842). Despite the advance being a mere seven seats, it was again difficult for moderate Liberals to oppose, because their own leaders had only offered two in 1860 and Gladstone only seven in 1866. Even the demand that increased Scottish representation should come from suppression in England, as under the 1866 scheme, was temporarily outflanked by an observation of the Lord Advocate that to be consistent the proposal should insist on suppression in Ireland, too. For partisan reasons the Liberals were not prepared to suggest such a course. Finally, the government held that, 'the mode in which that redistribution should be made...is a matter for the committee' (*Hansard* 190: 842). This latter concession effectively finessed the opposition, because it offered the strong possibility that the administration's redistribution proposals were a matter for negotiation, and the second reading of the bill passed without a division.

The Liberal forces, which had been divided and acquiescent on the early progress of the reform bill, began to coalesce on the eve of the committee stage. Prior to the committee proper, Baxter moved an amendment empowering the committee to disfranchise all boroughs in England with populations under 5,000, his motive being to provide ten extra seats for Scotland at the expense of England, although that was not an inevitable consequence of the instruction. A counter proposal from a Conservative, Sir Rainald Knightley, Northampton, supported the removal, instead, of one member from double-member English boroughs with populations of 10–12,000. On a largely partisan vote, though by no means exclusively so, Baxter's amendment was carried. Commenting on the result, McLaren, who preferred Knightley's motion, pointed out that having voted to remove rotten boroughs in England they should also deal with nomination constituencies in Scotland such as Sutherland and the Wigtown District. McLaren's own amendment 'supported by the convention of Royal Burghs [and] by the Town Council of Edinburgh' (*Hansard* 192: 466) to instruct the committee to increase Scotland's representatives by fifteen, on the Speaker indicating that if passed it would delay progress of the bill, was withdrawn.

The Liberals, having regained the initiative, pressed their advantage through an amendment proposed by Baxter outlining a comprehensive scheme of redistribution to replace that of the government. It involved an increase of ten Scottish members. Glasgow was to be divided into two divisions, each returning two members; Edinburgh was to elect three MPs; and the cities of Aberdeen, and Dundee, together with Lanarkshire, Ayrshire, Aberdeenshire and Perthshire, were each to receive one more member, but remaining undivided. The combined universities were to have a single member.

There was a distinct possibility Baxter's scheme would prevail because the government's proposal was not only unacceptable to moderate Liberals, but was even drawing criticism from some Scottish Conservatives. Consequently, Disraeli was forced to amend drastically his original ideas within the context of seven extra seats. The universities were still to get their two members, and there were still to be additional members for Glasgow, Lanarkshire, Ayrshire and Aberdeenshire, but the seat originally scheduled for the Clyde Burghs was lost to Dundee, and the industrial burghs of central Scotland, (including Govan and Partick), were to remain where they were. In an attempt to rescue the border counties from the consequences of the new franchise, however, a new burgh district of Galashiels, Hawick and Selkirk was to be established through the amalgamation of the Peebleshire and Selkirkshire. This new package was essentially a Tory embellishment on that presented by Gladstone in 1866.

On a division, Baxter's amendment was comfortably rejected by 261 to 221. Thirty five Scottish Liberals supported it, as did the Liberal front bench. Only McLagan, sticking to his position that the government's compromise should be supported to expedite matters, and Miller, probably irritated that the interests of Leith, his constituency, had been ignored, voted with the noes. Non-voting Liberals significantly included Traill (Caithness) and Leveson-Gower (Sutherland), whose counties were threatened not only by the taunts of Tories but also by the greed of their colleagues. Only one Scottish Conservative,

Smollett (Dunbartonshire), who particularly disliked the administration's desire to promote minority representation in Glasgow, where he feared, 'a trade unionist or a delegate representing those mischievous associations might get elected' (*Hansard* 192: 962), voted with Baxter.

The way was then open for Disraeli to press the government's own compromise plan. In commending his approach, he explicitly accepted Baxter's instruction on suppression, with the proviso that because only seven additional seats were required he would reprieve the three largest English burghs with populations under 5,000. Although various attempts were made by sundry Scottish Liberals to change Disraeli's proposals – particularly with respect to the electoral arrangements for Glasgow, and an attempt by Laing to associate Sutherland with Ross and Cromarty – they survived intact. Undoubtedly there was a general recognition, especially amongst English Liberals, that as with many aspects of the 1867 reform process, the revised Scottish redistribution scheme constituted a reasonable compromise between competing interests in a much divided parliament. Any shortcomings would be best considered by a new parliament following a reformed election.

The System

The Burgh Franchise

The burgh franchise established in 1868, while not revoking the clauses of the 1832 legislation under which £10 residents could claim the vote, greatly widened the electorate by extending the franchise to any person of full age and not subject to legal incapacity, (which included fatuous and insane persons, felons, women and aliens), and 'had been for a period of not less than twelve calendar months next preceding the last day of July, an inhabitant occupier as owner or tenant of any dwelling house within the burgh' (*Act*, 1868). The rights of £10 unfurnished lodgers, whose claims to register as joint-occupiers had been recognised by the registration courts in Scotland after 1832, were specifically enfranchised as £10 lodgers under the new law.

The interpretation of 'inhabitant occupier' continued to rest on the definitions established by sheriffs such as Cay after 1832. Inhabitancy was held to imply continuous residence at home in the burgh. Provided an *animus revertendi* could be established, short-term absences were permitted (e.g. as in the case of a commercial traveller or jobbing tradesman), but where employment compelled absence, as with sailors, registration would be refused. Furthermore, the new class of voters (ie sub-£10ers) could only claim on a dwelling house defined as 'any part of a house occupied as a separate dwelling, and (in any parish in which poor-rates are levied) the occupier of which is separately rated for the relief of the poor' (*Act*, section 3). Unlike the £10ers, therefore, the sub-£10ers had to live in the premises on which they claimed a vote. Also, joint occupancy for sub-£10ers was specifically excluded as a qualification in order to prevent the enrolment of 'several persons living together in the same house e.g. a father and his sons' (Nicolson: 8); and the courts refused to enrol those who could be turned out of their occupancy at any time by a landlord, which effectively denied the franchise to domestic servants. Movement from one house to another within the burgh, however, did not disfranchise an elector, unless his claim to the vote had changed, for example, if his inhabitant occupation was broken by a short period as a lodger.

The operation of the new inhabitant franchise was closely bound to the administration of the poor law, because (a) anyone in receipt of parochial relief in the year prior to revision of the register was excluded from the new list of voters; (b) non-payment of the poor rate, either through failure to honour the assessment or specific exemption from assessment in any year, also brought exclusion; and, most importantly, (c) no inhabitant occupier or tenant could receive the vote unless he was also assessed for rating under the poor law. (The only exception was in Anstruther Wester, part of St Andrews Burghs, where there was no poor law rating).

It followed that registration under the new act was closely associated with poor-rate collection, because it fell to the Assessor to prepare a list of electors based on the valuation roll once the poor rates had been received. Only then would it be placed in the hands of the town clerk and sheriff along with details of the poor-rate non-payment etc., for refinement and modification in the registration courts.

The new registration process caused a number of problems, especially during the early implementation of the act. In Greenock, for example, occupiers of part of a house were not liable to poor relief assessment, and were consequently denied the vote; while in Selkirk, where rates were levied on owners, it was decided that until changes were made in the method of assessment, that only occupiers of whole houses would qualify for registration. A more general difficulty, however, was the practice of a number of parochial boards not to assess households with a valuation under £4, (in some places it was £3 5s, and in a few as high as £5), because it was considered not worth the cost of collection. In such burghs, therefore, the poorer householders were denied the franchise because they failed to appear on the valuation roll. Although a remedy for erroneous exemption from the valuation roll lay within the reform act, it did not apply in 1868, and in requiring action on the part of the claimant, discouraged much registration under its provisions (Nicolson: 5–7). Consequently, while the franchise was in principle extended to all householders without a fixed-line rating limit, the organisation of poor law rating and collection almost certainly excluded a large number of the more indigent householders and tenants.

The £10 unfurnished lodger franchise, as has been indicated, was not new to Scotland, so that its inclusion in 1868 was merely a restatement of the *status quo ante*. Again, in contrast to England, change of lodgings within the same burgh did not constitute a disqualification, although the interpretation that if two lodgers occupied the same £10 lodging both were to be denied the vote, was less generous than the practise south of the border. In contrast to inhabitant occupation, the lodger franchise did not require a rating assessment, but the onus on the lodger to take action each year to get his name on the register was a discouragement, and the lodger franchise remained unimportant.

The increase in the burgh electorate from 55,515 in 1865 to 154,331 in 1868, enfranchised around one in nine of the male population, as against one in eight in England and Wales and one in sixteen in Ireland (Smith: 239). Thus, whereas the proportion of the burgh population enfranchised after 1832 had been smaller in Scotland than in Ireland, it was now twice as extensive, and more or less in conformity with the rest of mainland Britain. By 1874, the burgh electorate had risen to 188,156, one in eight of the burgh population, and reached 198,669 in 1880 (Table 7.2). The three and a half-fold increase between 1865 and 1880, however, was by no means uniformly distributed. In Dundee, for example, there were nearly six times as many electors in 1874 than there had been before the passing of the act, and in the Kirkcaldy Burghs their numbers grew five and half times between 1865 and 1880. At the opposite end of the scale were the burgh districts of Wick and Wigtown, in which the electorate barely doubled; and in Edinburgh and the burgh districts of Haddington, Dumfries and Inverness, the electorate grew by less than three-fold between 1865 and 1880. In Perth and the Montrose and Kilmarnock Districts, the register quadrupled over the same period. It is noteworthy, that with the exception of Edinburgh, the constituencies recording the smallest proportionate advances, (the districts of St Andrews, Inverness, Haddington, Dumfries, Wigtown and Wick), were also the smallest. Thus, an important consequence of the legislation was to magnify the differences in size between burgh constituencies: a phenomenon that was by no means peculiar to Scotland (Smith: 239–40; Seymour: 282–3). An analysis of the electorate in 1873 indicated there were only 179 lodgers out of more than 180,000 voters, 110 of whom where in Glasgow (PP. 1874). Eighty eight per cent of the remainder were registered as occupiers, and the residue as owners. Owners, however, constituted more than a third of the electors in the St Andrews Burghs, (41.4 per cent in St Andrews itself), around a quarter in the districts of Inverness, Haddington, Wick, and Wigtown, and a fifth in Edinburgh and the districts of Ayr, Dumfries, Elgin and Falkirk. In Glasgow, by contrast, 96 per cent of the electors were occupiers, as were more than nine out of ten in Greenock, Aberdeen, and the Kilmarnock Burghs.

The proportion of all burgh residents with the ballot in 1873 was 12.7 per cent overall, ranging from one in six in Aberdeen, and one in seven in Dundee, Perth, and the burgh districts of Montrose, Kilmarnock, Hawick and Stirling, down to one in nine or less in Glasgow, Paisley, and the burghs of Falkirk, St Andrews and Wick (Table 7.2).

Within the burgh districts the range was even greater. In the St Andrews constituency, for example, only 8.2 per cent were enfranchised in the head burgh, but 18.2 per cent, (the highest of all Scottish burghs), of the 484 inhabitants of Anstruther Wester, where there was a 'straightforward' household suffrage, had a vote. Similarly, in the Ayr District, while a respectable 13.6 per cent of the county town were enfranchised, only 7.6 per cent, (the lowest of all Scottish parliamentary burghs), enjoyed the privilege in Campbeltown. The variance in the proportion enfranchised was strongly associated with the ratio of owners to occupiers. If one excludes the Clydeside burghs of Glasgow, Paisley and Greenock, there was an inverse correlation of 0.78 between a high proportion of owners amongst the electorate and the higher levels of enfranchisement.

Variations in the proportion of the population enfranchised were a function of both contrasting social circumstances and registration practices which limited or extended the occupier franchise. In St Andrews, for example, with its dependence on the university, many people were employed in service, and such persons were expressly denied the vote. Registration was restricted in the expanding industrial burghs of the central lowlands because potential electors were less likely than elsewhere to satisfy the twelve months residential requirement, as they followed work opportunities, and occasional periods of unemployment left them excluded for having been in receipt of poor law relief and/or for having had the payment of the poor rate waived.

Table 7.2: Impact of the Second Reform Act in the Burghs

Burghs*	Increase in Electorate 1865-1880	Percentage Increase 1865-1880	Percentage of the Population Enfranchised, 1873	Percentage of All Burgh Electorate in each Burgh, 1880	Electorate 1880
Glasgow (3)	41,101	244	11.4	29.0	57,920
Edinburgh (2)	18,181	176	12.6	14.4	28,524
Dundee	11,527	379	15.0	7.3	14,566
Aberdeen	10,188	255	16.6	7.1	14,184
Leith D.	7,661	287	13.9	5.2	10,333
Montrose D.	6,537	362	14.6	4.2	8,343
Kilmarnock D.	6,055	368	14.4	3.9	7,700
Greenock	5,332	285	12.5	3.6	7,203
Falkirk D.	3,823	253	11.1	2.7	5,333
Paisley	3,618	266	10.5	2.5	4,979
Hawick D.	-	-	14.3	2.5	4,920
Stirling D.	3,545	281	14.5	2.4	4,807
Kirkcaldy D.	3,649	447	14.0	2.2	4,465
Ayr D.	2,957	221	11.6	2.2	4,297
Perth	3,018	307	14.4	2.0	4,000
Elgin D.	2,747	259	12.1	1.9	3,806
Inverness D.	1,968	193	10.5	1.5	2,990
Dumfries D.	1,807	161	12.4	1.5	2,931
St Andrews D.	1,703	203	11.3	1.3	2,542
Haddington D.	1,198	172	13.4	1.0	1,896
Wick D.	961	121	10.7	0.9	1,754
Wigtown D.	658	127	12.1	0.6	1,176
	138,234	249	12.7	99.9	198,669

* Ranked by size of electorate in 1880, after FWS Craig.

Equally important for the degree of enfranchisement were the consequences of rating customs. The absence of poor law assessment in Anstruther Wester simplified registration procedures, and removed a major cause of exclusion. By contrast, in most Scottish burghs, the routine exclusion of sub-£4ers from poor rate liability systematically operated against the enfranchisement of poorer households. In Greenock there was no assessment of houses, and alms were paid by custom. Despite the provisions made within the act to enable persons excluded from the parliamentary register as a consequence of quaint local practises to claim the vote *after* 1868, it is doubtful many did so, because it required personal initiative. It is instructive in this context to note that in seven burghs, (the Wick, Stirling, Falkirk, Kilmarnock and Wigtown Districts, Greenock and Glasgow), more than three quarters of the increase in the electorate between 1865 and 1880 had taken place as early as 1868. There is a strong suspicion, therefore, that in most of the burghs of central Scotland and Clydeside, that relatively small increases in their electorates after 1868 indicate under-registration of sub-£4 householders.

Political circumstances also seem to have played their part in determining the size of the register. In Aberdeen, for example, the greatly expanded electorate in 1874 followed an uncontested election in 1868 and the intervention of a Conservative for the first time since 1841. Also, in 1874, the presence of a Conservative candidate for the first time since 1837 in Dundee was associated with a particularly large registration of electors.

Although the mass electorates created by the borough franchise of 1868 contributed much to the development of political parties in the English cities, the caucus politics of Birmingham was not typical of most borough constituencies, where small electorates helped to sustain continuing aristocratic control (Ostrogorski; Seymour: 522). In Scotland, too, mass electorates shaped political life in only a small number of burghs. Only Glasgow and Edinburgh had electorates in excess of 20,000 by 1880, and there remained thirteen burgh constituencies with fewer than 5,000 electors, scattered, (with the exception of Perth), throughout groupings of three to seven different burghs. Thus, in most instances, the character of burgh politics was not fundamentally changed in 1868. In small constituencies politics could still operate on the basis of personal contact between individual voters and local notables, and it is not at all surprising that Scottish burghs of this period should have been described as 'member-ridden' (Hanham: 164). To that extent burgh politics after 1868 was more evocative of its immediate past than a harbinger of the modern system.

The County Franchise

Amendments to the county franchise were not so extensive as in the burghs, although they relaxed the value of the various property qualifications, and made minor technical changes. Interpretation of various qualifications (e.g. as to what constituted a heritable subject), continued to rest on the legal judgements as applied to the 1832 legislation. Under the new proposals the vote was extended to:

(a) Persons who had been for a period of twelve months preceding 31st July in any year, proprietors of lands and heritages, which were entered on the valuation roll as being of yearly value of £5 or more after 'deduction of any feu duty, ground annual or other consideration which he may have to pay or give or account for as a condition of his right, and after deduction of any annuity, life-rent provision, or such annual burden' (*Act*, section 5); and

(b) Persons who had been for a period of twelve months preceding 31st July in any year, a tenant of lands and heritages of annual value of £14 or upwards appearing on the valuation roll.

The major changes from 1832 were that the ownership qualification had been reduced from £10 to £5, and the annual rental value of tenanted property from £50 to £14. The definition of proprietor still continued to include life-renters, but also, after 1868, 57-year leaseholders, who under previous legislation had been classified as tenants. In the case of 'tenant proprietors' their annual rent was deducted from the yearly value of their property, as indicated on the valuation roll, in assessing their right to the franchise. Poor rates, however, were not deductible, nor was the payment of the poor rate assessment a condition of the new ownership franchise. Tenants claiming the vote had to be in 'actual personal occupancy' of their subjects, and were not, therefore, permitted to sub-let or assign their leases. On the other hand, tenants did not have to be in personal residence on their property, although in the case of those whose subjects were only marginally above £14, it would be unlikely that other residents would be other than sub-tenants.

Consequently, for poorer tenants, personal residence was probably also necessary if the franchise was to be claimed successfully. Payment of the poor rate was also attached to the new tenant franchise in those parishes where it was levied, (there were 100 parishes in which it was not). In contrast to the burgh sub-£4ers, however, the higher £14 lower limit meant that such potential electors were not excluded from the valuation roll. In an attempt to restrict the manufacture of votes under the new franchise, joint ownership and joint occupancy of the same lands and heritages was only permitted to yield a maximum of two votes, except in exceptional circumstances – e.g. where the persons 'shall be *bona fide* engaged as partners carrying on trade or business in or on such lands and heritages' (*Act*, section 14). Such limitations did not apply to those enrolled under the 1832 provisions, so that faggot voting continued to be a feature of county politics.

Initial responsibility for the construction of the electoral roll, as in the burghs, fell on the assessor in consultation with the collector of the poor rate. The sheriff-clerk and sheriff then dealt with appeals before producing the final version of the electoral roll. (In special cases a decision might rest with an appeal court.) As previously, the county register was revised each year, rather than reconstructed, as in the burghs.

Although the county franchise rose by 55 per cent between 1865 and 1868, and by 1880 was almost double what it had been on the eve of the Second Reform Act, there was little indication that the new franchise had tapped a greatly broadening social pyramid, as it had in the burghs. As in 1832, the sharp contrast with England remained, for whereas south of the border one in fifteen males in the counties was enfranchised in 1868, in Scotland it was a mere one in twenty four, barely in excess of Ireland's one in twenty six (Smith: 239). Consequently, whereas in England half as many county males proportionately were enfranchised as in the burghs, in Scotland it was only a third.

By 1874, an estimated 4.4 per cent of residents in the counties held the ballot, ranging from 1.4 per cent in Sutherland to 6.7 per cent in Bute (Table 7.3). Predictably, the Highland region, with an overall enfranchisement of 2.9 per cent, had the most narrowly based franchise, which was no better than in the other counties under the First Reform Act and below the 3.8 per cent reached by the Borders in 1865. By contrast, in the farming counties of the East and Borders, 5.2 per cent and 5.4 per cent of their respective populations had the vote in 1874. The mainly industrial counties of Clydeside (4.4 per cent) and Central (4.3 per cent) hovered around the mean, although across the Lothians (3.5 per cent) the enrolment was no better than in Caithness.

The biggest increases in the electorate, both proportionately and absolutely, between 1865 and 1880 were recorded in Lanarkshire and Renfrewshire, which intruded on the bulging suburbs of Glasgow. Together with Dunbartonshire they accounted for three in ten of all extra county electors throughout Scotland. In the Highlands, the electorate grew by one and a half times in Caithness and Orkney and Shetland, and doubled in Inverness. The Highland advances, however, were less a reflection of liberation under the 1868 Act than of an exceedingly low enfranchisement after 1832, which had only reached 1.6 per cent throughout the region by 1865. Remarkably, the proportionate growth in the electorate was actually below the national average in Ross and Cromarty, Sutherland, and Argyll, and there were only 5,005 more voters in the Crofting counties in 1880 than in 1865, almost 4,000 fewer than the increase in Lanarkshire alone. The smallest growth, however, was recorded in the Borders, where enfranchisement had been relatively high before 1868. Also, the creation of the Hawick Burghs out of Hawick, Selkirk and Galashiels, removed a number of former county electors from Peeblesshire and Selkirkshire and Roxburghshire. Elsewhere, there were substantial improvements in the north east, where the electorate doubled in Elgin and Nairn, Banffshire, and Aberdeenshire; and in Bute the number of voters grew one and a half times.

Despite expansion, the character of the county electorate does not appear to have been changed greatly in 1868, and by 1880 fourteen of the county constituencies still had fewer than 2,000 electors. Politically, the main developments were in the rural areas outside the crofting counties, where the influx of middling farmers assisted in the weakening of proprietorial control and the rise of a more progressive Liberalism. The working class of industrial Scotland and the northern crofters, however, remained largely unenfranchised.

Seats and Electors [1]

The electoral system established in 1868 was bound to produce a curious association between the distribution of seats and votes, for whereas the franchise in the burghs had been liberalised, in the counties it had been subject to less radical change. Furthermore, a reluctance to undertake redistribution preserved anomalies that had been protected in 1832; and in that context the allocation of only five extra seats, (apart from the introduction of university representation), produced a constituency settlement that gave scant regard to changes in the relative dispersal of the population over the intervening years. The deal which sanctioned the creation of an additional burgh district in the Borders, leaving Peebles and Selkirk with a combined electorate of less than 900 in 1868, would have been regarded by the 1832 reformers as a regressive development.

The recognition of the universities was a diversion that deprived more worthy candidates of representation; and in Glasgow the refusal of the Liberals to sanction the division of the city was no less a gerrymander than the Tory imposition of the Limited Vote. The refusal of parliament to throw industrial towns and villages into the burgh districts, however, prevented a nonsense being made of the political geography of central Scotland; but the most progressive feature of the redistribution scheme was undoubtedly the division of Aberdeenshire, Ayrshire, and Lanarkshire, because it not only pointed towards a more equitable way of allocating county seats, but also a fairer way of representing the diversity of opinion in the cities.

Table 7.3: Impact of the Second Reform Act on the Electorate in the Counties

County	Increase in Electorate 1865-1880	Percentage Increase 1865-1880	Percentage of the Population Enfranchised, 1873	Percentage of All County Electorate in each County, 1880	Electorate 1880
Lanark (2)	8,807	170	4.0 (N) 4.1 (S)	14.8	13,990
Aberdeen (2)	4,559	104	5.4 (E) 6.0 (W)	9.4	8,943
Ayr (2)	2,865	62	4.8 (N) 4.4 (S)	7.9	7,507
Renfrew	3,726	165	5.3	6.4	6,038
Perth	2,470	72	4.7	6.2	5,918
Fife	2,024	75	4.4	5.0	4,767
Forfar	1,526	72	5.6	3.8	3,634
Dumfries	1,282	61	5.4	3.6	3,379
Argyll	1,385	69	4.6	3.5	3,299
Stirling	1,385	71	4.1	3.5	3,328
Midlothian	1,604	97	3.6	3.4	3,260
Dunbarton	1,379	86	4.8	3.1	2,976
Banff	1,587	149	4.8	2.8	2,649
Kirkcudbright	851	63	5.8	2.3	2,204
Clack/Kinross	922	79	4.8	2.2	2,084
Roxburgh	339	21	5.2	2.1	1,978
Elgin/Nairn	1,028	119	4.4	2.0	1,891
Inverness	937	111	2.4	2.0	1,851
Kincardine	851	86	5.3	1.9	1,838
Berwick	583	47	4.7	1.9	1,830
Orkney/Shetland	1,019	149	2.7	1.8	1,704
Ross/Cromarty	731	78	2.1	1.8	1,664
Wigtown	570	52	5.3	1.7	1,657
Bute	798	156	6.7	1.4	1,311
Linlithgow	419	52	3.4	1.3	1,232
Caithness	751	147	3.5	1.3	1,263
Peebles/Selkirk	135	13	6.2	1.2	1,136
Haddington	375	56	3.2	1.1	1,040
Sutherland	146	81	1.4	0.3	326
All	45,143	91	4.4	99.7	94,697

* Ranked by size of electorate in 1880, after F.W.S. Craig.

As previously, not only was there a severe maldistribution of seats in relation to the dispersal of the electorate across all constituencies, (as would have been expected given the increased disparities between the franchise provisions for burghs and counties), but also within the various categories of seats. Indeed, the burgh constituencies were even less equitably distributed than in 1832, although there was improvement in the counties.

The coefficients of variation indicate that the differences in size between all constituencies had increased from 0.74 in 1832 to 0.91 in 1865, and that the reforms of 1868 did nothing to reduce the variation (Table 7.4). Amongst the burghs, the distribution of seats was marginally less equal than in 1832, and amongst burgh districts the degree of inequality increased from 0.44 in 1865 to 0.53 in 1868 because, as was indicated, the electorate grew by smaller proportions in the smaller burgh districts. Although significant disparities remained between the single burgh constituencies, due principally to the continuing gross under-representation of Glasgow and the small number of electors in Perth, the granting of increased representation to Dundee and Glasgow helped restore the 1832 position amongst constituencies in this category.

Table 7.4: Coefficients of Variation between the Distribution of Seats and Voters, 1832–1880

	Counties	Burghs	Single Burghs	Burgh Districts	All
1832	.75	.71	.47	.45	.74
1865	.76	.94	.62	.44	.91
1868	.52	.75	.48	.53	.90
1880	.65	.73	.48	.56	.90

The greatest progress towards equality took place in the counties, where the division of Ayrshire, Lanarkshire and Aberdeenshire, together with the amalgamation of Peebles and Selkirk, reduced the coefficient of variation from 0.76 in 1865, (a figure which had been stable throughout the operation of the First Reform Act), to 0.52 in 1868. It is, however, noteworthy that inequalities in the counties were increasing substantially by 1880 due in large measure to the virtual doubling of the electorate in Lanarkshire North and Renfrew, between 1868 and 1880, substantial increases in Dunbartonshire and Midlothian (all of them amongst the bigger constituencies), and the failure of the smaller counties to increase their numbers in similar proportions (Table 7.3).

In absolute terms, the average constituency in 1868 consisted of 3,989 electors, ranging by a factor of 45 from 358 in Sutherland to 15,591 per MP in Glasgow. Although the mean number of burgh electors per seat of 5,944 was predictably higher than the 2,401 in the counties, there were more voters in each of the ten largest county seats than in any of the nine smallest burgh constituencies. The discrepancy between the burgh districts and the single burghs was particularly marked. In the burgh districts 50,500 voters were distributed between fifteen constituencies, whereas the 104,031 single burgh electors were represented by only eleven MPs. A vote in Glasgow was worth only a seventeenth of a vote cast in Wigtown, and a vote cast in the Haddington District had seven times the value of one held in Edinburgh. There were more electors in Glasgow with its three members than in Perth and the fourteen smallest burgh districts put together. Similarly, the sixteen largest county seats each had an average of 3,340 electors, as against only 1,373 in the sixteen smallest, and, (setting aside the chronic case of Sutherland), a vote in Haddingtonshire had six times the value of one exercised in Perthshire.

The somewhat random relationship between the distribution of seats and voters in 1832 had appeared less irrational when expressed in regional terms, and even less so with respect to the regional distribution of the population. In 1868, however, a more distorted pattern emerged, because the new legislation gave only scant attention to demographic changes over the previous 36 years (Table 7.5).

The Highlands continued to be a favoured region, for although an exceptionally low level of rural enfranchisement argued for an allocation of only 2.5 seats, or no more than 6.5 constituencies on its share of the population, 8.1 seats were retained. Sutherland and the Wick District were the obvious candidates for suppression (Tables 7.2 and 7.3). Even more anomalous was the situation in the Borders, which retained 9.2 seats, but merited only 4.7 on the basis of population, or 4.3 with respect to the number of electors. The new constituency of Peebles and Selkirk had a combined population of under 17,000, (the national average being 58,000 per MP); Wigtownshire retained both a county seat containing fewer than 30,000 inhabitants, and a burgh district with a population under 10,000; and the new constituency of Hawick Burghs had only a modest 3,761 electors in 1874.

In the East, where the region's proportion of seats was in close accord with its share of the population, the division of Aberdeenshire might appropriately have been associated with the suppression of the Elgin Burghs to minimise over-representation; and the diminutive St Andrews Burghs might have been liberated to find a second member for the city of Aberdeen. Similarly, in the Central region, over-representation caused in part by the creation of two seats in Ayrshire, could have been reduced by the amalgamation of Bute with a neighbouring county.

Predictably, the most disadvantaged area was Glasgow, where there would have been at least eight members had its population been recognised, and fully a dozen had the measure been the electoral register. Clydeside also merited two more constituencies on account of its population in addition to the extra seat granted to Lanarkshire. It was, however, a measure of the under-representation of the working class in the west, that Clydeside's share of the seats accorded closely with its proportion of the national electorate. As a whole, Glasgow and Clydeside emerged with 7.8 fewer seats than deserved on the basis of population, in 1868, as against a shortfall on only 2.6 members in 1832. Had Glasgow's inhabitants been treated with the same generosity as those in Selkirk and Peebles, the city would have had 29 members of parliament.

The constituency settlement of 1868, therefore, was in many respects less credible than that of 1832. Additional seats were used to mollify the more populous areas, but with only five seats to dispose of, once the universities had pinched two, no significant moves towards proportionality were possible once redistribution had been ruled out.

Of course, such progress had never been intended by the framers of the legislation, who unlike the reformers of 1832 wanted to negate as far as possible the generosity of the new franchise. Nowhere were the priorities of the administration better illustrated than with respect to changes in the counties. Aberdeenshire and Ayrshire were more or less evenly divided because it was unclear how biases to the Conservative party could be manufactured; but in gerrymandered Lanarkshire there were nearly twice as many voters and more than twice the population in the industrial north division than in the rural south constituency, which fell to the Tories in 1874. Similarly, the newly combined counties of Peebles and Selkirk, having been divested of the burghs of Selkirk and

Galashiels, (half of which was in Roxburgh), constituted the third smallest constituency in Scotland, and had been devised simply to protect the Conservative interest. It is not inconceivable that had Disraeli's original redistribution scheme been adopted, the Second Reform Act as a whole, changes to the franchise notwithstanding, might have produced a more conservative outcome than the reforms of 1832.

Table 7.5 : Regional Impact of the 1868 Reform Act

	Electorate 1868	Percentage of Population Enfranchised	Seats	'Fair' Distribution of Seats by: (a) Population	(b) Electors
Aberdeen	8,312	9.4	1.0	1.5	2.1
Dundee	14,798	12.6	2.0	2.1	3.7
Edinburgh/Leith	27,002	10.6	3.0	4.4	6.8
Glasgow	47,854	10.0	3.0	8.3	12.0
Highland	9,943	2.6	8.1	6.5	2.5
East	38,964	6.4	11.8	10.8	9.8
Clydeside	29,929	6.4	7.2	9.7	7.5
Central	37,466	6.7	12.6	10.8	9.3
Borders	17,108	6.3	9.2	4.7	4.3
All	**231,376**	**6.9**	**57.9**	**58.0**	**58.0**

Conclusion

The Second Reform Act was a dog's breakfast because it was the product of a parliament over which the front benches had little control, and was pushed through by a minority Conservative administration that had plotted with the Whigs to defeat Gladstone's proposals and bargained with the Radicals to secure its own measure.

Clearly, the most notable feature of the new legislation was the introduction of household suffrage as it compromised the principle that 'property and intelligence' should be the basis of the burgh franchise. Although opening the door to a more democratic foundation, the residential and poor law qualifications were significant limitations to the general principal, imposing a test of respectability on putative working class electors. In the counties the underlying basis of the franchise remained unchanged, although the value of property confering a vote was reduced. As a result, the distinctions between the burgh and county electoral systems widened. In Scotland, where the burgh electorate tripled to establish virtual parity with England, and the county electorate was no more popular than that created south of the border in 1832, the divergence was particularly marked.

The distribution of seats continued to favour the more conservative elements in the polity, substantially neutralising the overall impact of the new burgh franchise, and the failure to recognise demographic change produced a greater distortion between the distribution of seats and population than in 1832. Thirty two of the 58 Scottish seats were located in the counties, and the fourteen burgh districts not only survived but were reinforced by the Hawick District. Only eleven MPs came from the single burghs. In 1880, the five constituencies with electorates over 10,000, (Glasgow, Edinburgh, Dundee, Aberdeen and the Leith Burghs), not only accommodated 63 per cent of all those enfranchised in the burghs and fully 43 per cent of all Scottish electors, but returned only nine members of parliament. Such prejudice served not only the interests of county Whigs and Tories, but also those of Liberals in the burgh districts. Consequently, Scotland's MPs continued to represent more a rural nation of the late eighteenth century than a modernising industrial state.

From a developmental perspective, the division of Aberdeenshire, Ayrshire and Lanarkshire was an important innovation because it introduced a principle critical to the evolution of equal electoral districts. Significantly, similar proposals for Glasgow proved more controversial and were strongly resisted by the Liberals, who feared it would favour the representation of minorities, (i.e. Conservatives), and by the Tory, Smollett, who foresaw the election of trade unionists. It was an early intimation of Liberalism's increasing vulnerability in single member constituencies based on socially segregated electorates in urban areas.

In Scotland, at least, the progressive features of the Second Reform Act flattered to deceive, and were potentially more threatening to the advanced Liberals in the big cities faced with swollen electorates, than to the Whigs and Tories in the countryside who could still mobilise faggot voters. To that extent, the measure was a triumph for the ingenuity of Disraeli, as he emerged triumphant from the Serbonian Bog (Smith: 7). It was, however, such a grotesque solution that even at the time it was not regarded as a settlement. Pressure to equalise the franchise was bound to increase, as it was patently unjust, for example, that a miner in a Fife burgh could claim a vote that was denied to one living in the county. Again, the cynicism of the redistribution scheme, which was hardly defensible in 1868, became even more manifestly absurd as industrial change gathered pace. In being too successful in 1868, Disraeli and the forces which supported him ensured the legislation would only last for a short time. It was unlikely that the Liberals would sustain indefinitely a system so biased towards the interests of rural landlords, particularly so once Gladstone had become the 'Peoples' William'. Decency precluded changes in the first reformed parliament, although it established the secret ballot; Conservative domination forestalled reform, 1874-1880; but the Liberal parliament of 1880-1885 could scarcely avoid the introduction of a comprehensive measure of electoral reform.

Notes

1   For the purpose of the discussion here, Glasgow is treated as three constituencies; and Edinburgh and Dundee as each having two constituencies.

References

An Act for the Amendment of the Representation of the People in Scotland, Cap, XLVIII, 1868.

Cockburn, H, *Memorials of His Time,* Edinburgh, 1874

Craig, FWS, *British Parliamentary Election Results, 1832–1885,* London, 1977

Hansard, (3rd Series).

Hanham, H, *Elections and Party Management,* Hassocks, 1978.

Nicolson, JB, *An Analysis of the Scottish Reform Act,* Edinburgh, 1869.

Ostrogorski, M, *Democracy and the Organisation of Political Parties,* 2 Vols., New York, 1902

Parliamentary Papers, Session 1874 (381) LIII, *Return, specifying for each Parliamentary city and borough in Scotland, the population in 1861 and 1871; numbers of electors, 1866, 1869, and in 1873, distinguishing occupiers, owners, lodgers, freemen &c.,*

Seymour, C, *Electoral Reform in England and Wales,* New Haven, 1915.

Smith, FB, *The Making of the Second Reform Bill,* Melbourne, 1966

8   The Operation of the System, 1868–1884

The lopsided character of the Second Reform Act created a system of politics that reflected its ambiguities. On the one hand, reform fundamentally changed the basis of the burgh franchise, stimulated the growth of political parties, and led to the introduction of the secret ballot in 1872, but by minimising the importance of the new mass electorates in the cities by denying them an equitable allocation of seats, and severely restricting franchise extension in the counties, the more radical consequences of reform were contained.

The main immediate impact of the reforms in Scotland was to strengthen the grip which Liberalism had established in both the burghs and counties by 1865. Indeed, the burghs remained Liberal virtually by definition and continued to drift towards radicalism. In the counties, however, not only was the trend against the Conservatives exacerbated, but Whig landowners also came under pressure as more agricultural tenants of middling means joined the roll and showed an increasing tendency to defy proprietorial interests. Nevertheless, although Whig influence in the industrial burghs weakened and businessmen began to secure county constituencies, landowners continued to dominate Scottish representation as a whole, and the ideological and social diversity of Scottish Liberalism remained as extensive as hitherto. Thus, while the politics of 1868 to 1880 indicate a further tilting of the balance towards the forces behind Liberalism, there was no fundamental restructuring of political power.

There were, however, underlying changes taking place post-1868 which were to become crucially important after 1885. Of these, the most critical was the institution of political parties on a national scale, because it effected the transition from the politics of the First Reform Act centred on individual constituencies, to the polarised British-wide campaigns that followed the rationalisation of voter alignment in the Home Rule crisis of 1886. Although both parties began to develop the rudiments of central organisations and constituency associations in Scotland after 1865, the dominance of Liberalism in the burghs and Conservative despondency in the counties minimised the impact of national political structures on the general elections of 1868, 1874 and 1880.

Even before the general election of 1868, the Conservatives created a Scottish National Constitutional Association following a visit by Disraeli to Edinburgh in 1867 (Urwin: 96). Although open to individual subscribers, it was never popular, most of its activities centred on a committee of Edinburgh lawyers, and was by-passed by local constituency associations, who preferred to conduct their external relations directly with London. It was, therefore, hardly surprising that a report undertaken on Disraeli's behalf in 1876 revealed a Scottish party which still relied heavily on aristocratic connection and the work of unpaid agents, possessed a demoralised rank and file, and had great difficulty in finding suitable candidates (Crapster: 355-60). In Glasgow, where in 1869 the first official Conservative Association had been formed north of the border, the local party considered disbanding altogether following the general election of 1880

(Urwin: 106). It was not until the appointment of Reginald MacLeod, the son-in-law of Sir Stafford Northcote, as Central Office agent in Scotland, in 1883, a year after the institution of the National Union of Scottish Conservative Associations, that a sense of general direction was given to the party's affairs (Hanham: 159). Nevertheless, in some county constituencies there was evidence of improved organisation after 1868, which played a part in the Conservative victories of 1874. Recognising the need to mobilise support beyond narrowly-based cabals of landowners, formal associations were instituted in counties such as Perthshire, (in which a network of 'twelve district committees with local agents and squads of enthusiastic local workers' was established), Stirlingshire, Wigtownshire and Kirkcudbrightshire, for the purpose of recruiting tenant farmers to the cause. Improved efficiency was also evident in re-registration drives undertaken in counties such as Dumfries and Roxburgh (Hutchison: 112). Thus, despite major deficiencies in many areas, there were indications of improved Tory activity, and the increasing number of Conservative candidates, 1868-1880, reflected the success of the central organs of the party in cajoling constituency 'associations'.

The impetus to Liberal organisation was delayed until after the general election of 1874, when the Conservatives had more than doubled the seats they won in 1868 (Kellas, 1965; 1968). In 1876, a West and South of Scotland Liberal Association, centred on Glasgow, was established, and the following year an East and North of Scotland Liberal Association, with its headquarters in Edinburgh, was inaugurated. The two merged in 1881 to form the Scottish Liberal Association, despite the reluctance of the Radical Glaswegians to be associated with a more Whig-oriented party. The main instigator of these various developments was William Adam, the Liberal Chief Whip, who together with his close friend, John Reid, first secretary of the East and North Association, used the new structures to influence constituencies in their choice of candidates, and to discourage the nomination of surplus Liberals. Thus, before the election of 1880, Reid made a tour of all constituencies, 'interfering with local committees to an extent which would hardly have been tolerated in England' (Hanham: 159). His powers of persuasion were assisted by the possession of a private political fund. It would, however, be mistaken to underestimate the continuing highly autonomous character of Liberalism in the constituencies, and the influence of powerful local politicians. Despite the formation of constituency associations, it was not until 1886 that the distinction between official and unofficial Liberal candidates, a *sine qua non* for the development of disciplined national parties, was of crucial importance. The main advantage to the Liberal leaders was that the new structures, linking the localities to the centre, facilitated communication between them and constituency powerbrokers.

In parallel with these institutional developments was the growth of a more popular style of politics and the emergence of Gladstone, whose charismatic appeal challenged the authority of traditional notables, both Whig and Radical, and curtailed the enthusiasms of the new constituency associations. Popular trust in the politically ambiguous Gladstone and candidates pledged to him provided a simple reference point for the emerging mass electorate, transcending the complexities of local Liberal factionalism.

Elections

It is not easy to characterise the elections of 1868 to 1880, partly because the electoral system drew an even sharper distinction between burgh and county than before, and partly because there was an insufficiency of elections under the Second Reform Act for a settled electoral culture to take root. The general election of 1868, the last to take place under the open voting system, found almost half the members returned unopposed, and Liberal 'primaries' in the burghs were four times more common than fights between the parties. The first secret ballot contest in 1874 was marked by a serious Conservative attempt to revive its fortunes; while the election of 1880, in which nearly all the seats were subjected to two-party confrontations, was dominated by Gladstone's Midlothian campaign. The appearance, therefore, is of a system edging towards nationally-focused two-party electoral competition. That, however, was only true of the counties, because in the burghs the Liberals were so dominant by 1880 that only in a formal sense did the Conservatives constitute an electoral force.

Participation

Perhaps the most important characteristic of politics in the two decades after 1868 was a quickening of public participation in the political process, which was associated with an increasing newspaper readership, and a flowering of all kinds of organisations and causes aimed at the moral improvement of society, of which the temperance movement was the obvious symbol.

According to Hanham, 'in the 1870s and 1880s everybody talked about politics...so that politics seemed to matter more than ever before' (Hanham: xv). That heightened intensity was reflected and stimulated by the more frequent publication of established newspapers and an expansion of the provincial press. In the whole of the period before 1830 only 131 newspaper titles had ever been registered in Scotland, and most of them in Edinburgh and Glasgow, but between 1831 and 1850 no fewer than 169 new newspapers were founded, and a massive 168 in the decade prior to 1860. Between 1861 and 1870, 109 more newspapers were established, 115 between 1871 and 1880, and 141 between 1881 and 1890 (Ferguson; Cowan). By 1870, the *Scotsman* was selling around 30,000 daily copies, and the *Glasgow Herald* 42,000 in the late 1880s (Hanham: 110). The bias of the press strongly favoured the Liberals, who enjoyed not only the backing of ten of the thirteen dailies by 1885 (Hanham: 112), but the burgeoning small town press was also favourable to progressive Liberalism, and contributed to the problems of both Tories and Whigs in the counties as landowners lost their monopoly over political communication. It was a measure of Tory weakness that as late as 1876 there was no Conservative newspaper published north of Aberdeen, where their organ, *The Aberdeen Journal*, had yet to appear on a daily basis (Crapster: 356). Conservative attempts to create a more favourable press proved difficult due to the disinterest of leading landowners in a medium which was urban-based and a political weapon with which they were unfamiliar (Hutchison: 114-5).

The widening dissemination of political and social ideas helped stimulate discussion and a participatory society not only in the cities and large towns but also in rural areas. In Kincardineshire, for example, a forum for political debate, the Laurencekirk Parliament, played a part in wresting control of the Liberal interest from a landed proprietor, Burnet of Leys, and placing it in the hands of tenant farmers and the small burgh bourgeoisie. More symptomatic of the increasing self-confidence and independence of the peasantry were the establishment in 1874 of the Chamber of Agriculture and the Scottish Farmers' Club, designed to articulate and advance the claims of tenant farmers (Hutchison: 106).

Such developments did much to change the character of rural politics, as they were part of a process which was undermining proprietorial control over parliamentary representation.

Table 8.1: Average Voter Participation in General Elections 1868–1880 by Region

	Counties				Burghs			
	1868	1874	1880	Average all counties	1868	1874	1880	Average all burghs
	%	%	%	%	%	%	%	%
Aberdeen					-	46	75	· 60
Dundee					71	57	77	69
Edinburgh					-	76	81	79
Glasgow					79	69	81	76
Highland	76	79	84	81	89	86	-	87
East	74	79	84	80	67	73	74	73
Clydeside	85	85	88	88	83	79	82	82
Central	83	81	85	84	74	83	80	79
Borders	82	86	89	86	91	89	88	89
All	**81**	**82**	**86**	**83**	**79**	**75**	**80**	**78**

All 57 Constituencies: 1868, 80 per cent; 1874, 78 per cent; 1880, 83 per cent.
All elections 1868-1880, 81 per cent.

The broadening of political debate inevitably enhanced voter interest in the outcome of elections, a process reinforced by the reduction of uncontested elections, thereby making voting more habitual. It is not, therefore, surprising to find that whereas between 1832 and 1865 turnout amongst registered electors was a somewhat modest 71 per cent, over the three elections, 1868-1880, it rose to around 81 per cent (Table 8.1).

Turnout in the counties (83 per cent) continued to run ahead of participation in the burghs (78 per cent) as it had done between 1832 and 1865. In the county seats of Borders and Clydeside the average turnout was 86 per cent, and 84 per cent in Central, underlining the strength and closeness of the two-party battle in these regions. Even in the East and Highland four fifths of the county electorate regularly voted, but an impressive increase of 11 per cent over 1832-1865 in Highland rendered turnout in the East weakest (just) of all the regions. Nevertheless, the range between all regions remained at only six per cent.

Differentials between levels of voting in the big cities, other single burghs, and burgh districts also continued to be a distinctive feature of electoral behaviour. Thus, comparing 1832-1865 with 1868-1880, despite an average increase in participation in the four big cities from 58 per cent on average to 73 per cent, and an impressive growth in turnout from an average of 66 per cent to 79 per cent in Paisley, Greenock and Perth, the burgh districts, with an average of 81 per cent of their electorates voting, continued to lead the field. As previously, turnout in Liberal burgh 'primaries' (85 per cent) remained higher than in elections where Conservatives intervened (80 per cent). Even when the 11 constituencies which had elections of both types are examined, participation was less when Tories stood. The essential point, however, is that despite a substantial increase in the burgh electorate, the willingness of those enrolled to cast a vote was greater than before.

Elections in the Burghs

The modernisation of electoral competition in the Scottish burghs continued to stall due to the inability of the Conservatives to establish themselves as a credible opposition to Liberalism. Of the 22 burgh constituencies, the Tories contested only four in 1868, fourteen in 1874, and sixteen in 1880 (Table 8.2); and their successes were confined to the capture of Ayr Burghs, 'an unexpected bonus' (Hutchison: 103) and a seat in Glasgow by default in 1874. Consequently, there were few pressures on the various Liberal factions to bury their differences through the creation of unifying party structures, a two-party electoral culture failed to mature, and the outcome of contests were determined as much by local loyalties and attachment to incumbents as ideologies and national questions. Change was barely detectable in the rural burgh districts, where Whig landlords continued to exercise considerable influence over representation, but in the cities and industrialised burgh districts there was a discernible shift towards Radicalism.

With the Conservatives only contesting Paisley, the burgh districts of Montrose and Wigtown, and one of the Glasgow seats, nine constituencies returning unopposed Liberals, and a further nine subjected to Liberal 'primaries', the character of the 1868 burgh elections was similar to that of the previous 30 years. Any assessment of the immediate impact of the new franchise, therefore, focuses on changes to the social and ideological profile of Liberal MPs.

Of the 23 burgh Liberals incumbent at the dissolution in 1868, two retired, two moved to new constituencies, and 19 sought re-election. The two retirals were occasioned by old age and infirmity. William Ewart (Dumfries Burghs 1841-68), was a sick man and died in January the following year. Similarly, Alexander Dunlop, a fellow septuagenarian, who left parliament after 16 years as a popular member for Greenock, passed away in September 1870.

Although there was clearly no connection between the new franchise and the retirement of Ewart and Dunlop, there is a suspicion that the reconstitution of the electorate had encouraged the two removals. Alexander Matheson, who moved to Ross and Cromarty, having spent 21 years representing the Inverness Burghs, was not only a businessman but also a local laird, and probably felt safer in a Highland county constituency, where the electorate remained peculiarly small. The other member to change his seat, James Moncreiff, was a former lord advocate, who had first been elected for Leith Burghs in 1851, but had moved to Edinburgh in 1859. The new franchise, however, had strengthened the Radical alliance of Dissenters and Free Churchmen in Edinburgh, and Moncreiff's support for the Annuity Tax, (a rate levied to support the stipends of established kirk ministers), had significantly weakened his chances of re-election in 1868. Consequently, he repaired to the newly-created and more conservative constituency of Glasgow and Aberdeen Universities. The wisdom of his move was confirmed when the Independent Edinburgh Liberals, McLaren and John Miller, (the latter having been defeated by an alliance of Whigs and Tories in 1865, who backed Moncreiff), were returned opposed 'neither by ancient Whig, modern Conservative, nor any combination of reactionary forces' (Mackie: Vol II, 52).

Table 8.2: Structure of Party Conflict in Burgh Elections, 1868–1880

Single Member Constituencies (19)	1868	1874	1880	All
Unopposed Liberals	8	7	5	20
Liberal v Liberal	8	3	1	12
Liberal v Conservative	2	8	11	21
Liberal v Liberal v Conservative	1	1	1	3
Liberal v Conservative v Conservative	-	-	1	1
All	19	19	19	57

Multi-Member Constituencies (3)	1868	1874	1880
Dundee (2 Seats) Each Elector 2 Votes	4 Liberals	4 Liberals 1 Conservative	2 Liberals 1 Conservative
Edinburgh (2 Seats) Each Elector 2 Votes	2 Liberals	3 Liberals 1 Conservative	2 Liberals 1 Conservative
Glasgow (3 Seats) Each Elector 2 Votes	3 Liberals 1 Conservative	5 Liberals 1 Conservative	3 Liberals 2 Conservatives

Six incumbent Liberals, a mixture of Whigs and Radicals representing constituencies in the eastern half of the country, were returned unopposed in Aberdeen, Perth, Edinburgh (1), and the burgh districts of Haddington, Kirkcaldy, and Elgin; while two newcomers, George Trevelyan, a disestablisher, in the newly-created Hawick Burghs, and Aeneas Macintosh (Inverness District), found themselves without opponents.

The advantages of incumbency, indicated by the unopposed returns, would seem confirmed by the fact that only three of the twelve seeking re-election in contested elections were defeated. In the Falkirk District, for example, E Horsman, who opposed the ironmaster James Merry, MP from 1859, was so unpopular that he suffered motions of no confidence passed against him at meetings organised by his own committee in Airdrie and Hamilton, and he received only 16 votes at the polls (*Scotsman:* 5 & 6.11.1868). Similarly, J Anderson, who challenged the landowner Edward Craufurd in the Ayr District, sustained a motion requesting him to retire from the contest at a meeting chaired by the Provost of Ayr, which 'ended amid indescribable confusion;' and at Irvine, where Anderson was criticised for not allowing non-electors to attend, a motion that he was 'a fit and proper person' to represent the constituency was defeated (*Scotsman:* 31.10.1868). Crum-Ewing, 'perhaps the most extreme Radical sent from Scotland' (*Scotsman:* 26.11.1868), easily held off his Liberal and Conservative opponents in Paisley. In the Kilmarnock District, Edward Bouverie, a Whig grandee, pushed aside Liberal opponents in the form of Edwin Chadwick, the controversial Utilitarian, who enjoyed the support of John Stuart Mill and the working-class dominated Scottish National Reform League, and the Reverend Robert Thomson of Kilmarnock, a non-established minister and 'rabid Protestant' (Hutchison: 133; Shedden: 37).[1] Another Whig, the baronet, Sir John Ogilvy, had no difficulty retaining a seat in Dundee, where four Liberals sought the two seats, although he came second to the merchant he had defeated in 1857; and the Radical, Baxter, overwhelmed his Conservative opponent in the Montrose District. In Glasgow, where the electors had only two votes each to return three candidates, 'the Conservatives plumped for their man, whilst the Liberals...adhered very rigidly to the scheme of voting up the two lowest of their three candidates' (*Scotsman:* 18.11.1868). All three Liberals were elected, including the former members, Dalglish and Graham, in a contest characterised by 'an almost entire absence of excitement' (*Scotsman:* 18.11.1868). It was, however, a sign of the emergence of a predominantly working class electorate in the city, that while Dalglish and Graham were 'somewhat Whiggish,' the new member, George Anderson, enjoyed the support of the Reform League (Hutchison: 134).

The most notable of the defeated incumbents was Samuel Laing in the Wick District, removed by George Loch, whose father Laing himself had expelled in 1852. Laing's defeat would seem a consequence of his attitude towards the Second Reform Bill, when he had offended both the Leveson-Gowers, who had influence in the constituency, by proposing the ending of separate representation for Sutherland, and the new voters for his opposition to household suffrage. Given the Whig credentials of both the candidates, and the peculiarly local nature of the battle, it is impossible to invest the outcome with any wider significance. A second disappointed incumbent was William Miller (Leith Burghs) defeated by Robert MacFie, whom he had beaten in 1859. The differences between the candidates do not appear to have been very great, although MacFie was probably the more Radical. Miller's election address was pro-Gladstone, supported the secret ballot and favoured the equalisation of the county and burgh franchises. MacFie's programme was very similar, but he enjoyed the support of the president of the Edinburgh Reform League, and whereas Miller's committee rooms were located in the Musselburgh Arms, MacFie's campaign operated from the Temperance Hotel. Miller was disadvantaged by a long absence from parliament due to illness, and his critics pointed out that he had voted only 21 times out of 366 divisions, and on five occasions had voted against Gladstone (*Scotsman:* 28.10.1868, 7 & 18.11.1868). Subsequently, Miller was returned for Berwickshire at a by-election in 1873.

The third defeated former member was John Ramsay, a Glasgow distiller, ousted from the Stirling Burghs by Campbell (Bannerman), who reversed the outcome of a by-election (under the old electoral law) held earlier in 1868. In the earlier contest, Ramsay, a philanthropist and Free Churchman, had enjoyed the national backing of both the Free and United Presbyterian churches and their ministers in the various burghs, which had been sufficient to carry him to victory by 565:494. Campbell had been further disadvantaged by the lack of a local agent, and had relied heavily on his father's business connections in Dunfermline. In anticipation of the new franchise, however, Campbell had taken care in the by-election to adopt a programme addressed to both 'electors and non-electors,' which was more advanced than that of his opponent, and following his defeat appointed a local agent and established 'an active and zealous committee' (Spender: Vol. I, 28). At the general election, Campbell added the cause of Irish disestablishment to his manifesto, which was popular with non-established Presbyterians, and 'pledged his allegiance firmly to Mr. Gladstone on that and other issues' (Spender: Vol. I, 29). After defeating his opponent by 2,201 to 1,602, he put his victory down to support from the Scottish working man: 'a stubborn chiel, / As hot as ginger and as true as steel' (Spender: Vol. I, 29). Although Campbell regarded his success as marking a shift towards a greater radicalism, the outcome was more ambiguous. Ramsay's supporters made much of the fact that Campbell's father and brother were both active Tory politicians. It is not, therefore, inconceivable that Conservatives in the constituency may have placed more trust in Campbell, on account of his family background and membership of the established Kirk, than in his Dissenter opponent. Significantly, the *Scotsman* favoured the outcome, 'especially as Mr Ramsay in his Parliamentary career several times showed an inclination to take as his leader Mr McLaren rather than Mr Gladstone' (*Scotsman*: 18.11.1868), indicating satisfaction at the defeat of a Radical by a more moderate candidate.

Although the 1868 elections were generally peaceful, it was not so in Greenock, which illustrated what a potentially heady brew had been created by the extension of the franchise and the retention of open voting. It also indicated how the larger employers could now mobilise a working class vote which had been unavailable to them during the First Reform Act.

> This was the bitterest struggle in the Parliamentary history of Greenock. It sundered lifelong friendships and even caused disunion and separation in families. While it lasted, ordinarily staid business men became restless, irritable, sometimes excited, and impulsive persons became irresponsible persons. It was the last election in Greenock by open voting...and for the last time the hustings were erected in Cathcart Square.

> The candidates were James Johnston Grieve, shipowner and Provost of the town, and William Douglas Christie, a former plenipotentiary for Brazil. Both were Liberals, but Christie claimed to be of the 'Independent' species.

> On the day of nominations (16th November), Grieve was proposed by John Scott, youngest, shipbuilder, seconded by David Johnstone, Belleaire (of Gourock Ropework Co.); and Christie by Bailie (afterwards Provost) James Morton, of Balclutha, seconded by William Birkmyre, of the Greenock Sacking Co.

> After the usual speeches, the show of hands was declared by the Sheriff-Principal Patrick (afterwards Lord) Fraser to favour Christie by a large majority, and on the demand of Thomas King, writer, on behalf of Grieve, a poll was fixed to take place on the following day (17th) between the hours of 8 a.m. and 4 p.m.

Grieve led from the start, and the state of the poll published by both parties hourly, showed a steadily rising majority for the Provost. As the figures mounted, general excitement increased. Trade processions paraded the town. When the rivals met in the Square, each side tried to capture the others' banners and a free fight resulted, which was not confined to the processionists.

Many amusing events occurred in the course of the day, as when big Charley Mulhern shouted to his men from a window of the Wheat Sheaf Inn: 'Who gives ye th'work?' 'You do.' 'An who gives me th'work?' 'Grieve.' 'An' who are ye goin' to vote for?' 'Grieve!' 'Grieve!' 'Away ye go, then, an' see that ye do, ev'ry gory wan o' ye!' or words to that effect.

Grieve beat Christie by 870 votes, the respective figures being: Grieve 2,962, Christie, 2092. The constituency numbered 6,223, and 5,054, or 81.2 per cent voted...

Three or four weeks later Christie presented a petition against Grieve's return on the grounds of 'bribery, treating and undue influence,' which was tried in Greenock and dismissed, with expenses against the petitioner. This, I may say, was the only occasion on which a Senator of the College of Justice (in this case Lord Barcaple) held a Court in this town (Donald: 37).

The contests of 1874 differed most from 1868 in that they were noted for an increase from four to thirteen in the number of Conservative candidates, and was the first conducted by secret ballot, which some Tories hoped would assist their cause in the burghs (Crapster: 357). Nevertheless, there were no contests again in the burgh districts of Elgin, Hawick and St Andrews; Greenock and Stirling Burghs produced no challenge to the victors of 1868; and the cotton manufacturer, William Holms, inherited Paisley without a fight on the retiral of Crum-Ewing. Surplus Liberals were still well to the fore in Dundee, Glasgow, Edinburgh, and the districts of Inverness, Leith, Kilmarnock and Wick. Consequently, national voting patterns remained difficult to detect.

Conservative candidates came forward in nine of the nineteen single member constituencies. Their best result was in the Ayr District, where a landowner/soldier/lawyer, Sir William Montgomery-Cunninghame bart., a Crimean War VC, ousted Craufurd, the member since 1852, with 51.6 per cent of the vote. The returning officer in the diminutive Wigtown Burghs also declared the Conservative elected, but his majority of only two votes was overthrown at a subsequent re-examination of the ballots, and the former Liberal member was awarded the seat with a majority of one.

Conservative candidates also did well in the Dumfries Burghs (44.1 per cent), where the new Liberal member, Ernest Noel, reversed his defeat against a fellow Liberal in 1868,[2] and in the Falkirk Burghs (43.1 per cent), where the Liberal victor, John Ramsay, following his defeat in the Stirling District in 1868, stood on the retiral of James Merry. The results in the Districts of Ayr, Wigtown, Dumfries and Falkirk were evidence of a move to the right amongst urban Protestant voters in the west of Scotland in reaction against Liberal concessions to Irish nationalism, that was to mature in the 1880s.

The Conservatives also did well to poll 41.1 per cent in Aberdeen, where Colonel Sykes had retired in favour of John Leith, who he had defeated in 1857, but the result hardly constituted a serious threat to Liberalism in the city.

Elsewhere in eastern Scotland, the Conservative performance was less encouraging. In the Montrose Burghs, later described by the Tory agent as 'Radical and demoralised in the extreme' (Crapster: 358), Colonel MacDonald had to be content with 36 per cent of the vote; and Conservative candidates performed hardly better in the Kirkcaldy Burghs (38.4 per cent) and Perth (36.3 per cent). In the Inverness District, where there were two Liberals standing, the Conservative candidate took only sixteen votes out of nearly 2,000 cast.

Developments in the smaller western burghs were also reflected in Glasgow, where a complicated seven-cornered contest occasioned the return of a Conservative, Alexander Whitelaw, son-in-law of the ironmaster, Baird of Gartsherrie, along with two Liberals. The election also illustrated the continuing autonomous character of burgh Liberalism at this time, and the added difficulties caused by the introduction of the secret ballot for a party seeking to return three members when each elector had only two votes (Table 8.3).

Table 8.3: The Glasgow Election Result, 1874

Elected		Votes	
C Cameron	(Radical Liberal)	18,455	Surplus Majority over Whitelaw, 4320
G Anderson	(Radical Liberal)	17,902	Surplus Majority over Whitelaw, 3767
A Whitelaw	(Conservative)	14,134	
Defeated			
J Hunter	(Conservative)	12,533	
A Crum	(Whig)	7,453	
Hon F Kerr	(Irish Home Ruler)	4,444	
J Bolton	(Whig)	169	

In 1874, two of the former Glasgow Liberal members, Dalglish and Graham, retired, but whereas in 1868 their Moderate Whig supporters had come to an agreement with the Reform League and Advanced Liberals to maintain party unity through the adoption of Anderson, a Radical, as the third candidate, the understanding broke down because both factions felt entitled to two of the three nominations. The Advanced Liberals backed Anderson, seeking re-election, and Dr Charles Cameron, the Radical proprietor of the *North British Daily Mail*, and the Moderates put forward Alexander Crum and John Bolton (Hutchison: 134). To further complicate matters, the Irish Nationalists, dissatisfied with Gladstone's Irish policy, urged Home Rulers to plump, (i.e. to use just one of their two votes), for their candidate, the Hon. F E Kerr. Liberal disunity was further exacerbated by the strengthening connections between Advanced Liberalism and the temperance movement, spurred by the 1873-4 Sankey and Moody revival campaign. Cameron was particularly involved with the temperance lobby, and sought its electoral support in 1874 (Hutchison: 139). On the eve of polling, in a belated attempt to retrieve the situation, the Whigs withdrew their official backing for Bolton, but it was too late for the divided Liberal factions to organise a voting up of the bottom candidate, now made more difficult with the introduction of the secret ballot.

Taking advantage of their opponents' squabblings, the Conservatives sought to maximise their vote by running just two candidates. As the result shows (Table 8.3), Liberal disunity produced surplus majorities for Cameron and Anderson that might well have been directed through proper organisation to elect Crum, Kerr's candidature notwithstanding. If only three Liberals had stood they would almost certainly have all been elected. As the *Scotsman* remarked, 'The defection of the Roman Catholic and publican Liberal voters, and the great amount of plumping on the Liberal side, more than accounted for the loss of the Liberal seat' (*Scotsman:* 6.7.1874). Nevertheless, with Whitelaw receiving the support of more than a quarter of the registered voters in Glasgow, the Conservatives had demonstrated they were a strong minority, as they began to mobilise Orangemen.

The extended franchise also placed Liberal unity under strain in Edinburgh, where new political forces emerged to challenge the authority of the Independent Liberal Committee, which had triumphed with the unopposed returns of McLaren and Miller in 1868. As in Glasgow, the Conservatives hoped to benefit from the squabbling.

In 1873, trade unionists in Edinburgh were opposed to a clause in the Criminal Law Amendment Act directed against picketing in unofficial strikes. Miller agreed to support repeal, but McLaren 'as an economist and Free Trader' was opposed to 'social tyranny,' and indicated publicly that he agreed with the legislation (Mackie: Vol. II, 53). As a result, the local secretary of the Amalgamated Society of Joiners formed an Advanced Liberal Association with the support of the Trades Council, to press working class interests within the party. The previous accord between McLaren and Miller was consequently broken, with the former entering the 1874 election as the nominee of the Independent Liberals, and the latter standing under the auspices of the Advanced Liberal Association. Encouraged by disunity amongst the Radicals, the Aggregate Liberal Committee (the Whig faction) put forward Lord Provost James Cowan, brother of a former member who had defeated McLaren in 1852.

The Conservatives advanced JHA MacDonald, a lawyer and 'popular Volunteer officer and leading Tory politician in the city' (Mackie: Vol. II, 56). Fortunately for the Liberals, each elector had two votes to return the two members, which reduced the disadvantage a multiplicity of candidates had caused in Glasgow. Predictably, McLaren (11,431) topped the poll because he attracted the second votes of those supporting both Cowan (8,749) and to a lesser extent Miller (6,281). MacDonald (5,713) was pushed into last place, although his share of the electorate (23 per cent) was within three per cent of Whitelaw's in Glasgow.

With an electoral system similar to Edinburgh, Dundee had four Liberals and one Conservative contesting the two seats in 1874. Seeking re-election, James Yeaman, a local shipowner and Lord Provost (1869-72) topped the poll with 6,595 votes. Defeated by Yeaman in a by-election the previous year, the second candidate elected was Edward Jenkins (6,048), a Liberal 'in advance of ministerialism' (*Scotsman*: 10.2.1874), who enjoyed the backing of the Scottish Permissive Billites, a militant teetotal organisation, (Hutchison: 138). Pushed into third place was the second retiring member, Sir John Ogilvy (4,401), 'a Whig nonentity of the highest respectability' (*Scotsman*: 10.2.1874), whose replacement by Jenkins indicated a leftward shift occasioned by the new franchise. Ogilvy was followed by the fourth Liberal, J Meiklejohn (2,231), and the

Conservative, J Gloag, whose derisory 573 votes established Dundee's claim to be the most Liberal of the major cities.

Straightforward intra-Liberal fights were much reduced in 1874, but they survived in the burgh districts of Kilmarnock, Wick and Leith. The shift against the Whigs was evident in the Kilmarnock Burghs, where Bouverie, having survived in 1868, found himself opposed by James Harrison of Sussex, a Lincoln's Inn barrister, who described himself as 'a thorough Liberal, in favour of the assimilation of the burgh and County franchise, a redistribution of seats, the abolition of the Game Laws, the repeal of the Law of Hypothec, and of tenant farmers being secured the full value of their improvements, and was opposed to all State endowments for religious purposes' (Shedden: 37). Despite increasing his vote, Bouverie was defeated by nearly 300 as the electorate had grown by 1,500 since 1868. Commenting on his victory, Harrison opined, 'We have got rid of a Tory...a man who sailed under false colours – Liberal colours from the masthead, and Tory notions guiding at the bottom' (*Scotsman:* 7.2.1874).

In Leith Burghs, the incumbent usurper, MacFie, found himself opposed by a formidable alliance of 'the beer and spirit trade, the Permissive Billites, the Good Templars, the Home Rulers, and Roman Catholics,' who backed Donald MacGregor, a local shipowner and merchant. 'The chief difference between them,' according to a contemporary, 'being that on great national and party questions, Mr MacGregor promises his undivided support to Mr Gladstone while Mr MacFie does not' (*Scotsman:* 7.2.1874). Ironically, a greater fire for Gladstone had been a cause of MacFie's victory in 1868, and his lack of it in 1874 helped MacGregor carry the seat by more than two to one.[3] More conservative and traditional influences prevailed in the Wick Burghs, however, where John Pender, 'a wealthy Whig mediocrity,' retained the seat he had won at a by-election in 1872, against Professor James Bryce, 'a man of brains and Imperial reputation' (*Scotsman:* 10.2.1874).

By 1880, the activities of the party managers had done much to reduce burgh elections to two-party confrontations. The Kilmarnock District was the only constituency fought by a surplus Liberal in the face of Conservative opposition, and St Andrews Burghs the only seat subject to a straightforward Liberal 'primary'. Only in Paisley and the burgh districts of Inverness, Wick, Leith and Montrose were Liberals unopposed, while in the Dumfries Burghs two Conservatives vainly sought to remove the Liberal incumbent.

The main problem for the Liberals had been the cities of Glasgow, Edinburgh and Dundee, where the multi-member constituencies had encouraged the disputatious Liberal factions to compete rather than co-operate. In 1880, therefore, Adam attempted to promote unity by persuading the various elements in the party to back incumbents, and to encourage the creation of over-arching electoral organisations.

A United Liberal Committee was established in Edinburgh under the presidency of George Harrison, (shortly to become Lord Provost), which unanimously endorsed McLaren and Cowan for the two seats. McLaren, however, although grateful to receive United Liberal support, had nothing to do with their committee, and would almost certainly have been re-elected had they nominated others to stand against him (Mackie: Vol. II, 57-8). The main function of Harrison's committee, it would appear, was to indicate to the Whig Aggregate and the Trades Council Advanced Liberals that any candidates they might put forward would not only offend the party consensus but almost inevitably fail.

In Glasgow, where the Liberals were divided between the Radical-dominated Glasgow Liberal Association, the Whig Committee, and the Liberal Workingmen's Electoral Union, (successor to the Scottish Reform League), the peculiarity of the electoral system and the fiasco of 1874 made co-operation particularly necessitous. By 1879, the Whigs and Radicals were reconciled through the appointment of Charles Tennant, 'a representative of the great Whig families in the city' (Hutchison: 144) as president of the Glasgow Liberal Association, which had been stripped of its ideological bias. Tennant even succeeded in becoming MP for the city in the same year at a by-election, when, following the death of Whitelaw, he received the nomination of the Workingmen's Electoral Union and the Liberal Association, in a coup which outmanoeuvred the Radicals (Hutchison: 145). Nevertheless, as in Edinburgh, under the prompting of Adam there as a disposition in 1880 to renominate retiring members, Anderson and Cameron, and the decision of Tennant to contest Peebles and Selkirk (successfully), removed the possibility of friction with the Radicals resulting from the by-election. Indeed, Tennant chaired the election committee of the third candidate, Robert Middleton, a fellow merchant, but a 'radical in the disestablishment-temperance mould' (Hutchison: 145). With peace returned to the Liberal camp, the way was then open for the committees of the three candidates to be co-ordinated through an election committee under the auspices of the Glasgow Liberal Association (*Scotsman:* 17.3.1880). It was a tribute to the Liberal electoral organisation in Glasgow that out of nearly 100,000 votes cast its three candidates were all returned separated by less than 700 votes.

Adam's pragmatic support for sitting members, so generally successful, drew criticism over his lobbying in favour of Yeaman in Dundee, because the latter had backed Disraeli's foreign policy, the very object of Gladstone's righteous condemnation in the Midlothian campaign (Hanham: 354). Yeaman in fact proved unable to retain a Liberal nomination, and was defeated as a Conservative by a Dissenter, George Armitstead, (a former member, 1868-73), and Frank Henderson, a local evangelical merchant fired with a social mission, who had chaired Jenkins' campaign before he retired from parliament in 1880 (Hutchison: 137). The rejection of Yeaman following the defeat of Ogilvy in 1874 completed the removal of Whig parliamentary representation in the city.

While factionalism within Liberalism was strongly evident and well organised in the larger urban areas by 1880, it is more difficult to assess the impact of popular Liberalism and the new Liberal Associations on the politics of the more numerous smaller towns and burgh districts. It does appear, however, that in such constituencies endorsement at public meetings played a part in discouraging a plethora of Liberal candidatures, as when Campbell-Bannerman received strong backing from a public meeting held at Dunfermline in 1880 (*Scotsman:* 17.3.1880). More critically, the Edinburgh architect, Dick Peddie, mobilised the new Liberal Associations in the Kilmarnock Burghs, where his fight against a Conservative Glasgow chemical broker, John Cuthbertson, was complicated by the intervention of a second Liberal, Malcolm Kerr of London, who had failed to win Peterborough in 1874. A motion passed by the Dumbarton Liberal Association 'that J Dick Peddie be adopted as candidate in whom the Association should concentrate its strength' (*Scotsman:* 17.3.1880) by 210 votes to nine (for Kerr), and a similar expression of confidence by the Kilmarnock

Liberal Association, undoubtedly helped to secure Peddie's return. It is, however, important to stress the distance between the embryonic local party structures and the candidates themselves. Peddie, for example, was not the candidate *of* the Dumbarton and Kilmarnock Liberal associations, but the one they chose to work *for*.

For all the openness of Liberalism in certain constituencies, one ought to be circumspect as to its general extent. It would appear, for example, that the party organisation in the St Andrews Burghs was tightly controlled by its long-serving member Edward Ellice (Hutchison: 142); the Wick District remained vulnerable to the patronage of the Duke of Sutherland (Hanham: 412); and a report regarding 'a meeting of the Liberal Provisional Committee...held last night in Provost Alexander's office' in Peterhead (Elgin Burghs), suggests a party whose power base in the smaller burghs, at least, was still concentrated in the hands of a few local notables (*Scotsman:* 16.3.1880).

Conservative attempts to improve their nominal presence in the burghs was realised in that eighteen candidates contested seventeen of the 26 burgh seats in 1880. Whether Conservative candidates were always the best is doubtful because there was little attraction for a Tory standing in a Scottish burgh. It is instructive to note that the Conservative agent in the Stirling Burghs hoped his party's candidate in 1880 would be the Provost of Stirling, George Christie, who was 'very popular and very rich' (Crapster: 358), but only a landed baronet, Sir James Gibson-Maitland, could be persuaded to come forward, and even he informally withdrew between nomination and polling day (Spender: Vol. I, 50). A more ambitious Conservative, Charles Fraser Macintosh, had found it easier to change parties, and in 1880 was an unopposed Liberal in the Inverness Burghs (Crapster: 368).[4] Perhaps the main consequence of the Conservative effort in 1880 was to unify their opponents by discouraging surplus Liberal candidatures.

The contrast between Conservative and Liberal approaches to burgh nominations, occasioned by their relative strengths and the weaknesses of formal party structures at this time, is well illustrated by the Greenock by-election of January 1878.

Early in December 1877, 'a [Conservative] deputation to wait on Sir Michael Robert Shaw Stewart, bart.' (Donald: 34-5), Lord Lieutenant of Renfrewshire and former MP for the county, failed to elicit a positive response, and the desperate search for a Tory candidate continued. On the same day, 6 December, the county Liberals, led by Councillor John Duff of Greenock, formed a Liberal Association, but it played little part in the by-election. By the time a mass meeting of Liberals was held in the town hall on 12 December, the merits of three candidates, Provost Lyle and James Stewart (both local merchants), and Donald Currie, a native of the burgh, but whose shipping interests were centred on London, were considered. Stewart indicated he would not oppose the provost. Lyle, however, withdrew, and on 17 December Stewart issued his election address. The next day Currie published his appeal. On 21 December, William Scott-Moncreiff, a Glasgow Radical, also threw his hat into the ring; and on 11 January, yet another Liberal, John Balgownie of Glasgow, threatened to stand, but he never appeared in Greenock and his challenge quickly faded. The main confrontation in the Liberal camp, therefore, was between Stewart, 'the choice of the temperance and disestablishment lobbies, who...were hostile to labour's demands,' and Currie, 'who was lukewarm on disestablishment,' backed by the local Workingmen's Liberal Association (Hutchison: 144). Meantime, on 27 December, the Conservatives had persuaded a second baronet, Sir James Fergusson, former member for Ayrshire, to represent their cause.

Despite calls for Liberal unity, even from the candidates themselves, none appeared willing to step down, and a suggestion by the *North British Daily Mail* for a Liberal primary fell on deaf ears. William Adam was asked to mediate. He suggested that Stewart and Currie, (but not, apparently, Moncreiff), should submit themselves to an impartial committee nominated by the two Scottish National Liberal Associations, which would decide who should stand. Representatives of the East and West Associations met Stewart and Currie, but were unable to persuade either of them to step aside. At the conclusion of the campaign, Stewart (2,138) only narrowly defeated Fergusson (2,124), because Currie (1,648) and Moncreiff (108), whose candidature 'was not taken seriously' (Donald: 37), divided Liberal support.[5] It was small wonder that Gladstone described Liberal disunity as 'a scandal and offence' (Donald: 38). At the general election of 1880, however, Stewart faced no opposing Liberal, which was just as well for them, because the Conservatives had secured as their candidate, John Scott, a Greenock shipbuilder, who had nominated the winning Liberal in 1868.

The burgh Conservatives were overwhelmed by the Liberal tide of 1880. The Ayr District, which had fallen to the Tories in 1874, was recaptured by the Liberals on a 13.5 per cent swing; in Glasgow the leading Conservative polled less than half the votes of the weakest Liberal; and in Edinburgh the Liberals both won more than three times the ballots cast for the lone Conservative. In the Falkirk Burghs, the Conservative share of the poll fell from 43.1 per cent in 1874 to 25.9 per cent in 1880, and collapsed from 41.1 per cent to 29.5 per cent over the two elections in Aberdeen. A new Liberal candidate in the Haddington Burghs, which the Conservatives had won in 1841, captured more than three fifths of the vote, and the Tories secured less than 15 per cent of the poll on their first foray in the Hawick District. In the Kirkcaldy Burghs, where a massive swing of 36.3 per cent to the Liberals left the Conservative only 2.1 per cent of the ballot, and Stirling Burghs, in which Campbell-Bannerman secured 95.7 per cent of the franchises, the Tory challenge completely fell apart. The best Conservative burgh result was in the Wigtown Burghs, where the Liberal majority increased from one to twelve: strong *prima facie* evidence that in this constituency of less than 1,400 electors, a more traditional style of management prevailed. The most improved Conservative performance was in Dundee, where Yeaman's change of allegiance increased the Tory vote from 573 in 1874 to 4,993 in 1880. Apart from Wigtown Burghs, there was no burgh constituency in which the Conservative won 40 per cent or more of the poll. It appeared, therefore, that the Second Reform Act had confirmed and deepened the overwhelming strength of Liberalism in the Scottish burghs, and rendered the possibility of a two-party system, threatened in 1874 and encouraged by an increase in Conservative interventions in 1880, a mirage.

Elections in the Counties

As has been discussed, the extension of the county franchise in 1868 was significantly less than in the burghs, and enfranchised as small a proportion of the population as in England under the First Reform Act. Nevertheless, in formal party terms, the Liberals made substantial gains in the counties, although most of their candidates were of the Whig variety, and probably had more in common with the county Tories than burgh Liberal MPs, whose anti-landlordism and disestablishmentarianism increased with each passing election.

A traditional style of politics was clearly evident (1868-1880) in those rural constituencies where there were no unopposed returns. The classic case, Sutherland, remained a nomination county still awaiting a contested election. In Ross and Cromarty, where the Liberal cause was dominated by 'a small group of lairds, big farmers or cattle breeders, and professional men' (Hanham: 164), the seat was uncontested between 1837 and a by-election in 1884, when Alexander Matheson easily slipped into the seat vacated by a kinsman, Sir James Matheson, in 1868; and in Banffshire, Robert Duff, a close relative of the Earl of Fife, was left unchallenged by the Earl of Seafield, who was responsible for advancing the Tory interest. Particularly illustrative of the survival of older practices is the case of East Aberdeenshire, where the incumbent Liberal laird, William Fordyce, having captured the former undivided county at a by-election in 1866, was unopposed in 1868 and 1874. On Fordyce's death in 1875, the by-election was comfortably won by the Tory, Sir Alexander Gordon, second son of the 4th Earl of Aberdeen. By 1880, Sir Alexander had changed party, but with the local Tory interest so closely associated with that of his family, no Conservative could stand against him at the general election.

In contested seats, too, proprietorial interests continued to play a dominating role. Argyllshire was strongly influenced by the 7th Duke of Argyll, a Whig, whose eldest son, the Marquess of Lorne, held the constituency without opposition from 1868 to 1878, when he was followed by his brother, Lord Colin Campbell, though not without Conservative intervention in 1878 and 1880. The Tory Baillies of Redcastle and Camerons of Lochiel presided over Inverness-shire politics, so that when Henry Baillie retired from parliament in 1868, having held the seat since 1840, Donald Cameron inherited the county without opposition, and was not pressed to the polls until 1880. To the south, Clackmannan and Kinross continued its historic domination by the Whig Adams of Blair Adam; and the Tory, Lord Elcho, having sat for Haddington from 1847-1883, handed over the constituency to his son (the new Lord Elcho) when he became the 9th Earl of Weymss and March. As Hanham points out, 'A number of counties were habitually contested by the partisans of two rival houses of different politics. In Wigtownshire the Conservative Earl of Galloway fought the Liberal Earl of Stair. The representation of Roxburgh was shared by two families over an even longer period. The two rival houses of Douglas...and Elliot, whose chiefs were the Conservative Duke of Buccleuch and the Liberal Earl of Minto, had fought each other since the seventeenth century' (Hanham: 164).

There were, nevertheless, signs of change. For example, although the Marquess of Bute continued to dominate the Tory interest in his county, his influence over the electorate, that had been overwhelming before 1868, was insufficient to prevent a Liberal victory in 1880. Similarly, the control which the Duke of Buccleuch established in Midlothian in 1841 could not prevent the defeat of his son in 1868 and 1880. The three unopposed returns of Sir Edward Colebrooke in North Lanarkshire was recognition by the Tories of a constituency beyond the reach of proprietorial manipulation; and the Conservative retention of the two Ayrshire divisions in 1880, (both Liberal in 1868), pointed more to a the growth of popular Conservatism in the west of Scotland than deference to leading landowners. Again, although many county Liberal interests were exclusive to or dominated by leading landowners, there were signs in counties such as Kincardineshire that power was passing into the hands of tenant farmers and the leaders of non-parliamentary burghs.

It would also appear that while the control over nomination in the counties still effectively rested with a narrow elite in most constituencies in both parties, the capacity of the proprietors to determine electoral outcomes in registration battles had passed. Even under the First Reform Act the manufacture of votes involved considerable time and expense, and not all landowners had the commitment of the Duke of Buccleuch (Brash: esp. intro.). Even before 1868, the weakening of Tory strength indicated the Conservative will to compete had much diminished, and the lowering of the county franchise qualifications by the Second Reform Act only deepened their loss of morale. By contrast, the Whig landowners, although fewer in number than the Tories, not only enjoyed the support of urban dwellers, but expected to benefit from the enfranchisement of £14 tenants. Although to a large degree their hopes were realised, the election results of both 1874 and 1880 demonstrated an increasing tendency of rural electors to express a preference in the secrecy of the polling booth at variance with the wishes of both Whig and Tory landlords, which would not have been made when voting was open.

The general election of 1868 in the counties was dominated by the Game Laws and other farmer grievances. So sensitive was the issue in Kirkcudbrightshire, that a possible Whig candidate was turned down because he was 'unsound [both on] Rabbits...and...on the Trinity' (Hanham: 166), and Liberals were already carrying seats with relatively short campaigns against well-established Tory members (Hutchison: 106-8).

The absence of contests in half the county constituencies in 1868 attested both to the survival of traditional practices as well as Tory reluctance to face the ire of the tenantry (Table 8.4). In addition to Sutherland, a culture of non-contestation lay behind unopposed Liberal returns in Forfar, Clackmannan and Kinross, none of whose representation had been challenged at a general election since the 1830s, and Banff and Ross and Comarty, uncontested since 1852.

More contemporary factors, however, appeared to have operated in Renfrew, Stirling and Kincardine, where the Conservatives, having lost all three seats in 1865 on the game issue, were loathe to test the water in 1868. Similarly, in East Aberdeenshire the Tories failed to challenge Dingwall Fordyce, who had carried the undivided county on the game question in 1866, and McCombie, a strong proponent of the tenant interest, was unopposed in Aberdeenshire West (Hutchison: 108). The Liberals were also unchallenged in the newly-created industrial constituency of North Lanark, where the Conservatives were distinctly weak, and in Berwick, which they had captured in 1859. Conservatives were the sole nominees in three seats: Elgin and Nairn, last fought in 1841, and

Dunbarton and Inverness, traditional Tory seats where the Liberals had vainly intervened in 1865.

Table 8.4: Structure of Party Conflict in County Elections, 1868–1880

	1868	1874	1880	All
Unopposed Liberals	13	9	7	29
Liberal *v* Liberal	3	-	-	3
Liberal *v* Conservative	13	17	25	55
Unopposed Conservatives	3	6	-	9
All	**32**	**32**	**32**	**96**

Three constituencies, Kirkcudbright, Fife and Linlithgow were subjected to Liberal 'primaries' in 1868, and the verdict in each case went to the sitting member. In Kirkcudbright, Wellwood Maxwell, whose family had been active in the politics of the stewartry since the sixteenth century, beat his opponent comfortably; and in Fife, the baronet, Sir Robert Anstruther, a retired lieutenant-colonel and lord lieutenant of the county, defeated John Kinnear, a Radical barrister.[6] The failure of the Tories to challenge Peter McLagan in Linlithgow demonstrated how their previously strong position in the county had collapsed. McLagan had been returned unopposed in 1865 as a nominee of the local Conservatives, but on arrival at Westminster took the Liberal whip (Hutchison, 107). Subsequently identifying himself strongly with tenant interests, the Tories felt unable to challenge his apostasy in 1868, when he easily defeated his Whig opponent, John Pender.[7]

Of the thirteen seats contested between the parties in 1868, five were in the Borders, five in Central, two in the Highlands, and only one in the East. The Conservatives prevailed in Haddington and the newly-joined counties of Peebles and Selkirk, and recovered Bute, which had been lost in 1865. A more significant result for the Tories, however, was the victory of Lord Gairlies over Agnew of Lochnaw in Wigtown, because it was the first time the Liberals had lost the seat since 1837, and it remained in Conservative hands until its demise in 1918. By contrast, the Liberals not only retained Caithness, Orkney and Shetland and Roxburgh, and captured both divisions of Ayrshire and Lanarkshire South, but for the first time narrowly gained Dumfries, where the tenants of the Duke of Buccleuch deserted their laird, removed the Tories from Perthshire for the first time since 1832, in another tenant farmer revolt (Hutchison: 106–7), and audaciously stole Midlothian from the Earl of Dalkeith with a majority of more than two hundred.

Compared to 1865, the Conservatives found their strength reduced from eleven to seven county seats. Peebles and Selkirk had been amalgamated (a net loss of one); Perth, Dumfries, Midlothian and a seat in Ayrshire (now split) were lost at the polls; and no Tory candidate was presented in either Aberdeenshire seat, to set against the gain of Bute and Wigtown. With Tory strength geographically split between Inverness and Elgin and Nairn in the north, Peebles and Selkirk and Haddington in the south east, and Bute, Dunbartonshire and Wigtownshire, divided by Liberal-held Ayrshire, in the west, the Conservative interest was in danger of losing the territorial coherence established by Buccleuch and his allies in the 1830s.

The Liberal victories of 1868, however, had been by no means overwhelming, and the increasingly popular character of electoral politics, which favoured Gladstone in that year, turned against his party in 1874, as tenant farmers, especially in the lowlands, became disgruntled with the government for its tardy response to their grievances (Hanham: 162). A low level in Liberal morale was reflected by unopposed Conservative returns in Wigtown, Bute, Haddington, Inverness, Peebles and Selkirk, and even in Ayrshire South, which had elected a Liberal in 1868. Dunbarton was retained somewhat narrowly by the Tories in the first two-party fight under the new act, but Liberals were defeated in Perthshire, Lanarkshire South, Berwick, Dumfries, Roxburgh, North Ayrshire, Midlothian and Stirlingshire.

The surprise and scale of the Conservative victory indicated that the recovery was as much a reflection of regional trends in public opinion as party organisation. The only county seats retained by the Liberals in southern Scotland were in Kirkcudbright (by a majority of four), Clackmannan and Kinross, where Adam secured two thirds of the vote, and in the uncontested seats of Linlithgow and Lanark North. On the other hand, despite defeat in Perthshire, there was a decisive regional shift to the Liberals in the East, where they carried all the other seats, (assisted by unopposed returns in Aberdeenshire East, Banff and Forfar), capturing Elgin and Nairn, (Tory since 1832), with 57 per cent of the vote. It was a sign of the increasing importance of the local press, that Brodie of Brodie, who should have been the Tory candidate in Elgin and Nairn, refused to stand because he claimed the lack of a pro-Conservative newspaper in the constituency harmed his chances (Hutchison: 109). The rural East was to remain a generally secure Liberal bastion until after the Great War. The Liberals also benefited from uncontested elections in Orkney and Shetland, Sutherland, Ross and Cromarty and Argyll, but only retained Caithness with a slender majority of thirteen.

The problems of the rural Liberals, and the ambivalence of their parliamentary leadership towards the tenantry, was nowhere better illustrated than in their failure to contest Inverness-shire in 1874. In that county, a local landowner, MacPherson Grant, whose grandfather had sat for Sutherland in the unreformed parliament, indicated his willingness to oppose the incumbent Conservative, Cameron of Lochiel. Some Liberal farmers, however, found him insufficiently receptive to their demands on the land question, preferring a Radical London barrister, Augustus Smith. In response, Grant withdrew his candidature, but the Whig business managers, Adam, a landed proprietor himself, and Craig Sellar, son of Patrick Sellar, the notorious executor of the Sutherland clearances, prevented Smith coming forward, leaving the field free for the incumbent Tory (Hutchison: 114). It was to be somewhat ironic, given the level of farmer grievances in the East, that MacPherson Grant was to become Liberal MP for Elgin and Nairn at a by-election held in 1879.

Presciently, the Conservatives were less impressed by their gains in 1874 than their failures, especially in the East. As a private Tory report of 1876 remarked:

> The Conservatives of Scotland have been so long excluded from power that very many of them seem to have lost hope. They appear to look upon the present

Conservative government as the result of accidental circumstances which may not occur again, and they seem to think the Party will do very well if they can hold on till the next General Election. The result is that they fail to make due preparations for the contest. The Conservatives of Scotland from their family traditions and social position could without difficulty exercise almost irresistible political influence, if they could be induced to use ordinary means of making themselves popular. They have lost much of their political power solely through their supineness (Crapster: 359).

The Tory lairds appeared particularly reluctant to adapt to the demands of the new politics. Colonel Grant, for example, who lost Elgin and Nairn, was criticised for having refused to address public meetings during the campaign, whereas the Earl of Fife, father of the Liberal candidate, did 'all he could to cultivate friendly feelings with the voters, by inviting them to dinner etc.' (Crapster: 358). The Earl of Seafield and Duke of Richmond were criticised for not having devised a means for carrying Banffshire, and it was generally concluded 'how desirable it is that the landowners of Scotland should be more genial with their tenantry, and mix more amongst them "at kirk and market"' (Crapster: 358).

The root of the Tory problem, of course, was the growing divergence of interests between the proprietors and the tenantry, as the franchise continued to slip down the social scale. The game question was a particular point of conflict, and 'in the whole of Scotland north of Aberdeen violent and extreme views seem to be held both in towns and counties. The farmers insist on having an absolute right to kill hares and rabbits, and it would appear that no candidate would have much chance there who would not go for this' (Crapster: 359). Indeed, the failure of the post-1868 Liberal government, perhaps out of deference to the Whig landowners, to meet such demands, contributed to their reverses in 1874. Disraeli made a number of gestures towards the Scottish tenantry by reforming the sheriff courts, enacting measures to prevent the pollution of rivers and improve roads and bridges. He even permitted the Liberal, Peter McLagan, to get through his Games Laws (Scotland) Amendment Act, but with revisions favourable to the landlords. Thus, rather than satisfying the tenantry, the Conservative government only underlined its difficulty in meeting their needs while at the same time retaining the allegiance of the landed magnates on whom its interest rested. By contrast, the agricultural tenants could rely on the vociferous support of the burgh Liberal MPs on land questions, even when the Whig county members were taciturn. It was, therefore, almost inevitable that once the Liberals had reunited in opposition to the Conservative government, and had more closely aligned themselves with the farmers, that they would establish a strong position in the counties. Agricultural depression, (1879-80), and the Midlothian campaign brought that consummation in 1880 (Hanham: 162).

With 25 county seats contested by both parties, the impact of central party managers was evident on the election of 1880. All Conservative candidates faced an opponent, and although the tide was flowing strongly to the Liberals, the Tories challenged them in two more divisions than in 1874. Four of the six unopposed returns were in the East (Aberdeenshire East, Banff, Elgin and Nairn, and Forfar), and two (Sutherland and Ross and Cromarty) in Highland. As in 1874, there were no intra-Liberal fights, partly in accordance with established practice and partly due to the influence of Adam. In Caithness, for example, it appeared that Traill of Hobbister was threatening to oppose Sinclair of Ulbster, which might have been disastrous for the Liberals, given their small majority in 1874. The Traills and Sinclairs had been traditional enemies, (in 1837 and 1852 representatives of each family had contested the seat), and in 1869, JC Traill, on the resignation of his father, had failed to win the constituency in a Liberal 'primary' against Sinclair. In bowing to Adam's request not to intervene, Traill drew the public comment from the Chief Whip that he hoped 'the excellent example by you in declining to divide the Liberal party...will be followed in other constituencies' (*Scotsman:* 16.3.1880). It was.

Liberals emerged strongest in a geographically contiguous area, linked by uncontested returns, extending from Linlithgow and Clackmannan and Kinross, where they won more than 70 per cent of the poll, through Fife, Kincardine, and West Aberdeenshire, in which each victorious candidate captured over 60 per cent of the votes. More than three fifths of the ballot went to the Liberals in Caithness and Orkney and Shetland, and 58.3 per cent of the electors backed the party in Berwick. Less convincingly, the Liberals carried Bute and the Border counties of Dumfries, Kirkcudbright, Roxburgh, and Peebles and Selkirk, with less than 52 per cent of the vote in each, as they deserted the Tories. The capture of Peebles and Selkirk was particularly notable because it had been a Tory gerrymander. Modest Liberal wins were also recorded in Perth, Renfrew, Stirling, Lanark South, Argyll, and Midlothian though Gladstone's famous win with 53.6 per cent of the poll was below the Liberal share of 1868.

The Conservatives held on in Dunbarton, Ayrshire North and Inverness with less than 51 per cent of the vote, and performed hardly better in Ayrshire South (53.6 per cent), Haddington (52.5 per cent), and Wigtown (51.5 per cent). Although reduced to six seats, it is significant, that in contrast to 1868, the Tories appeared to be establishing a regional base centred on Dunbarton, the two Ayrshire divisions and Wigtown. This development signified the emergence of a source of Conservative strength centred less on the influence of landed proprietors, than on popular Protestant reaction to Irish Home Rule in a region geographically proximate to Ireland noted for its Covenanting traditions.

Table 8.5: Regional Distribution of Liberal Support in County Constituencies at General Election, 1868–1880, compared to 1832–1865

	Highland	East	Clydeside	Central	Borders	All
Number of Liberal Wins, 1868–1880	15	22	8	13	10	68
Liberal Wins as a Percentage of all, 1868–1880	83	92	67	54	56	71
Percentage Liberal Gain 1868–1880 on 1832–1865	+11	+44	+23	+17	+12	+22

It was inevitable, given overwhelming Liberal dominance in the burghs since 1832, that partisan allegiances (1868–1880) changed most in the counties (Table 8.5). Over the three elections, the Conservatives won less than three out of ten county seats, compared to the 51 per cent they carried between 1832 and 1865.

The most dramatic developments were in the East, where in eight constituencies the Liberals lost only two contests, 1868–1880, to displace Highland as the most Liberal region. Elgin and Nairn, Conservative from 1832-1868, failed to elect a Conservative in the Tory apotheosis of 1874, and returned an unopposed Liberal in 1880; Aberdeenshire, which had only been Liberal in 1857 and 1859 due to exceptional circumstances, returned Liberals in all three elections in both its new divisions, the Conservatives failing to find a candidate in Aberdeenshire East (apart from a by-election); Kincardine, which had first become Liberal in 1865, stuck firmly to its new allegiance; and only Perth, bordering on the Central region, Liberal for the first time in 1865 since 1835, returned to the Tories briefly in 1874. The second most Liberal region was Highland, whose constituencies were uniformly Liberal with the exception of Inverness, where, apart from 1832, Conservatives were returned until the intervention of a Crofter in 1885.

In Central, Clydeside and Borders, the party battle was more balanced, and reflected the swings of national political fortunes, so that while in 1868 and 1880 the Liberals carried thirteen of the eighteen seats in these regions, the Conservatives were equally successful in 1874. Only a third of these constituencies were constant in their allegiance: Clackmannan and Kinross, Linlithgow, Kirkcudbright, Lanark North and Renfrew for the Liberals, and Dunbarton, together with Haddington and Wigtown, for the Conservatives. Bute, traditionally Tory, returned to the fold in 1868 after a brief flirtation with the Liberals in 1865, but fell from grace again in 1880; and Peebles and Selkirk was also lost to the Tories in the last contested election of the period. The quintessentially swing seats, however, were Midlothian, Stirling, Lanark South, Berwick, Dumfries and Roxburgh, Liberal in 1868 and 1880, but Conservative in 1874.

The electoral geography of the Second Reform Act, therefore, is of a Liberal Party overwhelmingly dominant in both the counties and burghs of the Highlands and Islands and East of Scotland, extending into Clackmannan and Kinross, Linlithgow, Leith Burghs and Edinburgh. Consistently Conservative Scotland, by contrast, was scattered between Inverness in Highland, to Dunbarton on Clydeside, Haddington to the east of Edinburgh and Wigtown in the south west. On less strict criteria, however, one can detect the emergence of a more coherent constellation of Conservative strength in the west, including Dunbartonshire, Bute, Ayrshire North and South, Wigtown, and to a lesser extent the burgh districts of Ayr and Wigtown. It was an early hint at the vulnerability of Gladstonian Liberalism to Unionist sentiment. Even so, Conservative Scotland rested on narrower foundations than hitherto.

Conclusions

The electoral system established in 1868, through the deepening of the franchise distinctions between burgh and county and the failure to tackle redistribution, sustained the essential features which had characterised electoral politics between 1832 and 1868. The severely restricted electorate in the Highlands ensured the survival of nomination seats and the control of representation by a very small number of mostly-Whig landowners; the Tories continued to rely heavily on the gentry to organise their affairs, and suffered when proprietors lost interest or changed their allegiance; Whig influence remained strong in the smaller rural-based burgh districts; and the larger burghs continued to assert their independence from national party leaders and their agents. Nevertheless, the expanded franchise, the increased incidence of contested elections, and a quickening interest in politics, led to a steady increase in the numbers of those voting (Table 8.6). In the counties, where fewer than 10,000 electors had participated in any general election from 1841 to 1865, almost 60,000 cast a ballot in 1880, though it was in the larger cities, particularly Glasgow and Edinburgh, that the change was the most dramatic. Even so, taking into account double voting in Dundee, Edinburgh and Glasgow, only around 200,000 Scots voted in 1880. Non-electors may have expressed their views at public meetings, but the ultimate choice remained that of a privileged minority.

Table 8.6 Number of Votes Cast in Elections, 1868–1880

	1868	1874	1880
Counties	26,924	37,313	57,767
Burghs	34,778	45,502	54,555
Dundee, Edinburgh & Glasgow*	86,004	127,437	155,397

* Each elector in Dundee, Edinburgh and Glasgow had two votes. They could, however, use only one if they so wished.

Paradoxically, the substantial expansion of the burgh electorate served to maintain existing forms because the Liberalism of the new voters prevented the emergence of a competitive two-party system, and inhibited the development of unified party structures. At the same time, the new electors were neither so numerous nor so lacking in respectability as to shatter the socio-political consensus betweeen themselves and the middle class, which underpinned Liberal dominance and marginalised the class appeal of Conservatism. Even in Glasgow, where the strains between the Liberal factions were at their greatest, a new accommodation, rebalancing power in favour of the Radicals, proved possible.

Continuities notwithstanding, there were signs of change. Most significant was the attempt by both party leaderships to exercise greater influence over the constituencies. Although embryonic national party structures failed to appear until after the 1880 general election, national agents played an influential role in establishing two-party competition across most constituencies, and (on the Liberal side) eliminating surplus candidatures. More important than party organisation in breaching the walls of endogenous constituency power structures, however, was the emergence of Gladstone, whose appeal to the electorate transcended the factionalism of local notables and provided both the press and public a simple yardstick by which the suitability of candidates could be measured. The significance of this development, however, was not to be fully realised until the Home Rule crisis of 1886.

In many respects, the modest franchise extension in the counties had as great an impact as the much larger growth in the burghs, because it was associated with the emergence of the tenant farmers as a more independent force, following the introduction of the secret ballot. The new electorate played a decisive role in shifting the allegiance of the East towards Liberalism. Much more significant, however, was the behaviour of counties in the central belt and southern Scotland, where the emergence of 'swing' constituencies indicated an electorate responding as much to changing political events and economic circumstances as the more settled allegiances of their lairds.

Although the 1868-1884 electoral system enabled Scottish Liberalism to retain much of its previous heterogeneity, with its flimsy 'alliance' of churchmen, free churchmen, voluntaries, landlords, tenants farmers, teetotallers, publicans and distillers, and add to it the bulk of respectable working class householders, it was an increasingly unstable coalition. Class-based politics, aided and abetted by burgh Liberals, was clearly emerging in the counties, and it was questionable how much land reform the Whig landowners would be prepared to concede to the tenantry before deserting to the Conservatives. In the burghs there were tensions between trade unionists and businessmen (often Radicals) over strikes and picketing, and between Advanced Liberalism, with its support for disestablishment, reform in Ireland, and teetotalism, and traditional Kirkmen, the drink interest, and the nascent Orange vote. It is difficult to see how even under the terms of the 1868 Act that the Liberals could have contained these contradictions indefinitely, particularly as the institution of national party structures created fora in which they would be debated.

To a large extent, therefore, the seeds of change which were to bear fruit in the crisis of 1886 were sown in the years immediately following the 1868 Act. Nevertheless, the old equilibrium (1868-1885) for all its problems had yet to meet its nemesis.

Notes

1 Hutchison classifies Thomson as a Conservative, Shedden as a Liberal.
2 Following the retirement of Ewart, Dumfries Burghs had been won in 1868 by Robert Jardine who defeated a fellow Liberal, Ernest Noel. In 1874 Jardine stood down and Noel won the seat. Jardine returned to parliament in 1880 as the member for Dumfriesshire.
3 MacGregor retired to the Chiltern Hundreds in 1878. He was to contest Leith as an Independent Unionist in 1886, though without success.
4 Fraser MacIntosh had deserted the Conservatives shortly before the 1874 general election. Although a landowner, he was returned as a Crofter for Inverness-shire in 1885, and returned unopposed as a Liberal Unionist Crofter in 1886. In 1892, he was defeated as a Liberal Unionist by a Crofter.
5 Donald became Liberal M P for Perthshire in 1880.
6 Kinnear became member for East Fife in 1885, but as a Liberal Unionist fell to Herbert Asquith in 1886.
7 John Pender was later returned to parliament by the Wick Burghs, following a by-election in 1872.

References

Brash, JI, *Scottish Electoral Politics*, 1832–1854, Edinburgh, 1974.
Cowan, RMW, *The Newspaper in Scotland: A Study of its First Expansion, 1815-1860,*

Glasgow, 1946.

Craig, FWS, British Parliamentary Election Results, 1832–1885, London, 1977

Crapster, BL, 'Scotland and the Conservative Party in 1876,' *Journal of Modern History,* Vol. XXXIX: 355–60.

Donald, J, *Past Elections in Greenock*, Greenock, 1933.

Ferguson, JPS, *Directory of Scottish Newspapers*, Edinburgh, 1984.

Hanham, HJ, *Elections and Party Management*, Hassocks, 1978.

Hutchison, IGC, *A Political History of Scotland*, Edinburgh, 1986.

Kellas, JG, 'The Liberal Party in Scotland, 1876–1895,' *Scottish Historical Review,* Vol. XLIV, No. 137, April, 1965.

_____, *Modern Scotland: the Nation Since 1870,* London, 1968.

Mackie, JB, *The Life and Work of Duncan McLaren*, 2 Vols., Edinburgh, 1888.

Scotsman.

Shedden, Sir Lewis, *The Parliamentary History of Kilmarnock*, Kilmarnock, 1929.

Spender, JA, *The Life and Times of The Right Hon. Sir Henry Campbell-Bannerman*, 2 Vols., Edinburgh, 1923.

Urwin, DW, 'The Development of the Conservative Party Organisation in Scotland until 1912,' *Scottish Historical Review*, Vol. XLIV, No. 138, October, 1965.

9   The Members, 1880

In 1880, with only three of the burghs and six of the counties retaining the members they had returned in 1865, no fewer than 49 of the MPs had only been associated with their current constituencies since the passing of the Second Reform Act. Nevertheless, changes to the social and occupational background of members between 1865 and 1880, though indicating a greater preference for MPs with business rather than landowner interests, were not dramatic. Thus, while those with a predominantly business background increased from fourteen to 21, the number of landowners only fell from 35 to 31. Lawyers and soldiers remained more or less as numerous as in 1865, but the other professions continued to be poorly represented. Most of the changes were confined to the Liberal parliamentary contingent, with the diminishing band of Conservatives continuing to draw their members almost exclusively from the land (Table 9.1).

The Liberals

A distinctive feature of Liberal representation, 1832-1865, had been the penetration of the burghs (especially the districts) by Whig landed proprietors. By 1880, the process had been arrested and reversed through defeat and the withdrawal of Liberal lairds from urban constituencies. Additionally, a number of Tory landlords, returned for county seats in 1874, were expelled by Liberal merchants in 1880, so that the Scottish Liberal contingent was a rough balance between landed proprietors and representatives of the urban bourgeoisie. The change, however, was not entirely to the direct benefit of Scottish-based enterprises, because a number of the businessmen had interests centred on the City of London rather than Glasgow or Edinburgh; and the mercantile background of most of the entrepreneurs meant that manufacturers continued to hold only the odd seat. Amongst the professions, law and soldiering (mostly linked to landowning) continued to dominate, almost to the complete exclusion of other occupations.

The Burghs

Four features characterised burgh representation: firstly, the dominance of locally-recruited members in the four major cities, Paisley and Greenock; secondly, the penetration of some burgh districts by big city influences; thirdly, the diminished but surviving landed presence in some burghs; and fourthly, the development of carpet-bagging.

The most impressive of the city notables elected in 1880 was the Radical Dissenting draper, Duncan McLaren, in Edinburgh. As a former city treasurer, he had been largely responsible for putting Edinburgh's finances on an even keel, and had subsequently held the post of lord provost and the presidency of the Chamber of Commerce. He was, however, past his sixty-fifth birthday when first returned in 1865, and age combined with a critical attitude towards his party leaders, especially Gladstone, to deny him office (Mackie). Elected alongside him in 1874 and 1880 was a second former lord provost, James Cowan, a paper manufacturer and brother of a former MP.

Table 9.1: Backgrounds of Scottish Members of Parliament Returned in 1880

	Counties	Burghs	All Libs	Conservatives (Counties Only)	All
Landowners	9	-	9	2	11
Landowner/Soldiers	6	1	7	1	8
Landowner/Lawyers	2	4	6	1	7
Landowner/Diplomat	-	-	-	1	1
Landowner/Businessman	1	1	2	-	2
Landowner/Businessman/Lawyer	1	-	1	-	1
Landowner/Academic	-	1	1	-	1
(All Landowners)	(19)	(7)	(26)	(5)	(31)
Soldier	1	-	1	1	2
(All Soldiers)	(7)	(1)	(8)	(1)	(9)
Lawyer	-	2	2		2
(All Lawyers)	(3)	(6)	(9)	(1)	(10)
Businessmen	6	14	20	1	21
(All Businessmen)	(8)	(16)	(24)	(1)	(25)
Academic	-	1	1	-	1
Academic/Architect	-	1	1	-	1
(All Academics)	-	(3)	(3)	-	(3)
Surgeon/Newspaper Proprietor	-	1	1	-	1
All	26	26	52	6	58

Aberdeen also returned an ex-chief magistrate, John Webster, scion of a well-established firm of advocates. Yet another councillor, Frank Henderson, a leather merchant, was re-elected in Dundee, where he remained a member of the corporation; and although the second Dundee MP, George Armistead, was a Yorkshireman, he was a resident of the city, having added Dundee and London to the mercantile interests his father had established in Hull and Riga. Similarly, Glasgow's members, Robert Middleton and George Anderson, had traded within the metropolis which returned them, although the latter was retired and lived in Fife. The third Glasgow MP, Charles Cameron, was also of local stock, although he had been educated at St Andrews and Trinity College, Dublin, where he became a master of surgery. He never practised his medical skills, however, and it was as the Radical proprietor of the *North British Daily Mail* he entered parliament at the tender age of 33. In Greenock, James Stewart, a local merchant and shipowner, sustained a strong tradition of indigenous representation; and in Paisley, William Holms, a spinner and thread manufacturer, with business interests in Edinburgh, Glasgow and London, had been raised in the town.

The influence of Glasgow was evident in the Falkirk Burghs, where one of its merchants, James Ramsay, had repaired in 1874 following his 1868 defeat at the hands of Campbell-Bannerman in the Stirling Burghs. Ramsay underlined the developing relationships between the merchant classes and the old aristocracy through his mother, a daughter of Lord Belhaven, and his wife, a daughter of the 19th Lord Torphichen. Campbell-Bannerman himself (although domiciled in Kent) came from a family of Glasgow merchants, and had been educated at Glasgow University before completing his studies at Trinity College, Cambridge. Campbell's elder brother, James, was also returned in 1880, but as the Conservative member for Aberdeen and Glasgow Universities. Big city tentacles were also evident in the Wigtown Burghs in 1880, when for a brief period John McLaren, lawyer son of the Edinburgh MP, and activist within the West and South of Scotland Liberal Association, was the member,[1] and in the Montrose Burghs, where the Dundee textile manufacturer, William Baxter, continued his long association with the constituency. The role of the big cities as sources of candidates was particularly evident in the Kilmarnock election of 1880. The successful Liberal, John Dick Peddie, was a native, architect and academician of Edinburgh, where his father was a Writer to the Signet, and his mother was the daughter of a professor at Glasgow University, while his opponent, John Cuthbertson (as has been noted) had strong connections with Glasgow (Shedden: 38-9).

Although traditional county Liberal interests in the burghs had much weakened by 1880, they were by no means extinct. Ayr Burghs, for example, expressed its Liberalism through a former pupil of Rugby School, Richard Campbell, who had fought during the Indian Mutiny as a captain in the 8th Madras Cavalry, and had subsequently become a major in the Ayrshire yeomanry and vice-lieutenant of his county. Elgin Burghs continued to place its affairs in the hands of Mounstuart-Elphinstone Grant-Duff, first elected in 1857. Kirkcaldy Burghs returned an Inner Temple barrister, the Fifeshire baronet and landowner Sir George Campbell, a former lieutenant-governor of Bengal and judge of the Supreme Court of Calcutta; and a local lawyer Charles Fraser Macintosh, who sat for the Inverness Burghs between 1874 and 1885, was also a Highland landowner. The last member of this group, a baronet, Sir David Wedderburn of Ballindean, Perthshire, who represented the Haddington Burghs from 1879 to its extinction in 1885, was also in the tradition of landowner/ lawyers that had sat for Scottish burgh constituencies.

The long line of English-based carpet-baggers in the burgh districts continued to thrive. Ernest Noel, for example, who sat for the Dumfries Burghs, was a resident of Haywards Heath, Sussex. The most well-known of the 1880 crop, however, was the English landowner/historian, George Trevelyan, former member for Tynemouth, inserted into the newly-created Hawick Burghs in 1868. His claim to a Scottish seat would seem to have been that his uncle, Lord Macaulay, had sat for Edinburgh. John Pender, former MP for Totnes, was introduced to the Wick Burghs in 1872. Although his father was Scots, and he, himself, owned a residence in central Scotland and was a justice in both Argyll and Linlithgow, he lived in the south east of England, where he chaired the affairs of several London-based companies. It was a measure of his wealth and interests that he was also a JP in Kent, Middlesex, and Denbigh, and a deputy lieutenant of Lancashire. Similarly, weak Scottish links were exhibited by the three other carpet-baggers, who seemed more associated with Liverpool than Scotland. The member for Perth, Charles Parker, was the son of a Liverpool merchant and a fellow of University College, Oxford. His suitability to be MP for Perth seemed to rest on a home in Ayrshire, and his earlier election (and subsequent defeat) as MP for Perthshire. Stephen Williamson, returned for St Andrews Burghs in 1880, was connected with the constituency through his father's interests in Anstruther. He, however, was a Liverpool merchant, vice-president of its Chamber of Commerce, and lived in the salubrious pastures of Cheshire. His selection as a 'zealous disestablisher' (Hutchison: 146) replacing a Churchman, Ellice, was regarded by his opponents as a triumph for 'the extreme wing' (Hutchison: 144) of the party in one of the more conservative burghs. Lastly, the son of an Oxford clergyman, Andrew Grant, who sat for Leith Burghs, was a former East India merchant in Bombay and Liverpool. His possession of property in Perthshire, however, enhanced his claim to sit for a Scottish constituency, and his earlier education at Edinburgh High School and university made his selection not entirely inappropriate.

The Counties

Liberal members in the counties continued to be firmly biased towards traditional landowning interests, often with strong military connections. Nineteen of the 26 county Liberal MPs were principally landed proprietors, seven of them being members of aristocratic families. Reflecting the increasing Anglicisation of the Scottish upper classes, and an establishment that had consolidated its power through the Treaty of Union and the Highland clearances, they combined long-established family connections and interests in the constituencies they represented with an English education and service in the armed forces. These traditional landed proprietors were reinforced by a smaller group of business magnates with commercial interests encircling the globe, who had adopted the style of the gentry through the acquisition of extensive rural properties. It was quite fitting that William Gladstone, whose Tory brother had become the leading landowner in Kincardineshire, and who himself had commercial antecedents and an estate at Hawarden, through marriage, should have been returned along with them.

The aristocrats included the eldest son of the 3rd Duke of Sutherland, the Marquess of Stafford, a former lieutenant in the 2nd Life Guards and a captain in the Staffordshire yeomanry. His constituency, Sutherland, was no more than a family fiefdom. Aberdeenshire East was represented by the second son of the 4th Earl of Aberdeen, the Honourable Alexander Gordon, who had been elected as a Conservative in 1875 before changing sides. An Equerry to the Queen, he had been decorated for his services in the Crimea and had subsequently served in India, rising to the rank of lieutenant general. Neighbouring Banffshire was held by Robert Duff of Fetteresso, a Kincardineshire landowner and relative of the Duke of Fife, a leading county proprietor. Argyll returned Lord Colin Campbell, the youngest son of the 8th Duke of Argyll; and Fife was represented by an old Etonian and graduate of Balliol, Robert Bruce, a grandson of 1st Earl of Durham and heir presumptive to the 8th Earl of Elgin. In the Borders, Berwickshire was held by Edward Marjoribanks, a barrister at the Inner Temple, eldest son of Lord Tweedmouth and son-in-law of the 7th Duke of Marlborough; while Roxburgh, in 1880 elected the Honourable Arthur Elliot, an Inner Temple barrister and second son of the Earl of Minto.

The second rank of landowning Liberals was hardly less well established. One baronet, Sir John Sinclair of Ulbster, a former officer in the Scots Guards and vice-lieutenant of Caithness, continued a family history of parliamentary service in his native county dating back to 1678. Clackmannan and Kinross returned the barrister/landowner and Liberal Chief Whip, William Adam of Blair Adam and Kincardine. Educated at Rugby and Trinity College, Cambridge, and former Private Secretary to the Governor of Bombay, Adam belonged to a house that had played an important part in the development of the Indian Empire, and had rendered faithful service to the Scottish Whigs during the suzerainty of Dundas. In Lanarkshire, too, Liberalism deferred to the gentry, despite the impact of economic change. Sir Thomas Colebrooke, a baronet, and member for the north division was a lord lieutenant of the county; and John Hamilton, who won the south constituency in 1868 and 1880, had military/landowning antecedents, his father having fought in the Peninsular War and at Waterloo, while he himself had served as a captain in the Second Lifeguards. Hamilton was also a vice-lieutenant of Lanarkshire, and connected by marriage to the Earl of Leven and Melville. From August 1857 to 1859 he had sat for the Falkirk District, following the unseating of Merry on a petition. In 1859, however, he had stood aside to allow Merry's reinstatement. The third Liberal seat on Clydeside, Renfrewshire, also went to a landowner/soldier, William Mure, who had fought in the Kaffir War, 1851-3, and in the Crimea at Balaclava and the siege of Sebastapol. His father, a sympathiser of the Non-Intrusionists had sat for the same constituency as a Conservative from 1846 to 1855. Bute briefly returned Thomas Russell of Ascog, and Linlithgow was held from 1865 to 1893 by Peter McLagan of Pumpherston, a member of the Council of Edinburgh University and a strong supporter of tenant farmers' rights.

In the north east, West Aberdeenshire enjoyed the services of Robert Farquharson of Finzean, who before returning to his tenantry had been an assistant surgeon in the Coldstream Guards, following medical training in Edinburgh. A moderate Gladstonian, his volumes on parliamentary life, containing a number of pertinent remarks on the medical undesirability of female MPs, (especially as ministers), are singularly revealing of the values of a Scottish backbencher at this time (Farquharson). Another landowner/soldier, Sir John Maxwell of Kirouchtree, a former captain in the 1st Royal Regiment, held his county, Kirkcudbright, for Liberalism in 1880. In the north east, a fellow baronet, and a founder of the Church Defence Association, Sir George MacPherson-Grant of Ballindalloch, with landholdings in Inverness-shire and

Banffshire, where he was convener of the county, sat for the intervening counties of Elgin and Nairn. His grandfather had been MP for Sutherland, 1809-1812 and 1816-26, and he, himself, had contested Inverness-shire in 1865. Ross and Cromarty returned the absentee landlord, Alexander Matheson of Ardross and Attadale, a director of the Bank of England and a commissioner of the lieutenancy of London. To this company might be added Joseph Laing, who had repaired to Orkney and Shetland following defeat in the Wick Burghs, for although a barrister in England and chairman of the Brighton Railway Company, his claim to the seat rested on family property on Papdale, Orkney.

The most important development in the structure of Liberal representation in the counties, 1868-1880, was the arrival of MPs whose interests did not rest traditionally or principally in land, and whose local qualifications were recent and/or weak. It was a trend that was to continue more strongly after 1885. The change signified less the reluctance of Liberal Associations to nominate local landowners, (although there are hints that was becoming the case), than the increasing unwillingness of landed proprietors to support a party whose national leaders were becoming more sympathetic towards tenant farmers and crofters. Most of the county businessmen, however, were to the Whig rather than Radical wing of the party, and to a certain extent their emergence in the counties reflected their difficulties in securing burgh nominations.

Amongst this new business group we may include Gladstone, who in 1880 had defeated the Earl of Dalkeith in Midlothian, the lair of his father, the Duke of Buccleuch, although a streak of populism makes him less typical of the class as a whole. More representative was Charles Tennant, the first Liberal to sit for Peebles and Selkirk, a Glasgow merchant and manufacturer, who had sat for his native city between 1879 and 1880. His translation to the joint counties was a recognition that his Whiggish sympathies were not acceptable to the Glasgow Radicals he had finessed in 1879, and was locally justified through his acquisition of property in Peeblesshire. Similarly, in Stirlingshire, another Whig merchant and former vice-chairman of the Glasgow Chamber of Commerce, John Bolton, who had polled miserably in Glasgow in 1874, ousted a Conservative, Sir William Edmonstone, whose family had periodically sat in Scottish and United Kingdom parliaments from the sixteenth century. More notable was Robert Jardine, a partner in Matheson's, a major player in the development of trade between London and Hong Kong, who, having sat for the Whig nomination burgh of Ashburton (1865-68), in 1880 broke an almost uninterrupted Conservative hold on Dumfriesshire. Likewise, the 1880 victor in Perthshire, Donald Currie, although locally resident at Farth Castle, was a lieutenant of the City of London and had made his money as a London-based shipowner. Another shipowner and merchant, though with farming interests as well, James Barclay, a former Aberdeen town councillor, represented the neighbouring county of Forfar. Barclay's selection in 1872 was a deliberate snub by Angus farmers to the ambitions of a relative of the Earl of Dalhousie 'in order to establish the rejection of the political control of Brechin Castle' (Hutchison: 106). The newer type of Liberal MP also included Sir George Balfour, who replaced a Liberal landowner as Kincardineshire's MP in 1872, for although a soldier he was not of the gentleman/soldier variety. His father, a resident of Montrose, had been a captain in the Royal Navy, and he himself had served as a professional soldier in India following his training at the military academy in Addiscombe. Balfour's selection as Liberal candidate in Kincardineshire rested not on the traditional military/landowning connection, but his marriage to the daughter of Joseph Hume, the surgeon and reformer who had sat for Montrose Burghs from 1842 to his death in 1855. His adoption was secured by pro-tenant views on the land-question.

The Conservatives

Only six Conservatives were elected in Scotland at the general election of 1880. Five of them were from established landowning families, and all sat for county constituencies. Donald Cameron of Lochiel, representing Inverness, was a high-land proprietor, whose mother was a sister of the 5th and 6th Earls of Buckinghamshire, and his wife a daughter of the 5th Duke of Buccleuch. Following an English education at Harrow, he entered the diplomatic service before finding a parliamentary seat in 1868. In 1874 he was appointed as groom-in-waiting to Queen Victoria. With similarly impeccable credentials was Lord Elcho, son of the 8th Earl of Weymss and March, who, having sat for East Gloucestershire from 1841 to 1846, was returned unopposed in 1857 in Haddingtonshire, which he held until his elevation to the peerage in 1883. He served as a lieutenant-colonel in the London Scottish Volunteers, was ADC to the Queen, and ensign-general in the socially prestigious Royal Company of Archers.

The gentry included the seventh in a line of baronets, Sir Herbert Maxwell, who sat for his county, Wigtownshire, from 1880 to his retiral in 1906, and the Ayrshire members, Claude Alexander and Robert Cochran-Patrick. Son-in-law of Alexander Speirs, Liberal MP for Paisley, 1835-6, Alexander, the member for South Ayrshire, was in the tradition of soldier/landowners, having joined the Grenadier Guards following an English education at Eton and Christ Church. He had been decorated while on active service in the Crimea. Cochrane-Patrick, MP for North Ayrshire, was somewhat atypical of his class, for although receiving his LL.B. from Cambridge, he had taken his first degree in Scotland at Edinburgh University. Furthermore, although a magistrate in both Ayrshire and Renfrewshire, where he held property, he was 'an admirer of the co-operative movement who had been approached by Ayrshire miners for help in exposing evasions of the Truck Act because of his reputation as a sympathiser of the working classes' (Hutchison: 200). Only one of the Conservative MPs, Archibald Ewing, who sat for Dunbartonshire from 1868 to 1892, was connected with trade – his father having been a Glasgow merchant. Even he, however, held landed property in various parts of Scotland, so that his adoption reflected less a gesture towards new social forces than the assimilation of those elements into the old ruling class.

Conclusions

Even as late at 1880, three decades after Britain had ceased to be a predomi-nantly rural society, and 50 years since the Liberals had emerged as the major political force north of the border, rather more than half of Scotland's MPs con-tinued to be drawn from the landowner class. This situation was largely due to

the survival of a constituency system which continued to favour the smaller agricultural counties and rurally-based burgh districts at the expense of the larger
urban areas. Nevertheless, minor changes to the county franchise appeared to
have modified somewhat the overall characteristics of rural MPs. With only
seven of the county members the sons or sons-in-law or aristocrats, noble families were less dominant than before 1868 as the balance of rural representation
shifted firmly towards the gentry. The greatly expanded urban franchise occasioned a significant increase in the number of MPs with a non-landed background in the burghs, so that only seven of the twenty six burgh members were
landowners, and only one closely related to the aristocracy. Consequently, the
sharpened distinction in 1868 between the burgh and county franchises was
clearly reflected in the contrast between urban and rural representation.

In some respects the increased number of burgh businessmen, (who continued to include only a scattering of manufacturers), indicated the slow emergence
of the business class as a national political force promised by the reforms of
1832, but their presence in the counties also pointed to a deepening ideological
conflict within Liberalism. A radical stance on land questions had become
almost *de rigeur* for political survival in the burghs, and backing for disestablishment an increasingly necessary credential to secure the support of middle
class Liberal activists. On both these issues most landowner Whigs were lukewarm, if not hostile, so that they were less likely to seek or receive burgh nominations than in the past. That ideological development was also reflected in the
kinds of businessmen who were becoming burgh MPs. Representatives of the
old commercial aristocracy with imperial and landed connections were under
increasing pressure to give way to new money, which was more urban-based
and culturally centred on those social forces associated with religious dissent
and the disruption. By contrast, businessmen representing counties in 1880
tended to come from more established backgrounds than their urban colleagues,
and included Churchmen who were no longer acceptable to urban Radicals.
Consequently, the penetration of counties by businessmen reflected not only an
extension of urban power, but also the increasing conservatism of some sections
of the commercial upper middle class, whose political values were closer to
those of rural Whigs than those of advanced city Liberals.

Although Scottish MPs were less socially homogeneous than in 1865, and the
differences between some urban and rural members more marked, one would
not wish to overstate the point, partly because the association between class,
status and ideology was by no means perfect, partly because carpet-baggers and
representatives of landowner families continued to hold around 40 per cent of all
burgh seats, and partly because individual members frequently straddled social
and ideological categories. It was, therefore, still the case that Scottish members
as a whole continued to emphasise integrating rather than conflicting values
within the evolving political elite. As in 1865, Scotland's Westminster ranks
underlined the socially unifying cause of Britain's imperial venture through
landowners as soldiers, lawyers as administrators, and businessmen as traders.
The role of the English public schools and universities in reconciling the
traditional ruling class with the urban haute bourgeoisie was particularly
evident, especially amongst those Anglo-Scottish MPs whose parents or
grandparents had extended their business interests to Liverpool and London. The
social integration of the old and new political elite was also reinforced by the

increased number of lawyer-MPs from a business background who joined those from landed families at the Inns of Courts, and the tendency of businessmen to acquire country estates through purchase and marriage. At the same time, although deriving status and income from their estates, traditional landowners were by no means strangers to the world of commerce and trade.

The dominant characteristic of Scottish MPs in 1880, therefore, continued to be their membership of an imperial British establishment based on land and commerce, supported by their allies in the military and legal profession. The leitmotif was the emergence of a more parochial group of Radical businessmen in the industrial burghs. That nearly all the MPs were Liberals of one sort of another emphasised the close relationship which had developed between Liberalism and both urban and rural elites by the third quarter of the nineteenth century. 1880, however, marked the last hurrah for that increasingly unstable coalition, because the consensus it represented, already under considerable pressure from voters and party activists, hardly survived the election of 1885, and broke irrevocably in 1886, with far-reaching consequences for the subsequent social recruitment of Liberal MPs.

Notes

1   On his appointment as Lord Advocate, John McLaren lost his seat in the consequent by-election (May, 1880), and failed again at Berwick-on-Tweed. His father, however, stood down in Edinburgh to make way for him at a by-election in Jan. 1881, (Mackie: Vol. II, 224-6).

References

Forster, J, *Members of Parliament, Scotland, 1357-1882,* London, 1882
Hutchison, IGC, *A Political History of Scotland*, Edinburgh, 1986.
Mackie, JB, *The Life and Work of Duncan McLaren*, 2 Vols., Edinburgh, 1888.
Shedden, Sir Lewis, *The Parliamentary History of Kilmarnock*, Kilmarnock, 1929.

10 Conclusion

The evolution of Scotland's representation in the United Kingdom parliament rested heavily on the electoral system established in 1707, which had its roots in Scotland's ancient constitution. Before 1832, continuity with the pre-Union arrangements was particularly evident in the structure of the franchise, the distribution of county constituencies, and the social background of members of parliament. Even the restructuring of burgh representation, which was most disturbed in 1707, deviated in few essentials from past practices.

In 1832, a large element of standardisation with England and Wales was introduced with respect to the franchise, but Scottish backbenchers, as much by accident as design, had considerable influence over the distribution of seats. Consequently, although the First Reform Act replaced the old franchise, it achieved little by way of redistribution, when only the acquisition of extra seats introduced a degree of modernisation. The precedent was repeated in 1868, when additional seats were again found from England, not only to satisfy the urban electorate but also to protect rural interests. To a large degree, therefore, redistribution was hardly a feature of Scottish reform either in 1832 or 1868: a defect which weakened the impact of the new franchise, and helped sustain the highly traditional social characteristics of Scotland's parliamentary representatives.

Despite a different inheritance, the broad conclusions of Charles Seymour regarding the impact of electoral reform in England and Wales were generally applicable to Scotland. As in England after 1832: 'the introduction of the new borough franchise...furnished an opportunity to a large class of the community for expressing its opinions at the polls,' although, 'the rural...constituencies were in possession of far greater electoral power than the industrial disticts,' and 'small boroughs, generally representative of aristocratic interests, held the balance of power in the Commons' (Seymour: 519–20). It took the 1868 Act to 'break down aristocratic control in many [burgh] constituencies,' where the Whigs had resisted Radical pressures, but even so 'the redistribution of 1867...failed to grant to the large industrial centres the representation they claimed was due to their wealth and importance...and the representatives of the small rural boroughs could still outvote the members for the great textile, mining and shipping districts' (Seymour: 522).

There were, however, points of contrast between the two parts of Britain. Whereas in England boroughs continued to dominate representation over the counties by a ratio of two to one, (1832–1865), and by three to two, (1868–1884), in Scotland the counties remained more numerous, despite an increased number of burgh constituencies. In England and Wales the need to extinguish borough corruption continued to pose problems for reformers down to 1883, but in the Scottish burghs, where the changes of 1832 had removed traditional forms of electoral manipulation and Liberal hegemony minimised inter-party rivalry, the relevant legislation was hardly necessary. The main post-1832 problems for

Scotland arose from attempts to merge the franchise qualifications north and south of the border, because property ownership and land tenure, which remained the basis of the system, were quite different. In the burghs, the obstacles appear to have been surmounted without too much difficulty, but in the counties the 1832 Act created abuses and strengthened the influence of large landed proprietors for a further fifty years.

The proportion of the Scots with the franchise before 1885 remained substantially below that in England, which was a reflection both of the relative poverty of the Scottish people and a constituency system biased towards the counties, where the franchise conditions were less generous than in the burghs. With the Scottish tenantry significantly less able than their English counterparts to secure enrolment, the lairds were distinctly advantaged. Other differences, such as the willingness of Scottish sheriffs to enrol lodgers as early as 1832, were of minor importance.

Despite the rather conservative features of the Scottish reforms, compared to England Wales, the character of politics and elections perhaps changed more in Scotland than elsewhere in Britain, (though less so than in Ireland), because the politics of ministerial patronage, based on the private needs of individual electors, could no longer be sustained. Political leadership passed to local elites, whose control over the electorate varied from nomination in a small number of counties to almost none at all in the larger cities. The level of popular participation in elections, even of the registered electorate, was not very high before 1868, but following the Second Reform Act there was a distinct raising of the political temperature as the new electorate strengthened the Radical challenge in the burghs, and tenant farmers grew more independent in the counties.

In partisan terms, the 1832 Act created a Liberal hegemony that virtually monopolised burgh representation down to 1886, and changes in the counties progressively aided the advance of Whig interests. During the reform debates, 1830-32, the Scottish Tories seemed to go out of their way to alienate middle class opinion by commending Scotland's prevailing electoral system as a bulwark against democratic influences. After 1832, the Conservatives remained closely linked to the more unpopular features of Scottish life from intrusionism and the close corporations to the game laws. At the same time, there were important issues, of which free trade was by far the most salient, where prominent Conservatives identified more with the Liberal position than that of their own party leaders. As a result, the Liberals had little difficulty in establishing themselves as the custodians of the national (Scottish) consensus and institutional renewal.

To a considerable degree Scottish electoral politics, 1832-1884, exhibited features more in common with the one-party American South, as described by VO Key, than the domestic system which was established after 1885. The hegemonic position of Liberalism sustained a political culture in Scotland that was quite distinctive from elsewhere in the United Kingdom; and the Liberal Party, like the Democratic Party in the Old American South, had little social, ideological, and organisational coherence. That was particularly the case in the burghs where political conflict was focused on disputes between the various factions in the Liberal coalition, and elections were little more than open 'primaries' between competing Liberal candidates. Inevitably, the Conservatives also became incorporated within the Liberal universe due to the weakness of their own alignment and the courting of their support by the competing Liberal election committees. Even in the counties, where a more conventional two-party system was sustained, the attraction of Palmerston for a number of Tory families also caused a blurring of partisanship. Although by 1880 the form of a two-party system was emerging, the substance of the Scottish political struggle remained focused on a hegemonic Liberalism.

The breadth of the Whig/Liberal coalition is exemplified by backgrounds and attitudes of the members of parliament it returned. There were Established Churchmen, Free Churchmen, Dissenters, and even the odd Anglican; descendants of noble lines and urban arrivistes; supporters of the Highland clearances and critics of the game laws; wine merchants, whisky distillers, and teetotallers; imperialists and opponents of the Opium War; sympathisers with trade unionists and those who saw combinations as a restraint on trade; supporters and opponents of the Maynooth Grant and state aid to religious establishments; and even varying shades of opinion on free trade. It held together largely because the political system established in the 1830s had drawn a sharp distinction, (recognised in the electoral system), between burghs and counties, which had enabled the urban middle class to achieve emancipation while leaving rural power structures largely undisturbed.

The degree of political integration achieved through the electoral system between 1832 and 1885 was mixed. Although Scots reform required separate enactments, the Scottish franchise had become largely compatible with that of England and Wales. The continuing distinction between the burgh and county franchises, (exaggerated in 1868), however, sustained functional representation at the expense of a common national citizenship on both sides of the border. Although Scottish members of parliament were less a coherent national (Scottish) cohort of ministerial supporters as they had been in the past, and identified with United Kingdom-wide parties and tendencies, the claims of national party allegiances and objectives were less important than local power bases and interests. While the campaigns of 1874 and 1880 had the rudiments of nationally-focused contests, the particular weakness of Scottish Conservatism delayed the process of modernisation north of the border. There were, however, sufficient signs, not least the growing assertiveness of tenant farmers following the introduction of the secret ballot, to suggest a major realignment in Scottish politics was about to take place. The Third Reform Act was to make it certain.

References

Key, VO jnr, *Southern Politics in State and Nation,* New York, 1949.
Seymour, C, *Electoral Reform in England and Wales: the development and operation of the parliamentary franchise, 1832-1885,* New Haven, 1915.

Bibliography

A. Government Publications

Statutes

Acts of the Parliament of Scotland, Vol. XI, 1702–1707, Edinburgh, 1824.

An Act for the Amendment of the Representation of the People in Scotland, 31 & 32 Victoria, Cap. 48, 1868.

An Act for the more effectual Registration of Persons entitled to vote in the Election of Members to serve in Parliament in Scotland, 4 & 5 William IV, Cap. 88, 1834.

An Act to amend an Act of the Second and Third Years of King William the Fourth, for amending the Representation of the People in Scotland, in so far as relates to the Procedure in County Elections in that country, 18 & 19 Victoria, Cap. 24, 1855.

An Act to amend the Law as to taking the Poll at Elections of Members to serve in Parliament for Scotland. 16 & 17 Victoria, Cap. 28, 1853.

An Act to amend the Law for the Registration of Persons entitled to vote in the Election of Members to serve in Parliament for the Burghs in Scotland, 19 & 20 Victoria, Cap. 58, 1856.

An Act to amend the Law relating to Procedure at Parliamentary and Municipal Elections, 35 & 36 Victoria, Ch. 33, 1872.

An Act to amend the Representation of the People in Scotland, 2 & 3 William IV, Cap. 65, 1832.

An Act to explain and Amend an Act passed in the Second and Third Year of the Reign of King William the Fourth, for amending the Representation of the People in Scotland; and to diminish the Expenses there, 5 & 6 William IV, Cap. 78, 1835.

House Occupiers Disqualification Removal (Scotland) Act, 41 Victoria, Ch. 5, 1878.

Parliamentary and Corrupt Practices Act, 43 Victoria, Ch. 18, 1880.

The County Voters Registration (Scotland) Act, 24 & 25 Victoria, Cap. 83, 1861.

Parliamentary Papers

Hansard, *Parliamentary Debates.*

Minutes of Evidence taken before the Select Committee in the Roxburgh Election Petition: with the Poll Books, 1837-8, (152), XII, 227.

Municipal Corporations (Scotland), Local Reports of Commissioners, Part I, From Aberbrothwick to Fortrose, 1835, (31), XXI, 1.

Number of registered electors in each county in Scotland, 1861 and 1862; and the number of names that were struck off or added to the register in the revision, in 1862; 1863, (252), L, 801.

Reports from Commissioners, 1836, (32), XXIII, appendix, *A Report of the State of Royal Burghs of Scotland, 1691,* 17.

Reports from Commissioners upon the Boundaries of the Several Cities, Burghs, and Towns of Scotland in respect to the Election of Members of Parliament, 1831–2, (408), XLII, 1.

Return, specifying for each Parliamentary city and borough in Scotland, the population in 1861 and 1871; numbers of electors, 1866, 1869, and in 1873, distinguishing occupiers, owners, lodgers, freemen &c., 1874 (381) LIII, 53.

Return of Registered Electors, 1844, II, xxxviii, 427.

Return showing the distance of each contributing burgh in Scotland from the other contributing burghs in the same district of burghs, &c. 1866 (314) LVII, 791.

Summary, showing the state of the Population and Representation in the Counties and Burghs in Scotland, Proportion of Electors to Population; Number of Members returned from each to serve in Parliament; Number of Males Twenty Years of Age and Upwards, 1834, (591), ix, 600

B. Commentaries

Cay, J, *An Analysis of the Scottish Reform Act with the Decisions of the Courts of Appeal,* Edinburgh, 1850.

Dyer, M, 'Mere Detail and Machinery: The Great Reform Act and the Effects on Redistribution on Scottish Representation, 1832-68,' *Scottish Historical Review,* Vol. LXII, 1983.

Ferguson, W, *Electoral Law and Procedure in Eighteenth and Early Nineteenth Century Scotland*, (Ph.D., Glasgow, 1957).
Ferguson, W, 'The Reform Act (Scotland) of 1832: Intention and Effect', *Scottish Historical Review*, Vol. XLV, 1966.
Nicolson, JB, *An Analysis of the Scottish Reform Act*, Edinburgh, 1869.
Wight, A, *Inquiry into the Rise and Progress of Parliament, chiefly in Scotland, and a complete System of Law concerning the Election of Representatives from Scotland to the Parliament of Great Britain*, Edinburgh, 1784.

C. Letters and Journals

Cockburn, H, *Life of Jeffrey*, Edinburgh, 1852.
Cockburn, H, *Journal*, Edinburgh, 1874.
Cockburn, H. *Letters Chiefly Connected with the Affairs of Scotland from Henry Cockburn to Thomas Francis Kennedy*, London, 1874.
Cockburn, H, *Memorials of His Time*, 1856.
Lockhart, G, *The Lockhart Papers*, London, 1817.
Marchmont, AH, *A Selection from the Papers of the Earls of Marchmont*, London, 1831.

D. Elections

Aberdeen Poll Book, 1847. (Manuscript in Aberdeen Central Library.)
Aberdeen Poll Book, 1852. (King's Collection, Aberdeen University.)
Aberdeen Poll Book, 1857. (King's Collection, Aberdeen University.)
Adam, Sir CE, *A View of the Political State of Scotland in the Last Century*, Edinburgh, 1887.
Brash, JI, 'The Conservatives in the Haddington District of Burghs, 1832–1852,' *Transactions of the East Lothian Antiquarian and Field Naturalists' Society*, Vol. XI, 1968.
Brash, JI, *Scottish Electoral Politics, 1832–1854*, Edinburgh, 1974. (Incorporating Horne, D, *Election Surveys.*)
Craig, FWS, *British Parliamentary Election Results, 1832-1885*, London, 1977.
Crapster, BL, 'Scotland and the Conservative Party in 1876,' *Journal of Modern History*, Vol. XXXIX, pp. 355–60.
Dod, CH, *Electoral Facts Impartially State*, 1852.
Donald, J, *Past Elections in Greenock*, Greenock, 1933.
Ferguson, W, 'Dingwall Burgh Politics and the Parliamentary Franchise in the Eighteenth Century,' *Scottish Historical Review*, Vol. XXXVIII, 1959.
Hanham, HJ, *Elections and Party Management*, Hassocks, 1978.
Inverness Poll Book, 1859, (Kings's Collection, Aberdeen University).
Shedden, Sir L, *The Parliamentary History of Kilmarnock*, Kilmarnock, 1929.
Wilkie, T, *The Representation of Scotland: Parliamentary Elections since 1832*, Edinburgh, 1895.

E. Members of Parliament

Adyelotte, WO, 'The House of Commons in the 1840s,' *History*, Vol. 39, October, 1954.
Forster, J, *Members of Parliament: Scotland, 1357-1882*, London, 1882.
Stenton, M, and Lees, S, *Who's Who of British Members of Parliament: a biographical dictionary of the House of Commons, Vol. I, 1832-1885*, Hassocks, 1976.
Woolley, SF, 'The Personnel of the Parliament of 1833,' *English Historical Review*, Vol. 53, April, 1938.

F. Miscellaneous (Scotland)

Aberdeen Banner.
Aberdeen Free Press.
Aberdeen Herald.
Aberdeen Journal.
Ballard, A, 'The Theory of the Scottish Burgh,' *Scottish Historical Review*, Vol. XIII, 1916.

Cowan, RMW, *The Newspaper in Scotland: A Study of its First Expansion, 1815-1860*, Glasgow, 1946.

Defoe, D, *The History of the Union between England and Scotland*, London, 1786.

Ferguson, JPS, *Directory of Scottish Newspapers*, Edinburgh, 1984.

Ferguson, W, *Scotland: 1689 to the Present*, Edinburgh, 1968.

Fry, M, *Patronage and Principle*, Aberdeen, 1987.

Hutchison, IGC, *A Political History of Scotland*, Edinburgh, 1986.

Keith, A, *The History of the North of Scotland Bank, 1836–1936*, Aberdeen, 1936.

Mackie, JB, *The Life and Work of Duncan McLaren*, 2 Vols., Edinburgh, 1888.

Mackie, JD, and Pryde, GS, *Estate of Burgesses in the Scots Parliament and its Relation to the Convention of Royal Burghs*, St Andrews, 1923.

MacLaren, AA, *Religion and Social Class: The Disruption in Aberdeen*, London, 1974.

Pagan, T, *The Convention of the Royal Burghs of Scotland*, Glasgow, 1926.

Pryde, GS, *The Burghs of Scotland: A Critical List*, London, 1965.

Pryde, GS, *The Treaty of Union of Scotland and England*, London, 1950.

Rait, RS, *The Parliaments of Scotland*, Glasgow, 1924.

Ross, JA, *Record of Municipal Affairs in Aberdeen Since the Passing of the Burgh Reform Act in 1833*, Aberdeen, 1889.

Scotsman.

Scottish Censuses, 1831 and 1871.

Smout TC, *A History of the Scottish People, 1560–1830*, Glasgow, 1969.

Spender, JA, *The Life and Times of The Right Hon. Sir Henry Campbell-Bannerman*, 2 Vols., Edinburgh, 1923.

Sunter, RM, *Patronage and Politics in Scotland, 1707–1832*, Edinburgh, 1986.

Terry, CS, *The Cromwellian Union*, Edinburgh, 1902.

Terry, CS, *The Scottish Parliament: Its Constitution and Procedure, 1603–1707*, Glasgow, 1905.

Urwin, DW, 'The Development of the Conservative Party Organisation in Scotland until 1912,' *Scottish Historical Review*, Vol. XLVI, No. 138, October, 1965.

Walker, WM, *Juteopolis*, Edinburgh, 1979.

G. General

Gash, N, *Politics in the Age of Peel*, London, 1952.

Key, VO jr., *Southern Politics*, New York, 1949.

Moore, DC, 'The Other Face of Reform,' *Journal of Victorian Studies*, Vol. V, 1961.

Moore, DC, 'Concession of Cure: The Sociological Premises of the First Reform Act,' *The Historical Journal*, Vol. XI, 1966.

Moore, DC, *The Politics of Deference*, Hassocks, 1976.

Oldfield, THB, *Representative History of Great Britain and Ireland*, 6 Vols., London, 1916.

Ostrogorski, M, *Democracy and the Organisation of Political Parties*, 2 Vols., New York, 1902.

Porritt, E & A, *The Unreformed House of Commons*, 2 Vols., London, 1903.

Rokkan, S, *Citizens, Elections, Parties*, Oslo, 1970.

Seymour, C, *Electoral Reform in England and Wales*, New Haven, 1916.

Smith, FB, *The Making of the Second Reform Bill*, Adelaide, 1966.

Index